Management in English Language Teaching

Ron White

Mervyn Martin

Mike Stimson

Robert Hodge

The right of the University of Cambridge to print and sell all manner of books was granted by Henry VIII in 1534. The University has printed and published continuously since 1584.

CAMBRIDGE UNIVERSITY PRESS

Cambridge
New York Port Chester
Melbourne Sydney

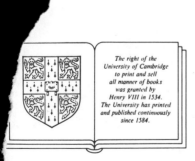

Published by the Press Syndicate of the University of Cambridge
The Pitt Building, Trumpington Street, Cambridge CB2 1RP
40 West 20th Street, New York, NY 10011, USA
10 Stamford Road, Oakleigh, Melbourne 3166, Australia

First published 1991

Printed in Great Britain
by Bell and Bain Ltd, Glasgow

Library of Congress cataloguing in publication data
90–27574

British Library cataloguing in publication data
White, Ron
Management in English Language Teaching.
1. English language. Teaching

I. Title
420.71042

ISBN 0 521 37396 4 hardback
ISBN 0 521 37763 3 paperback

CONTENTS

THANKS

It would not have been possible for us to write this book without the help and support of staff and students in the many and varied EFL institutions in which we have worked and gained experience. We would like to extend our thanks to all of them.

In particular we would like to acknowledge the generous help of David Allen, Andy Hopkins and Richard Rossner of the Bell Educational Trust; the British Council; Cultura Inglesa, Sao Paulo; and Reading University. Thanks are due to Nora White for her encouragement and support during the writing and editing of the book, and to Fiona Davies and Lynda Stimson for their constructive comments on the manuscript and for typing and re-typing. Thanks are also due to Helena Martin for her promotional work on the seminars associated with the book.

Finally, there are many ideas in the book which have come from diverse sources. Where possible we have tried to acknowledge such sources and we hope that nothing remains unacknowledged.

ACKNOWLEDGEMENTS

The authors and publishers are grateful to the authors, publishers and others who have given permission for the use of copyright material. While every effort has been made it has not been possible to identify the sources of all the material used and in such cases the publishers would welcome information from the copyright owners. Apologies are expressed for any omissions.

Blackwell publishers for the figure on p. 176 from R.V. White (1988) *The ELT Curriculum*; The British Association for Commercial and Industrial Education for the figure on p. 8 from J. Adair (ed) (1978) A *handbook of management training exercises* Vol. 1; Paul Chapman Publishing Ltd. for the extract on p. 182 from K.B. Everard and G. Morris (1990) *Effective School Management* (second edition); Harper and Row Ltd. for the extract on p. 12 from T. Bush (1986) *Theories of Educational Management* and for the figure on p. 169 from M. Skilbeck (1984) *School-based Curriculum Development* (second edition); "Hierarchy of needs" on p. 10 from *Motivation and personality, 2nd ed.* by Abraham H. Maslow. Copyright 1954 by Harper and Row Publishers, Inc., © 1970 by Abraham H. Maslow. Reprinted by permission of HarperCollins publishers; L.E. Henrichsen for the figure on p. 182 from *Diffusion of Innovations in English Language Teaching: The English Language Exploratory Committee's Promotion of C.C Fries's Oral Approach in Japan, 1965–1968* PhD dissertation, University of Hawaii at Manoa, 1988; The Institute of Personnel Management for the figure on p. 71 based on P. Long (1986) *Performance Appraisal Revisited* and for the extract on p. 110 from M. Megranahan (1989) *Counselling: A Practical Guide for Employers*; Longman Group for the figures on pp. 12 and 13 from A. Paisey (1981) *Organisation and Management in Schools*; C. McCabe for the extract on p. 179–80 from 'The External Evaluator – Inspector or Management Consultant?' in *Evaluation and Research in Education* Vol. 1, No. 1 pp. 1–8 (1987); the figures on pp. 18, 19, 20 and 21 from Charles B. Handy *Understanding Organisations* (third edition) © Charles B. Handy 1976, 1981, 1985. Reproduced by permission of Penguin Books Ltd; Pergamon Press and the British Council for the figure on p. 176 from R. Bowers (1983) 'Project planning and performance' in *ELT Documents 116: Language Teaching Projects for the Third World*; Pitman publishing for the extract on p. 11 from L.L. Mullins (1985) *Management and Organisational Behaviour*.

INTRODUCTION

Who is this book aimed at?

Teachers making the transition from the role of classroom practitioner to that of manager will find shelf upon shelf of books on management in any well-stocked bookshop. None of them will be on management in ELT, however, and it is precisely to fill this gap that this book has been written. Furthermore, because it deals with ELT, the book should be more relevant and more accessible than those management books which are based on manufacturing industry.

Aiming at newcomers to the field of management, at administrators and at those who are curious to know how a teaching organization might be run more effectively, we have set out to provide a clear, practical guide to the management of English language teaching schools both in the United Kingdom and elsewhere in the world. Taking many of our examples from good current practice drawn from our own experience in ELT institutions, we hope that the principles exemplified can, with adaptation and sensitivity, be transferred internationally.

We recognize that in a book of this size and scope, it is not possible to cover everything. For instance, we have not dealt with the management of co-operatives because very few schools are organized in this way and none of us has any direct experience of such organizations. Nor have we dealt with the question of cross-cultural and international differences in management styles because this is an area which requires considerably more attention than could be discussed within the confines of this book.

How should the book be used?

It is not intended that you should work through the book sequentially, starting at Chapter 1 and ending with the final chapter, although it can be read in this way. Rather, you may find it preferable to refer to chapters which are of immediate interest and relevance. Each chapter contains a set of follow-up activities which reinforce and develop the content of the chapter by relating it to practical issues. We do not anticipate, though, that you will work through all of the follow-up activities. Instead, a choice can be made from the activities available, ranging from practical exercises to small group discussions to simulations, all of which make it possible to use the book for individual self-study, for a programme of staff development involving a group of colleagues or as the basis of an ELT management course.

How is the book organized?

The book is in three parts, each focusing on a different management theme. Part One deals with people and organizations. Part Two is concerned with marketing. Part Three covers accounting and finance.

Part One

In Part One, the introductory chapter on organizations and the final two chapters on organizing resources and managing curriculum development and innovation were written by Ron White who, as Associate Director of the Centre for Applied Language Studies at the University of Reading, has confronted the practical problems associated with all of these areas, from which it has become clear that professional and pedagogical issues have management needs and consequences. In his chapter on organizations he emphasizes that organizations are primarily about people and that each organization has a cultural character of its own. The implementation of any kind of change in teaching objectives, content, methodology or assessment will involve not only matters of pedagogical principle; it will also involve people's views and values so that change is not only a question of introducing new technology, but of changing people's behaviour, and these are issues which are addressed in the chapter on managing innovation. The smooth running of an organization depends both on people and on the setting up and operating of routines and systems which promote efficiency, and his chapter on organizing resources and information looks at how this can be achieved.

The chapters on staff selection and development and communication are based on Mike Stimson's experience as Director of Studies at the Cultura Inglesa Sao Paulo and subsequently in the Personnel Management Department of the British Council. This practical on-the-job experience has been deepened by studying for a Personnel Management qualification with the Institute of Personnel Management.

In many ways, his chapters cover ground which you will probably be familiar with, having yourself experienced selection interviews, looked at advertisements, enjoyed (or suffered) training courses, and wondered how to cope with some of the conflicts that have arisen in the schools you have worked in. While this experience should be drawn upon to provide a frame of reference and a basis for the follow-up activities, there will be a need to make some order out of such disparate experience and it is the function of these chapters to give coherence to this aspect of management.

The first chapter deals with the process of selecting staff and all that this entails, while the next chapter moves on to consider training and career-planning in schools, with particular reference to performance appraisal. Inevitably, the problem of poor performance has to be faced in the issues of discipline and dismissal. Finally, the theme that underlies all three chapters – communication – is considered and he emphasizes the importance of nurturing all forms of communication so as to avoid grievances and conflict. The increasing need for negotiating skills, for both management and trade union representatives, is also covered in some depth.

Part Two

Mervyn Martin's chapters on marketing draw on his experience as Marketing Co-ordinator for the Bell Educational Trust, combined with the academic training acquired as part of his MBA. He begins by looking at marketing, which is not just another word for selling or advertising, but is a separate approach and a discipline in itself. Fundamentally, marketing in the ELT world is concerned with why customers should choose one school's services in preference to another's. All businesses – and schools are businesses – have to market themselves, and everything and everyone that has an impact on the client using the school is part of and falls within the ambit of marketing. What is important is how consciously and professionally they do so, which means that marketing needs to work to a strategic plan. These chapters deal with devising and operating such plans.

Part Three

All aspects of an organization's activities, whether recruiting staff or introducing new methods and equipment or finding out what the public wants, involve planning, and in his chapters on finance, Robert Hodge deals with what is, for many ELT specialists, the most esoteric aspect of management. With a career which has combined financial training and ELT, he relates the principles and practice of financial planning and control to the ELT context and shows why financial records are necessary and how they are organized.

So as to be able to use financial statements intelligently, it is vital to know where they come from and what they mean. Chapter 10 provides an introduction to double-entry book-keeping, which is the conventional way of recording and summarizing financial transactions in financial statements. Although most people will not have to do their own book-keeping, it is important to understand the principles involved. While the double-entry convention is excellent for recording transactions, it can be misleading when transactions are summarized in a profit and loss account and balance sheet. Chapter 10 tries to show why.

Chapter 11 concentrates on three areas that are of major importance to managers: planning, decision-making and cash flow. For each area, the chapter presents a way of looking at a business, and shows how managers can manipulate each component.

Chapter 12 restores the human element by dealing with the kind of information a manager may be given or should obtain, and how it can be interpreted. Not least, it shows how information can affect behaviour, often in unpredictable or undesirable ways.

The area of accounting and finance involves practical activities. Although it involves numbers, it is not like the arithmetic we learned at school. It seldom offers 'right' answers or 'correct' methods. It is a response to practical problems and anyone can do it if they are prepared to experiment. However, it helps to have some instruction, if only to avoid puzzling over problems that others have faced and solved before.

Most accounting and finance textbooks are aimed at present and future specialists. Ours is aimed at readers with an interest in the general problems of management accounting, specifically in language schools. The approach taken in this book is, therefore, different from that of the conventional accounting and finance textbook. We assume that readers are interested in principles rather than the manipulation of numbers. This doesn't mean that the Chapters 10 to 12 are theoretical. All of the points are illustrated with examples, though where strictly life-like numbers (e.g. 8¾% of £157) would obscure principles, we have opted for simpler numbers (e.g. 10% of £100). This makes some of the examples slightly forced, but the pay-off should be a clearer focus on logic rather than on fine detail.

If you are employed in a school and have access to financial information (which is often confidential), you will have a wealth of data to work on, and the activities at the end of each chapter are intended to stimulate real and practical analysis. If you don't have access to detailed financial information, a number of activities with simulated financial information have been provided. As the subject essentially involves a way of looking at things, the activities include a number of general questions which are intended to stimulate a mind set. If you require more extensive practice in techniques, you can study the books referred to in the bibliography.

Finally, we have used conventional words like 'business' and 'profit' for convenience' sake. If you are involved in non-profit making or public sector organizations, you will be aware that their activities are businesslike, even if they do not in legal terms produce a 'profit'. You can substitute 'operating surplus' or a similar term instead without any change in the underlying meaning.

Whether we like it or not, all schools – including increasingly those which are part of the state-maintained sector – are businesses. Marketing aims to make the business grow profitably. Finance controls the running of the business. Personnel administers the business and looks after staff. Organization provides the structure. It is our hope that this book will provide a better understanding of all these aspects of ELT management.

There is, however, a word of caution. As we noted at the beginning of this introduction, a well-stocked bookshop will contain dozens or even hundreds of books on management. There is, however, no such thing as perfection in management, in spite of what many of the more racey management titles may suggest. Like teachers, managers are constantly having to work at ways of improving what they and others do together. This book is a contribution to that improvement.

Ron White
Mervyn Martin
Mike Stimson
Robert Hodge

PART ONE: PEOPLE AND ORGANIZATIONS

1 ORGANIZATIONS

Aims

The aims of this chapter are:

1 to define some key management terms and concepts and provide a conceptual framework for ideas and procedures which will be presented in subsequent chapters.
2 to review the main characteristics of organizations.
3 to set up a scheme of organizational needs.
4 to categorize and describe organizational cultures and relate them to differences within and between organizations.
5 to identify elements of structure in a school organization.
6 to evaluate different approaches to organizational structure.
7 to consider management styles and functions.
8 to define the features of effective delegation of authority.
9 to outline a systematic approach to management as the basis for the effective management of a school.

1.1 Organizations

Schools are simultaneously two things: *institutions* and *organizations*. The school as *institution* will have a legal status, with governors or shareholders (depending on whether it is state or privately owned), a board of management, staff and students. As an institution, the school will have to conform to whatever legal requirements are laid down for such institutions, and it will normally be registered with the appropriate authority as an employer and tax payer. As an institution with a legal entity, the school assumes legally defined responsibilities, and it will be the school as institution which can be held accountable for fulfilling these obligations.

Schools are also *organizations*, which is to say, they consist of a network of relationships among the individuals who regard themselves as belonging to that organization. These relationships will be variously directed towards the achievement of the goals of the organization, towards maintaining the organization as a social unit, and towards fulfilling the personal needs of the individuals. Organizations have no existence other than through the people who make them up, even if, as we shall see, it is possible to describe the relationships among their members in terms of structures and functions. Without people, there is no organization – just as, without students, a school has no existence as a living and functioning organization, even if it may still have a legal existence as an institution.

Because all of us as individuals combine a mixture of the rational and irrational, so, too, organizations contain both rational and irrational elements. It is as well to bear this in mind, since neat descriptions of organizational structure can obscure the volatile and all too human aspects of organizations and, although we may talk of organizational goals, it is not the organization as such which has the goals, but the individuals within it. Given the fact that everyone is different, it is scarcely surprising that there will often be a diversity of goals among members of an organization, and one of the problems which management has to face is reconciling such differences and helping to establish a consensus as regards goals and the means of achieving them.

In addition to people, there is another vital aspect of an organization: its technology. Technology constitutes the means by which various operations are carried out in pursuit of organizational goals. It includes both *hardware* (things like computers, typewriters, reprographic equipment, video recorders) and *software* (printed material, video tapes, computer programs). An important part of organizational technology is the communication systems which enable information to be circulated around members of the organization (see Chapter 4). Another important part of the educational technology of a school is the curriculum itself (see Chapter 6), since it is the curriculum which embodies not only the pedagogical aims of the school, but the methods and materials employed in realizing those aims. In short, then, the technology of an organization consists of both tangible and intangible means whereby organizational goals can be achieved.

Finally, organizations, like any social unit, are characterized by belief and value systems which influence, sometimes very profoundly, the relationships, practices and achievements of the organization. That is, organizations have a *culture* by which they can be characterized. The culture of a school is expressed in the attitudes and behaviour of people towards each other, and it is something which we pick up from what people say and do. For instance, in one school all decisions about the choice of textbooks may be made by the academic director or Director of Studies without consultation with teachers. In such a school, the culture would tend to be based on the idea of a hierarchy of command and professional status. In another school, such decisions might be jointly arrived at through discussion involving all tutorial staff as well as feedback from students. Such a school would have a collegiate culture in which teachers are seen to have as equally valid a contribution to make as senior tutorial staff.

Other examples can be drawn from the kinds of routines and systems which staff and students are expected to conform to and from the relationship between staff and students. To take an instance, a school which values the student as an individual will tend to put a lot of emphasis on pastoral care, while one which sees students in less humanistic terms may keep them at arm's length and encourage distant and impersonal contacts between teachers and learners.

It is also not uncommon for different sections of an organization to have cultural differences. Typically, there will be a difference between the administrative and tutorial staff, the former tending to value set routines and ways of doing things, the latter often preferring variation and originality. One of the roles of management is to promote a satisfactory cultural mix so that the organization can both achieve existing goals and adapt to changing circumstances.

1.2 Needs and the organization

A school exists to provide an educational service to its clients (i.e. the students) and other stake holders (i.e. people having an interest in the school, such as parents, members of the community, employers, governors, shareholders). There is some ambiguity as to the status of the clients within any educational organization: are they raw materials in the process of being converted to finished products; are they co-participants with teachers in a process of discovery and growth; are they consumers of a service provided by the school; or are they something else? Different schools may give different answers to these questions, depending on their own goals and culture.

As an *organization*, a school will have to fulfil and maintain in balance three broad sets of needs, as depicted in Figure 1.1.

Figure 1.1 Organizational needs (from Adair 1983, BACIE 1978)

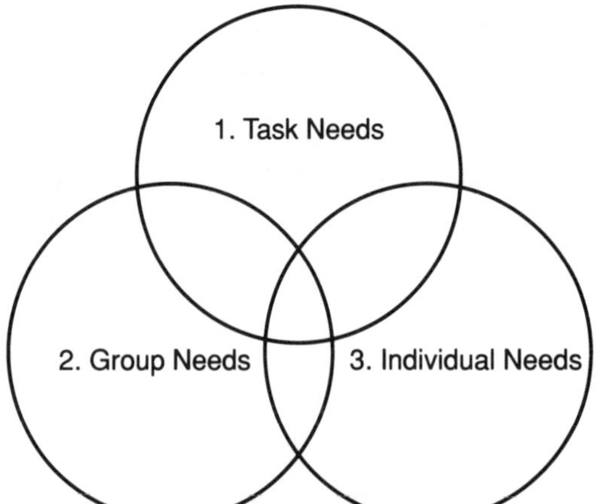

The *task* needs are those which have to be satisfied in order successfully to carry out the work of the organization. If, for instance, we take a private language school, one of its goals will be to stay in business and to generate a profit. To achieve this, students will have to be recruited, so marketing and selling the school's services will be a key task, which will involve planning a marketing strategy, allocating work to people assigned to marketing, and providing finance so that, for instance, publicity material can be prepared, printed and distributed while the person in charge of marketing can be enabled to make contact with potential clients and agents through visits abroad. Carrying out the work of marketing and selling will have to be monitored so that mailings are sent out on time, marketing tours are made at the best time to recruit students, and projected student numbers are realized. If for some reason, such as a postal strike which delays mailing, planned activities fall behind schedule, the plan will have to be adjusted and alternative procedures put into operation. For instance, a marketing tour might be brought forward so as to circumvent delays caused by a postal strike.

The second set of needs, those concerned with the *group*, are to do with the organization as .a social unit. For the organization to meet task needs, successful group maintenance is vital, because, if it becomes split into antagonistic factions – as can happen given cultural differences between different parts of the organization – it will be swept off target. Satisfying group needs gives rise to such group functions as:

setting standards
maintaining discipline
building team spirit
encouraging, motivating and giving a sense of purpose
appointing sub-leaders
ensuring communication with the group
training members of the group

All social groups have standards of behaviour both for work and interpersonal relationships. Often these standards are unspoken and it is only when they are violated that people become aware of them. For instance, a school with a particularly dedicated staff may have very high expectations of staff as regards the amount of time they devote to out-of-class activities. Teachers who give less time to such activities will be seen to have infringed work standards and the group may then impose some sort of pressure – or discipline – on the teachers concerned to bring them into line with group norms in this aspect of their work.

The successful creation and maintenance of team spirit is also important and it is a mark of a successful organization that this social need is fulfilled. It is in an attempt to do so that people will engage in what may be seen as being purely social relationships. A happy and harmonious staff room is one sign that such group maintenance needs are being met, while such activities as meeting for a drink after work are further examples of the same thing.

Finally, there is a third set of needs which have to be met – *individual* or *personal* needs. If they are not met, there will be a loss of morale and motivation among the individuals who make up the group or team. Meeting individual needs involves:

attending to personal problems
praising individuals
giving status
recognizing and using individual abilities
training the individual

Basically, all of us like to feel valued and a successful organization is one in which people feel that their worth as individuals has been given appropriate attention. Indeed, the kinds of individual treatment which good educational practice advocates for students apply equally well to teachers and other staff.

It can be helpful to match these individual needs against Maslow's hierarchy of needs (Maslow 1970). His theory of individual development and motivation was originally published in 1943, and he proposes that people are wanting beings. They always want more; but what they want depends on what they already have. He proposes that human needs are arranged in a series of levels, with physiological needs at the lowest level, and proceeding through security needs, affiliation needs and esteem needs, to the need for self-actualization at the highest level. This hierarchy is often depicted as a pyramid (Figure 1.2), with the highest needs at the top.

Figure 1.2 Maslow's hierarchy of needs

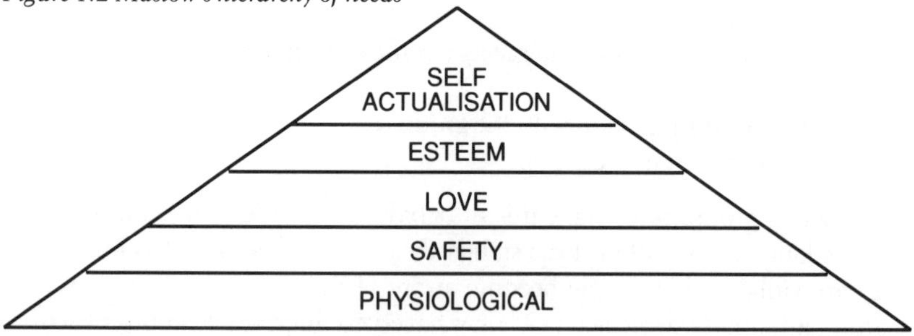

The principle behind this hierarchy is that, beginning at the lowest level, the needs of each level have to be satisfied to some extent before people think about needs at the next level above, and only unsatisfied needs motivate a person. Problems can arise in an organization if such needs are overlooked. Assuming that physiological and security needs are normally met, the social, esteem and self-realization needs may so motivate individuals within the organization that they may become more concerned with the fulfilling of individual or personal needs than with the realization of group and task needs. In other words, individuals may become concerned with 'me' rather than 'us' and it can be this which is at the heart of staff motivation problems.

1.3 The structure of organizations

A fundamental concept of organizations is the notion of structure. Basically, structure is an inventory or list of what has to be organized. The models of organization and management to be outlined in this section are attempts to explain what goes on in organizations with regard to decision- and policy-making and implementation. While some models (e.g. formal and democratic) attempt to provide prescriptions for what *should* be done, others (e.g. political and subjective) try to account for what is believed to happen. Obviously, it would be unwise to take any one model as a way of explaining what is going on in one's own school, any more than it would be sensible to take one model as a recipe for successful management. As should become clear from the diversity of models postulated, organizations and management are highly complex. What the models may do is to provide insights into aspects of school organization which have hitherto proved baffling, while also enabling the manager to take pre-emptive action to avoid creating difficulties through inadvertently setting up the very conditions which can lead to misunderstanding and conflict.

Organizations, as we have seen, consist of relationships between people who have come together for a purpose. Just as relationships have no existence other than through the people who engage in them, so, too, organizational structure has no separate existence other than through the roles and relationships through which the structure is expressed. Thus, although it is possible to describe organizational structure in diagrams showing hierarchies and functions, such representations are themselves simply a kind of abstraction, a way of depicting the organization in order to understand it better. It is important, though, not to confuse the picture with the organization it attempts to portray.

What is structure? According to Paisey (1981: 64)

> Structure is the deliberate patterning of relationships between organization members.

Mullins (1985:72) defines structure as:

> the pattern of relationships among positions in the organization and among members of the organization. The structure defines tasks and responsibilities, work roles and relationships, and channels of communication. The purpose of structure is the division of work among members of the organization, and the co-ordination of their activities so they are directed towards achieving the goals and objectives of the organization. Structure makes possible the application of the process of management and creates a framework of order and command through which the activities of organizations can be planned, organized, directed and controlled.

What may be clear in Mullins's definition is the normative view of structure; that is, the belief that through structure an organization defines what *should* be done by its members. Such a view is implicit in a role culture and is in line with the idea that organizations are rational, goal-directed and relatively stable – all of which are characteristics of *formal* models of organizations (Bush 1986:22–47). Formal models also emphasize the official and structural elements of organizations, and Bush (1986:23) has defined them as follows:

> Formal models assume that organizations are hierarchical systems in which managers use rational means to pursue agreed goals. Heads possess authority legitimized by their formal positions within the organization and are accountable to sponsoring bodies for the activities of their institution.

Before considering what the limitations of formal models of organizations might be, let us look at what a description of organizational structure can tell us, whether our interest in organizations is as an academic exercise or whether, as an employee, we are trying to understand the institution by which we are employed. Basically, as Paisey points out, when we ask the question, 'What is the structure of a school?', we are trying to understand the distribution of jobs, authority and position within the organization. In other words, the questioner is interested in finding out who is who, who does what, and what the limits of their powers are. Paisey has summarized this in Figure 1.3.

Figure 1.3 The elements of structure (from Paisey 1981)

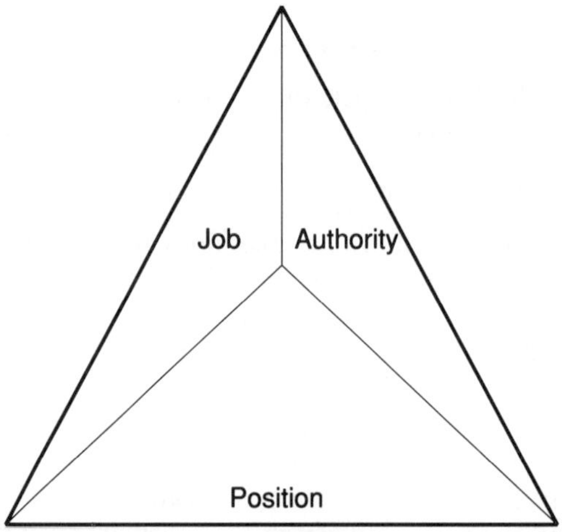

Jobs, authority and positions will be labelled. That is why such titles as Director of Studies, Marketing Manager, Bursar, Secretary, and so on exist. A list of such titles in a school provides a kind of snapshot of organizational structure at one point in time and it will show the observer where – in theory at least – occupants of each position stand in relation to one another. What such a structural list does not include, however, is the dynamic aspect of the organization. Nor does it indicate the *informal* structure of the organization as realized through the relationships which are not actually specified in formal titles and procedures. As we noted earlier, such models specify what *should be* rather than what actually is.

Traditionally, the organizational structure of a school will be depicted as a variant of a pyramid, the pyramid being either flat or tall, according to the levels of authority and the distribution of jobs. (See Figure 1.4 below and see Chapter 5 for an organizational diagram of an actual school.) A tall pyramid will have a long chain of command from top to bottom, whereas a flat one will have a short one. In fact, more than one pyramid may exist within an organization, each reflecting both the culture of different parts of the organization as well as the functions carried out by these different sections. Thus, the bureaucracy, which is concerned with controlling the organization in such areas as finance, employment and promotion, may be characterized by a tall pyramid, with several intermediate levels of command, while the operations side, which will be concerned with day-to-day teaching, may be depicted as a relatively flat pyramid. The height of the pyramid and the chain of command are factors to be considered in delegation.

Figure 1.4 Flat and tall pyramidical forms (from Paisey 1981)

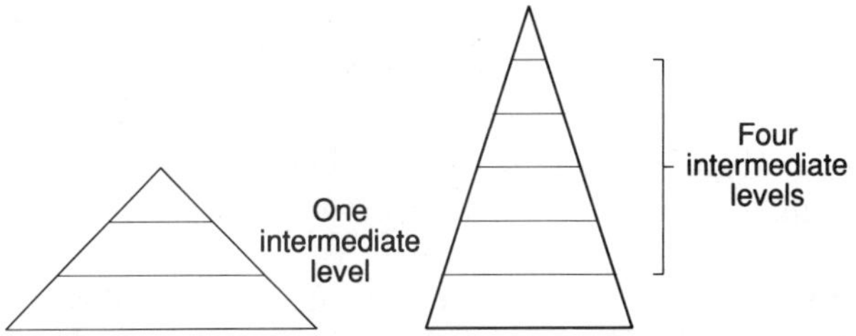

Necessarily, the pyramidical view of organizational structure tends to promote a top-down, hierarchical picture of a school, with considerable importance being given to the Principal and other authority figures, as in a club or power culture. Although there is considerable evidence for the importance of the Principal's leadership role in a school, particularly with regard to the implementation of innovation, such a hierarchical model gives priority to authority and an essentially mechanistic view of structure, with prescribed and somewhat inflexible modes of operation. As will have already become obvious, such a view does not sit happily with a more organic and egalitarian philosophy, as realized in a task culture. Not surprisingly, therefore, formal approaches to organizational structure have been open to criticism. Both Bush and Paisey discuss the weaknesses of formal models, the former listing the following:

1 It is unrealistic to characterize schools and colleges as *goal-directed* organizations because few educational organizations actually have a formal – or even informal – statement of their objectives. Indeed, it would be interesting to know how many teachers, let alone Principals, are aware that their school or department has a 'mission statement' and if it does, how many of the staff would agree with it.
2 The portrayal of decision-making as a *rational* process is fraught with difficulties. Bush, like other writers concerned with educational management (e.g. Everard and Morris 1985), points out that decision-making is both an intuitive and a rational process. This, no doubt, will come as a relief to many people who would be hard put to give a rational account of the process by which decisions – pedagogic or administrative – are made.
3 Formal models focus on the organization as an entity and ignore or underestimate the contribution of *individuals* within organizations. Such models give primacy to the organization, subordinating individuals to organizational requirements. Yet, as we noted in section 1, organizations are made up of highly varied, individual human beings. Formal, structural models of schools ignore such individuality, and a style of management which is based on a formal approach will tend to ignore those aspects of individual motivation which, as we noted earlier, are so important.
4 A central assumption of formal models is that power resides at the apex of the pyramid, and that acceptance of managerial decisions by those lower down in the hierarchy is unproblematic. Yet, in schools, there is a built-in conflict between the authority of expertise (as exemplified by the skills that classroom teachers bring to their work) and positional authority (as exemplified in the role of Director of Studies or Head of Department). There is an inherent tension here between the teachers' claim to autonomy in pedagogical matters, and the responsibility and accountability of the Principal for the quality and efficiency of the work carried out by the school.
5 Formal approaches are based on the implicit assumption that organizations are relatively *stable*. However, as Bush observes, 'it can be argued that assumptions of stability are unrealistic in many organizations and invalid in most schools and colleges.' Indeed, a moment's reflection will reveal how tenuous is the assumption of stability in any organization, especially an educational one, given the volatility of personal relationships and the constantly changing wider environment (economic, political, demographic) in which schools exist. This is especially the case for language schools, whose clientele can change almost overnight according to economic and political changes. So, in reality, stability is a false assumption.

Clearly, in view of the criticisms of formal models of organizations and management, alternatives have been proposed, among which are democratic, political, subjective and ambiguity models. The first of these, the democratic, is, like formal theories, strongly *normative* in orientation. Advocates of *democratic models* have the rather utopian belief that decision-making should be based on democratic principles, while also emphasizing the *authority of expertise* (rather than the authority of position characteristic of formal models). Furthermore, consensus rather than conflict is valued by the democratic model, being realized in organizational terms through collegiality – that is, group discussion involving maximum participation by all members of the organization – and through committees.

The *political model* emphasizes groups rather than the larger organization, stressing also the prevalence of conflict and of interest groups. Not surprisingly, goals and aims are seen as being unstable, ambiguous and contested (Bush 1986: 70). Bargaining and negotiation are the means whereby decisions emerge, while power is seen as a central feature. The process of negotiation may be revealed in the management of resources, particularly in times of shortage. Emphasizing as they do the less attractive aspects of group behaviour, political models may seem intrinsically unappealing to teachers: but they do highlight some of the processes which are present in most schools at some point, and they also draw attention to what can happen when, through external pressures or internal developments, members of an organization are drawn into factions competing for power and resources.

As is implied in its name, the *subjective model* focuses on the individual's interpretation and understanding of organizational structure and processes. What interpretation and meanings do individuals place on events? Such interpretations reflect each individual's background, experience and values, while structure, as was suggested in the introduction to this section, is seen as being a product of human interaction rather than something which is fixed and predetermined (Bush 1986:91). Finally, subjective models deny the existence of organizational goals, emphasizing the significance of individual purposes and aims (cf. the introduction to section 4).

The fourth, *ambiguity model*, emphasizes uncertainty and unpredictability. Organizational goals are considered to be unclear and ambiguous, organizations themselves are seen to be fragmented, and structure is felt to be unclear and uncertain. Decision-making is seen to be unplanned, while decentralization is considered to be advantageous. In many ways, the ambiguity model reflects the characteristics of a person culture as described on page 21.

As may be clear from these brief descriptions, no model fully accounts for organizational structure and management processes. Bush (1986:131f.) suggests that the validity of the various models depends on five overlapping considerations, and that the applicability of each model will depend on how significant each of these factors is in any given situation.

1 The *size* of the institution. Large size leads to specialization and fragmentation.
2 The nature of the *organizational structure*. Participative structures, for instance, enhance democratic and political dimensions.

3 *Time*. Participative, democratic decision-making requires more time of teachers than centralized decision-making. One reason why moves towards a participative style of management can fail in schools is because it eats into teachers' free time. 'Oh, no, not another meeting about computerization,' is the kind of cry which may be heard in the staff room when out-of-class time is to be given up to a staff meeting.
4 The availability of *resources*. Basically, it is easier to be democratic in times of plenty; retrenchment and political action tend to go together as subunits and individuals try to retain existing resource levels. 'Of course, we'll be exempted from the cut backs' is the kind of statement which can be heard when retrenchment is proposed. But if everyone regards themselves as a special case, implementing cut backs will rapidly become a political issue when budgets (see Chapter 12) are being set.
5 The nature and rate of change in the *environment*. Stability and democracy go hand in hand; with change and instability, the ambiguity model may be more appropriate.

Following Enderud (1980) and Davies and Morgan (1983), Bush outlines a four-phase model for policy formation, which brings together many of the characteristics of the models just described. The four phases suggested are as follows:

1 The *anarchic* phase, during which issues are identified and potential solutions are considered.
2 The *political* phase, when a broad consensus is reached through a process of bargaining and negotiation.
3 The *collegial* phase, when an attempt is made to persuade colleagues to accept the compromise reached during the previous political stage.
4 The formal or *bureaucratic* stage, during which agreed policy may be changed in the light of administrative or practical considerations, and subsequently put into operation.

It is suggested that 'attempts by leaders to omit certain stages or to hurry issues through the process may lead to subsequent breakdown or create the necessity for loopback to earlier phases' (Bush 1986:134). Indeed, the same warning can be applied to many other aspects of management, and most notably to the development of that sense of corporate identity which is a feature of an effective organization.

1.4 Organizational cultures

We have seen that organizational structure can give rise to quite different relationships among parts of an organization, while different management models can lead to very different styles of management within an organization. Such management styles will, in turn, result in distinctive kinds of organizational culture, and it is to this aspect of organizations that we shall now turn.

Why is it that there are aspects of a school – the climate, character or culture – which can be picked up as soon as one crosses the threshold? What is it that a new teacher has to adapt to on joining the staff of a school? And why is it that conflicts arise among staff and between different sections of a school? The short answer to these questions can be found in the heading to this section: organizational cultures.

All organizations have a history and traditions, rules and regulations (often unspoken), ways of doing things, and conventions governing relationships, which together constitute the culture of that organization. Charles Handy (1978) has suggested four types of *organizational culture* and he has applied his classification to the characterization of schools as organizations (Handy 1984). His discussion of the organizational culture is concerned with looking at the way in which attitudes and relationships give rise to a climate or culture that can be highly successful in achieving organizational goals on the one hand, or very unsuccessful in working productively towards shared aims on the other. Organizational culture will also give greater or lesser emphasis to the maintenance of social, task and individual needs. Since schools as organizations have been established in order to achieve both specified and unstated goals, it is important to consider in what ways organizational culture or climate can help or hinder the accomplishment of goals, whether these be commercial, educational or – as might be assumed in many language schools – a combination of both.

Handy names the four organizational cultures as follows:

1 Power or 'club'.
2 Role.
3 Task.
4 Person.

He takes some pains to point out that

> there are no wholly good cultures and no wholly bad cultures. All cultures are OK, in the right place, because each culture is good for some things, and less good at others. (Handy 1984:10)

He goes on to say that

> Few organizations have only one. They are more often a mix of all four. What makes each organization different is the mix they choose. What makes them successful is, often, getting the right mix at the right time. (ibid, 13)

1.4.1 The power or club culture

What Handy has called the power or club culture is characterized as a spider web with a power source at the hub, surrounded by concentric circles of intimates and influence. Those nearer to the hub or spider have more power than those at the periphery. The lines radiating out from the centre indicate the lines of responsibility and functions of the organization. In such a culture, the organization is led rather than managed.

Figure 1.5 The club or power culture (from Handy 1978)

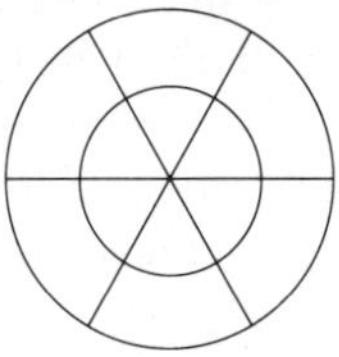

The priority of such a culture is meeting the aims of the head, and the organization exists primarily for this purpose. Handy (1984) observes that organizations based on this principle have very personal cultures, 'rich in personality' and abounding 'with almost mythical stories and folklore from the past' and they 'can be very exciting places to work *if* you belong to the club and share the values and beliefs of the spider'. By implication, if you don't, they aren't.

Communications within a club culture tend to be informal and personal. If minutes are kept or memoranda sent (and they are not, because face-to-face communication will tend to be preferred), they go from one individual to another individual (e.g. Bob to Betty or RW to BT) rather than from job title (or position) to job title.

Such cultures depend on a strong and capable head who can pick a good team. Indeed, selecting a group of compatible people is an important consideration in such an organization. If the spider is not strong and capable, the organization will reflect the head's weakness. Handy suggests that power or club cultures are a *convenient* way of running things when the organization is small – around twenty people. But once things become bigger, a more formal and less personal style of communication and organization becomes essential.

Anyone who has worked in a small school, either public or private sector, will recognize this type of culture. Owner-managed schools, in particular, tend to embody a club culture, with the owner-principal occupying a central role at the centre of the spider's web. Problems can and do arise, however, when such an organization grows beyond the size where it is possible to sustain the kind of intimate, face-to-face communication which is the hallmark of such a culture in a small organization. Similarly, there can be problems of succession when a particularly charismatic central figure is replaced by one who lacks the particular leadership skills of the retiring Principal.

1.4.2 The role culture

The role culture is quite different, resembling a pyramid of boxes, each box being a job which exists independently of whoever occupies it. The underlying organizational idea of such a culture is that 'organizations are sets of roles or job-boxes, joined together in a logical and orderly fashion so that together they discharge the work of the organization' (Handy 1984:11). In fact, such an organizational culture resembles closely the stereotyped organizational chart, arranged as a hierarchy, and with roles rather than individuals as the titles for each place on the chart. In such a culture, the organization is managed rather than led.

Figure 1.6 The role culture (from Handy 1978)

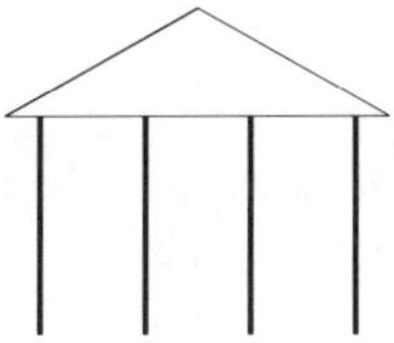

Communication within a role culture, in contrast to that within a club culture, will follow prescribed conventions, and memoranda go from role to role (e.g. Principal, Director of Studies, Bursar) and not to individuals. The roles, like other aspects of the organization, will be defined by job descriptions, and procedures will be specified in rules and handbooks.

Mature and larger organizations 'have a lot of role culture in them' (Handy 1984:12). There is within schools a range of tasks which require routine and uniform handling, and the absence of routine procedures can be bothersome. Conformists rather than individuals are required as role occupants in such a culture, and new occupants of a role can be trained to fit the role they will occupy.

The administration within an organization will often be characterized by a role culture. It is easy to see why this is so. The administration is that part of an organization which is set up to operate the kinds of routine procedures and systems without which the actual work of the organization would be impossible. In schools, the registration of students is one such example, involving as it does in the private sector, the collection of fees, as well as assignment of students to classes. A school which lacks a system for registration will soon find itself in trouble. Other routine aspects of a school include the ordering of and payment for materials, books and equipment. Textbooks, class sets and readers have to be ordered in time for incoming courses, while suppliers have to be paid on receipt of their invoice. Services, such as electricity and water, also have to be paid for at times specified by the service providers. And, most importantly, staff have to be paid at regular intervals. All of these services require routinization to be efficient, and consequently, the administrators who provide these services within any organization will tend to inhabit a role culture.

This can sometimes lead to conflict because teachers tend not to subscribe to the same set of values as characterize members of a role culture. Thus, administrators who require time sheets to be completed in a particular way and submitted by a specified date will become exceedingly irritated by teachers who fail to conform to their system, while such teachers, for their part, will resent having to do such 'boring paperwork'. Likewise, the senior management of a school might wish to implement a staff appraisal scheme as a way of improving the efficiency of the school through close monitoring of staff, whereas teachers may see such a scheme as potentially threatening. It can help both sides of the culture divide if they can be brought to see that their differing viewpoints are not simply expressions of personality quirks but represent cultural differences which actually have a functional purpose.

1.4.3 The task culture

Contrasting with club and role cultures is the task culture, which is job- or project-orientated. Its members are able to respond to change in a less idiosyncratic or individualistic way than members of a club culture, and more quickly than occupants of a role culture. Indeed, role cultures may be very slow indeed to respond to change since, by their very nature, role cultures are based on the principle of uniformity and routine. Change is unwelcome.

Handy suggests that the 'organizational idea' of the task culture is 'that a group or team of talents and resources should be applied to a project, problem or task. In that way each task gets the treatment it requires . . . and the groups can be changed, disbanded or increased as the task changes' (Handy 1984:12). Diagrammatically, a net, in which the cords can be pulled in various ways and which can regroup, represents the task culture.

Figure 1.7 The task culture (from Handy 1978)

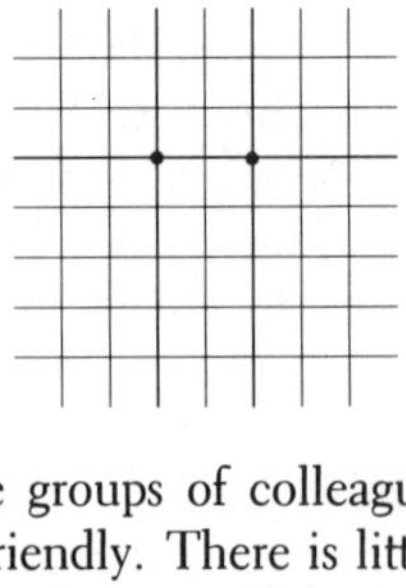

Built around co-operative groups of colleagues making up a team, task cultures can be warm and friendly. There is little hierarchy, there are plans rather than routinized procedures, and 'reviews of progress rather than assessment of past performance' (Handy 1984:12). Handy notes that such cultures thrive in situations where problem-solving is the job of the organization, and that there are 'team leaders' rather than managers. Organizations characterized by a task culture will be expensive to run and may not, therefore, offer job security, even if they offer excitement and challenge and call for commitment and imagination.

Clearly, a task culture provides an exciting work environment and it may well be the case that a good school is one in which a task culture predominates. Indeed, some small, specialized schools, such as those offering tailor-made courses for specific clients or groups, would tend to require a task culture since no two courses will be the same and small, flexible teams of staff would be needed to respond to constantly changing client needs. Even larger schools, offering a standard service, will have a need for the sort of flexibility that a task culture promotes when it comes to responding to new demands and initiating change.

1.4.4 The person culture

The last type of culture defined by Handy is what he terms the person culture in which, unlike the other three, the priority is the individual's talents rather than the organization's purposes. The 'organizational idea' behind this culture 'is that the individual talent is all-important and must be serviced by some sort of minimal organization' (Handy 1984:13). 'Stars, loosely grouped in a cluster or constellation, is the image of a person culture', while the management is subservient to the professional stars.

Figure 1.8 The person culture (from Handy 1978)

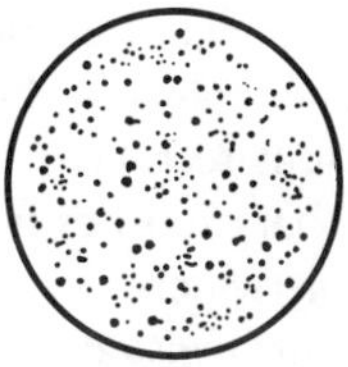

It is difficult to imagine an effective school operating within a person culture because schools depend upon teams of people collaborating together for a common purpose rather than serving the needs of one individual member. Indeed, the evolution of a person culture in a school could give rise to conflict, since it would tend to be identified with the setting up of differentiation among people who would otherwise regard themselves as peers. The result could be that a staff member comes to be perceived as a prima donna. Although most people are prepared to accede to someone for a limited time when something crucial is at stake, it becomes irksome and divisive if it continues once the situation which gave rise to this cultural development is over.

The cultural mix which characterizes any organization will be the product of four factors:

size
work flow
environment
history

In general, large size and role cultures go together. When work is organized on an interdependent sequential basis, a role culture is typical, whereas organization into separate units where groups or individuals are responsible for the whole job goes hand in hand with task or person cultures. As Handy (1984:14) says, 'a lot depends on what the job of the organization is seen to be'.

The environment will have an important influence on the development of organizational cultures. In general, a stable environment promotes the evolution of a role culture, whereas a changing or demanding environment requires a culture responsive to change, i.e. a task or a club culture. Members of an organization which has been run by a powerful head, around whom a club culture has evolved, will find difficulty in changing to a task culture in which greater participation of members is called for. Conversely, people who are at home in a task culture will tend to resist the development of a role culture, whose requirements for standardized and routinized procedures will be at odds with existing ways of doing things.

1.4.5 Culture conflict

Why, then, are some organizations more successful than others? And how do conflicts arise within an organization? The answer will be determined, in no small measure, by the cultural characteristics of the organization and its sub-groups. As may have been obvious from the earlier description of organizational cultures, different sections within a large organization may have quite different cultural characteristics from one another. For instance, the administration of a school, which, as we have noted, deals with such aspects as financial management, registration and examinations, will usually be characterized by a role culture. Indeed, any other culture will not be as efficient in terms of the kinds of functions which the administration is required to carry out, as will be obvious in financial matters in which there are fixed conventions and systems which those concerned with the financial management of an institution are obliged to follow (see Part Three). However, teachers concerned with the operations side of the organization – particularly curriculum development, course design and actual teaching – will tend to see themselves as operating within a task culture. The basis for conflict between the two organizational sub-cultures is obvious, and may help to explain why relations between the administrative and tutorial sides of a school can be so fraught. An appreciation of why and how these cultural differences exist can assist in reaching an understanding of others' viewpoints and of the mutual interdependence of these two complementary aspects of the organization.

1.5 Styles and functions of management

It will be obvious that there is likely to be a relationship between the structure of an organization, the kind of decision- or policy-making processes which are followed, the style of management exhibited by those who occupy management roles and the culture of an organization. Formal models of organizations emphasize control, while democratic ones stress participation. Likewise, managers adopt different 'theories' or views of management according to the beliefs which they bring to their management role – beliefs which, incidentally, will be strongly influenced by their own national cultural background as well as their previous experience as employees.

Contrasting two very different belief systems about the nature of work – and consequently of management – McGregor (1960) termed them 'Theory X' and 'Theory Y'. Managers adopting 'Theory X' believe that (Everard and Morris 1985:29):

1 Work is inherently distasteful to most people.
2 Most people are not ambitious, have little desire for responsibility, and prefer to be directed.
3 Most people have little capacity for creativity in solving problems.
4 Motivation occurs only at the physiological and security levels (cf. Maslow's hierarchy of needs in section 2).
5 Most people must be closely controlled and often coerced to achieve organizational objectives.

By contrast, 'Theory Y' managers believe that:

1 Work is as natural as play, if conditions are favourable.
2 Control of one's own work activities is often indispensable in achieving organizational gains.
3 The capacity for creativity in solving organizational problems is widely distributed in the population.
4 Motivation occurs at the social, ego and self-actualization levels as well as at the physiological and security levels.
5 People can be self-directed and creative at work if properly led.

It takes only a moment's thought to relate this dichotomy to views on teaching as well as to beliefs about management. As managers of people and resources in the classroom, teachers may approach their task with a 'Theory X' or 'Theory Y' set of beliefs and related set of practices. Yet, ironically, the 'Theory X' teacher may resent being treated in the same way by a 'Theory X' manager, such as a Principal or Academic Director.

In fact, what goes on in the larger organization of the school will probably be reflected in what goes on in the smaller setting of the classroom. Thus, management style will set a tone from which the classroom will not be immune. In other words, the organizational culture will tend to influence all parts of the school. Where management and tutorial styles are in harmony, the one will reinforce the other; where they are not, teachers can experience conflict and difficulty which cannot help but influence the work and relationships with their students. It is in recognition of this relationship that the British Council Recognition Scheme for language schools in the United Kingdom includes among its criteria for inspection both management and administration as well as academic management. Whatever the style of management, there are certain functions which management will carry out, even though 'the essential nature of managerial work is not easy to describe' (Mullins 1985:123). Mullins, like many writers on the subject, draws a distinction between

> those whose main occupation is the carrying out of discrete tasks and the actual doing of work themselves; and those who spend proportionally more of their time in determining the work of other people, the planning and organizing of their work, issuing them with instructions and giving advice, and checking on their performance.

By making such a distinction between 'managing' and 'doing' (which parallels the distinction commonly made between management and operations), Mullins suggests that management can be seen as

> the planning of work, organizing the distribution of activities and tasks to other people, direction of subordinate staff and controlling the performance of other people's work.

This leads to a generalized definition of the common activities of management as:

clarification of objectives
planning
organizing
directing
controlling

In addition to these functions, Everard and Morris (1985:10) believe that the manager's mission should be:

1 to utilize and integrate resources economically in the definition and pursuit of organizational goals;
2 to facilitate beneficial change (see Chapter 6);
3 to maintain and develop resources (see Chapter 5).

The style with which these functions are carried out will depend on the theory or view of management entertained by the individual in the role of manager. As we have seen, style of management and organizational culture are closely integrated, while environmental conditions will also influence management style so that, in times of stress brought about by external factors, a more autocratic style of management style may emerge in response to need for rapid and decisive action. The continuation of such a management style when conditions have stabilized may prove to be difficult or even harmful, however.

What even the most autocratic manager will have to learn is the art of delegation, and no more so than if a democratic and participative style of management is to be successful. What is delegation? And how is it to be practised?

Mullins (1985:181) defines it at two levels:

> At the organizational level, delegation involves consideration of centralization/decentralization and divisionalization or departmentalization. At the individual, or personal, level delegation is the process of entrusting authority and responsibility to others. It is the authorisation to undertake activities that would otherwise be carried out by someone in a more senior position.

Authority is defined as 'the right to take action or make decisions that the manager would otherwise have done', while *responsibility* involves 'an obligation to the subordinate to perform certain duties or make certain decisions and having to accept possible reprimand from the manager for unsatisfactory performance' (Mullins 1985:171). Mullins points out that it is not practical to delegate authority without responsibility, while also warning that no manager can delegate ultimate responsibility, as was so cogently indicated by the sign on President Harry Truman's White House desk: 'The buck stops here.'

Efficient delegation depends on three things (Everard and Morris 1985:49):

1 Clearly defined objectives with a timetable.
2 Clearly defined criteria which should be borne in mind in achieving the objectives.
3 Review procedures or check points.

An important means of *permanently* delegating authority and responsibility is through job descriptions (see Chapter 2, section 1).

1.6 A systematic approach to management

Although in some respects, as in utilizing resources, management is concerned with *things*, for the most part management is concerned with *people* and *ideas*, especially in the context of educational management. Whether clarifying objectives or controlling activities, managers – like teachers – are involved with people. And, as with classroom life, the irrational tends to impinge on the rational in ways which make nonsense of strictly systematic approaches to management. The importance of taking account of the individual, idiosyncratic and irrational is built into some management models, as we noted in section 4. Thus, the political, subjective and ambiguity models make allowance for the unstable and volatile nature of individual and group behaviour.

Management has to face a conflict between the unstable on the one hand and the need for systematization on the other. In spite of the recognition of the volatile and ambiguous nature of relationships and understandings among members of an organization, most approaches to management advocate being reasonably systematic, and the procedures outlined below conform to common management practice within a basically democratic frame of reference.

The first step in any project – whatever its extent or scope – is to clarify aims and purposes. It is important to distinguish between clarification which involves selling an idea that has already been decided upon (as when a central authority, such as a ministry, transmits a decision on some aspect of school practice), and clarification which involves consulting the views of others and taking these into account before a decision is actually taken. In the former, the policy decision is not open to negotiation, whereas in the latter, the whole point of the exercise is to inform the decision-making person before a decision is taken. Whatever form of decision-taking is used, it should be open and clear to all involved and consistent with the reality of the situation itself. There is very little point, for instance, in operating a consultative process if, as will be the case in an autocratic system, none of the views expressed can have any effect on outcomes.

Clarification as to eventual aims and outcomes will involve all those concerned with the implementation of objectives, whether these have been decided in advance or are the outcome of negotiation. Whatever the case, it is important to 'lay things open', for perceptions and understandings to be revealed. Questions such as the following will be discussed. Some of them may even give rise to uncomfortable and unsettling discussion:

Why are we doing this?
What is it for?
Who is it for?
What do we want to achieve when the task is completed?
What will it be like?
How can we evaluate the end product to be sure that it is what is required?

This stage matches the anarchic phase described by Bush, and although it may be uncomfortable and messy, out of it should emerge a clearer view of what people think and feel about the issues concerned. Suppression of doubts or alternative views will tend, in the long run, to be counter-productive, particularly if difficulties subsequently arise, when recriminations will give expression to hitherto unvoiced or ignored doubts or suggestions.

The process of reaching consensus is essentially a political one, arrived at through bargaining and negotiation, which should involve all interested parties, while the outcome of bargaining may be rather different from that originally envisaged by the individual or group who initiated the process. Such change in the final realization of a policy is an important aspect of the implementation of innovation, as will be noted in discussing the management of change in Chapter 6.

The clarification of aims and purposes leads to the next stage, that of planning and organizing, which will begin with assembling relevant facts, ideas, skills, experience and resources. Two questions to be answered here are:

What facts or information do we already know or have?
What do we need to learn or obtain?

Information subsequently obtained will have to be interpreted and processed, and the options and choices that have been revealed will have to be considered and the costs and risks evaluated.

Information gathering is followed by planning, in which an agenda for action and a list of responsibilities and deadlines will be established. Basically, planning involves specifying in detail what will be done, how, where, when and by whom and with what outcomes. It is at this point that we move into the formal or bureaucratic stage, in which administrative and practical considerations determine the shape of what is to be done.

Once the plan has been specified, the group moves into action, during which individuals carry out agreed actions. It is at this stage that the monitoring process is carried out, outcomes are matched against planned aims, and changes to plans are made to accommodate shortfalls and the responses of those involved in the process of implementation. Reviewing the process of implementation, and analysing successes and difficulties, are important inputs to planning for improvement or changes which will ensure successful outcomes. Such monitoring will help to take account of the unplanned, unforeseen or irrational, and it is an unwise manager who ignores such feedback during the action phase.

The above account is necessarily a digest of what may occur in reality and it may be helpful to consider an actual instance – the setting up of a computer laboratory. The first thing to consider is 'Why are we doing this?' The answers may include 'because our competitors have introduced computers', 'because it will motivate and interest students', 'because it will make possible greater individualization', and so on. From such discussion, we proceed to consider how the installation of a computer laboratory would be evaluated. Clearly, there would need to be some ways of measuring the effects of such an installation on students' motivation and language achievement. How this might be done would have to be considered. For instance, to find out how popular the laboratory would be, an easily administered record of student use would need to be maintained.

Once clarification of such basic issues has been reached, responsibilities need to be assigned (if they have not already emerged in the earlier discussion) and relevant information would need to be gathered. This would involve finding out what the experience of other schools has been with computer installations, surveying the available hardware and software in terms of price, flexibility, types of software, and so on. Such information would be essential in order to make an informed choice of equipment and material – or even to make a decision not to go ahead with the installation of a computer laboratory because of expense, the limitations of the available software or the unsuccessful experience of schools which have already gone down this particular path.

If, however, a decision is made to install a computer laboratory, the planning stage will follow and this will involve specifying, among other things, who does what and when and within a budget. Since a room will be required for the laboratory, various changes and the installation of appropriate wiring and plugs will be required, plus the purchase of furniture, the computer equipment itself and software with which to operate it. Someone will have to be responsible for co-ordinating all this and making sure that, for instance, when the equipment arrives, it is checked and the Bursar or financial controller is informed, so that the bills are paid. Someone, presumably the same person (or persons), will also have to supervise the actual installation and testing of the equipment. And, once the laboratory is ready, the designated person will have to set up a system for using it. This will include a system for booking the laboratory, storing and retrieving software, trouble-shooting and maintenance, not to mention monitoring the use of the facilities so as to be able to evaluate its success in relation to objectives.

This account smooths over the variations which characterize projects, and anyone involved with management will find that their work brings encounters with views, attitudes, beliefs and practices very different from their own, as a result of which, management decisions can rarely, if ever, be effected in a pure and unmodified form. It is highly unlikely, for instance, that the setting up of a computer laboratory in our example above will be accomplished in a way which matches completely the aims of the people who agreed to go ahead and install such a facility in the first place.

It is also important to keep in mind that even when management operates on a democratic and consultative basis, it is up to the management to ensure that resources are available and that they are used economically and effectively. Members of an organization are entitled to expect that there will be support – both in morale and material terms – for agreed actions. In a school, such support will involve not only making material resources available, but also making appropriate administrative or organizational provision as well as giving people that most crucial of resources – time. Thus, the management of a school will be under an obligation to ensure, for instance, that timetables and classes are organized in accordance with new requirements – an important consideration if, for instance, the use of an expensive installation like a computer laboratory is to be optimized. Furthermore, the management is responsible for seeing that paid time is made available for in-service training of teachers – or, if not paid time, teachers are given remission for time spent on courses. Thus, if teachers are expected to spend time learning how to use the new computer laboratory, it may be necessary to make extra paid time available for this purpose. Even when proposals for innovation come from teachers themselves, support from the management hierarchy is needed if the changes are to be implemented successfully.

Finally, it is only management who, in general, has an overview of the situation. Individuals may be concerned with their own areas of responsibility, but management will be looking at the complete picture. Such an overview is vital if adequate monitoring of progress on a project is to be maintained. The manager cannot and should not, once a project has been set under way, then assume that all will be well. It is necessary to maintain contact with all levels and stages, particularly as it is unlikely that any one other individual within the organization will have assumed such a role. Monitoring does not mean interfering; nor should the manager stand back from intervening if problems arise. Such a role is not an easy one to carry out successfully, but the members of an organization are entitled to expect that management will maintain a grasp of events for the wellbeing of all concerned.

Conclusion

School management is concerned with practical results in the context of the school. Considerations of theories and models may, therefore, be given low priority. Yet, as we have seen, no theory or model of management provides a complete explanation of how an organization works. Even less, no theory of management can give a fool-proof recipe for success. This is because management is, above all else, concerned with people, who are themselves so diverse and varied that no two combinations of individuals will ever be the same. Schools are highly complex organizations, containing as they do two sets of people – staff and students – who interact in diverse ways. Added to these is the relationship of the school to its social, economic and political environment. The school is, therefore, subject to internal and external forces which greatly complicate the manager's job.

All managers have a responsibility to be as well-informed as possible and to provide adequate resources and facilities for carrying out agreed aims. Part of this responsibility is some understanding of organizations, how they work, and how they are structured. Such understanding should help the manager in processes like setting objectives, planning, controlling and delegating. Above all, the successful manager will attempt to involve everyone in the organization in decision-making, planning and implementation, and will provide the conditions in which such a participative style of management and action will flourish.

Follow-up activities

1 What are the legal requirements which a school as an *institution* has to fulfil in your country? Does a school have to be registered? If so, with which authority? What financial requirements must be fulfilled? What regular and repeated requirements have to be met, such as the auditing of accounts?
2 What are the goals which your school has been set up to achieve? Are these goals expressed in a written document or a mission statement? To what extent are these goals known by and agreed upon by staff and students?
3 Do the functions and activities carried out by your school actually match its goals? Survey in detail the services which your school provides under these headings, to which more can be added.

Language courses
- aims
- content
- methods

Social activities
- excursions
- visits
- films
- discos
- concerts

Accommodation
- with host families
- other

Travel
- to and from the school from the home country
- to and from the school and local accommodation

Publications
 publication of own materials
 sale of own or other materials

Catering
 snack bar
 morning and afternoon tea or coffee
 lunch
 other meals

Counselling

Other services
 sports facilities
 making contacts for students with other bodies
 other (specify)

What proportion of the school's time, resources and effort is put into these? What proportion of the income from fees is derived from these? How does the proportion of organizational input into these activities match the goals of the organization? Are you, in short, in the business which you thought you were in? How could a mismatch between activities/services and goals lead to problems?

4 How do you and your colleagues regard the clients of your school? How does your view of the clients influence the goals or the organization and relationships between staff and between staff and clients?

5 Take each of the three sets of needs – task, group and personal – and discuss them with colleagues with regard to your own school. What task, group and personal needs exist within your organization? Is there a mismatch between them, e.g. is there a mismatch between personal needs on the one hand and group and task needs on the other? Or between task needs and group needs? How could such a mismatch be resolved?

6 Take Handy's characterization of organizational cultures, and apply them to your own organization. Do you find a mixture of cultures? Are there any conflict points within your organization which might be explained by such internal cultural differences? Is there a mismatch between the culture of the school (or sections within the school) and the functions which the school sets out to serve?

7 Draw an organizational chart of your school. Refer to the organizational chart in Chapter 5. Your diagram should indicate
 titles and functions
 the flow of communication (both hierarchically and laterally).

To what extent does your chart reveal
 specialization (i.e. one person, one job or area of responsibility)
 areas of authority
 areas of responsibility

span of control (i.e. how many people are supervised by any one person in the organization)
balance (i.e. is there a match between units and areas of responsibility)?

The chart may reveal illogicalities or difficulties. For instance, you may find that one position/role has too much responsibility. Or you may find that an individual unit has become too large in relation to the functions it performs. A language school which has as many administrators as teachers may well be over-staffed on the former.

8 The spreading of decision-making and the devolution of power is a democratic ideal. However, it can result in unexpected political action. For instance, a teacher development group supported by management could become a political group which sees itself as being in opposition to management; or specialized units can compete for power and resources within the organization. Review any such cases within your own or another organization and relate the events to the four management models described in section 1.3. Consider how any problems which resulted could have been avoided.

9 Organizations are affected by factors in the environment, and schools are especially subject to such influences. Recall the effects of environmental changes on your school and analyse the response of individuals and the organization to these influences. Examples of such influences are changes in the number, age, or type of students because of economic or demographic changes. In some countries, because of economic conditions, fewer adults are enrolling for language courses. One response of schools has been to recruit more younger learners. This change in student recruitment has repercussions on the organization, and it is the effects of such changes that you should consider.

10 Consider what the effects on individuals within an organization will be if a 'Theory X' or a 'Theory Y' management style is adopted.

11 In schools, the distinction between 'management', 'administration' and 'operations' sections is often blurred, and different functions may be assumed by one and the same people as part of their jobs. Review the distribution of roles and functions within your own school. To what extent is there overlap? To what extent is there specialization by functions? Could the running of the organization be improved by more or less demarcation between 'management' and 'operations'?

12 Review job descriptions in your organization. If there aren't any, draw them up (see Chapter 2). Compare the job descriptions with your organizational chart (activity 7). Are there 'holes' in the range of jobs covered by the descriptions, such that some organizational functions are no one's responsibility? Is there overlap, so that more than one person is responsible for a particular area? With your colleagues, discuss how such gaps and overlaps can be dealt with. One outcome will probably be rewriting job descriptions to match the revised scheme agreed upon.

13 For this task, you will need to work with a group of your colleagues, preferably as many of them as possible, but certainly with no fewer than six. Set a team task to be carried out within a specified time. Examples are given below. It is up to the team to define objectives and end product, that is, to agree upon a viable reason for doing the task. One person should observe the group carrying out the task, and should lead a process review at the end in which the group goes back over how they carried out the task. Such reflection by the group on what happened is most important to ensure that the activities are a learning experience. Questions to guide observation and to ask in the process review are:

Were objectives discussed and agreed upon?

- Were success criteria agreed before the team went into action on the task itself?
- Were the talents of group members drawn upon?
- Were all members of the team given a chance to participate and contribute?
- Did some contributions get lost?
- Were there any 'critical incidents' which either moved the team forward or hindered its task performance?
- How did the group manage itself in the allocation of roles and distribution of work?
- How did the group establish a set of norms to guide its work?
- Was a plan of action prepared, with responsibilities and deadlines clearly specified?

Such exercises can be revealing and at times disturbing. It is very important to attempt to create an open atmosphere in which discussion of the group processes can be carried out, without resorting to criticism or praise of individual personalities in the group.

Below are examples of tasks (each, with the exception of the first one listed, to take 30 to 40 minutes, depending on the setting). The process review will take as much time again. It is suggested that the first task be used initially to get people thinking about how to plan a project, and that one or two of the other tasks are done as part of a staff development programme.

- Describe the separate stages that should be followed in carrying out a work project of any kind.
- Survey the fire appliances in the building.
- Survey the communication facilities in the school.
- Survey the sports coverage in a representative selection of the day's newspapers.
- Survey the car parking facilities in the immediate environment of the school.

More extensive tasks, such as the following, can be used for further work of this kind.

> Make a map of an interesting and enjoyable 15-minute walk starting at the school. The end result is to be a map indicating 10 or more features likely to be of interest to those who take the walk. A further success criterion is that the whole group completes the walk within the time allocated for the task.

The understandings about group organization and dynamics, not to mention planning and organizing, which emerge from such tasks (which are safely removed from directly professional or pedagogical activities) can be applied to the actual work of the school.

2 STAFF SELECTION

Aims

The aims of this chapter are:

1 to consider job descriptions.
2 to look at how the qualities needed to do jobs are established.
3 to review the selection process from advertising through to appointment.
4 to outline procedures that might be used for the induction of new employees.

Introduction

For a small English language teaching school with a stable staff that expands only temporarily at peak periods, the question of selection of staff might appear to be of little relevance. And yet underlying any selection process, no matter how limited, should be a careful definition of why the post is necessary and what duties are needed to undertake it efficiently. In turn such job descriptions, as will be seen, may serve as the basis not just for selection, but for performance reviews, training and promotion (Chapter 3).

The careful selection of a candidate for a well-defined vacancy can be of great benefit to a school. Not only is a good fit between person and job ensured, but the procedure itself demonstrates an openness and integrity that can improve morale. And the more successfully the person chosen is trained to take on the duties of the post through an induction programme, the more productive and content will be the individual, the Principal and the school generally.

The starting point for any selection process is, however, not the job description but the question 'Is the job really necessary?' It is usually assumed that if somebody leaves and there is a vacancy, it must be filled. It may be the case that the duties can be redistributed or that the post is not really necessary. However, assuming that this critical question has been asked and answered positively, the starting point of any selection process has to be either the creation of a new job description or the revision of a current one.

2.1 Job descriptions

All organizations attempt to define the group of tasks that constitute specific jobs. If this were not done, both management control and the employee's work would be arbitrary and there could be no guarantee that all were working to the same end. In a larger company, individual job descriptions should be seen as fitting into departmental plans and they in turn will link into the objectives of the company. At school level a job description will fulfil this function for the Principal, while for the individual it will indicate the tasks to be accomplished and even perhaps the priorities to be accorded to individual tasks.

At its basic level, then, a job description becomes a concise description of normal duties as well as a clear statement of occasional subsidiary activities. It also serves broader purposes, such as:

1 To define tasks undertaken by individuals.
2 As a basis for recruitment, selection and transfer.
3 To indicate the performance levels expected.
4 To identify training needs.
5 To help with transfer and promotion.
6 To establish the grades of jobs.
7 For location and equipment design.

2.1.1 Form of job descriptions

Any number of formats is possible as Figure 2.1 (opposite), together with the job descriptions in the Activities section at the end of this chapter, reveal. It is probably necessary to consider at least some of the following features.

TITLE OF JOB

At first sight it might appear pedantic to single out for attention the title of the job, but often this indicates the salary band and implies the duties to be undertaken and provides comparisons with other schools.

LOCATION

Since travel to the place of work may well be an important element for a candidate to consider, it is important that the location as well as any anticipated travel is mentioned here.

PRINCIPAL OBJECTIVES OF THE JOB

This should be an accurate but brief statement of the overall aims of the job. It is often easier to do this once the rest of the form has been completed.

JOB DESCRIPTION FORM

1. Title of job: Department:

Location:

Current postholder: Postcode:

2. Principal objectives of the job:

3. Responsibilities (indicate briefly the number and titles of posts, and the resources directly managed):

3.1 Personnel: 3.2 Financial:

3.3 Organization chart (Overleaf please show in chart form how this post relates to the unit and department)

4. Main duties of the post	Approx % of time	Skills required

5. Special conditions of service (e.g. regular overtime, shift work, unsocial hours, special allowances etc.)

Figure 2.1 A job description form

MAIN DUTIES AND SKILLS EMPLOYED

The objectives defined above can only be achieved through undertaking specific tasks. It is helpful at this stage to define up to about ten of these tasks along with the skills needed to ensure that the tasks are accomplished effectively.

RESOURCES MANAGED

It should be quite clear how many staff are managed and what job titles they have. Equally, responsibility for equipment and the extent of the budget handled should be indicated.

WORKING ENVIRONMENT

If you are advertising a post internally, staff will have a clear idea of the working environment but for outside recruitment it is helpful to indicate the facilities, such as the staff canteen, which the school has to offer.

TRAINING REQUIREMENTS

Some posts require further training on appointment and this should be noted so that the appointees are clear about what is expected of them and what the school will provide. In order to avoid future misunderstandings, the regular in-service courses that are a normal part of some schools' activities should be indicated.

CAREER OPPORTUNITIES

Travel is often something that can be cited as a bonus of the job in many language schools in Britain. In larger schools there are opportunities for promotion to advisory posts or to posts on the administrative side. Overseas work, discounts on lessons for staff and family may be other unexpected benefits.

ANY SPECIAL TERMS AND CONDITIONS OF SERVICE

It may be worth putting down the hours of work particularly if these are unusual. It is easy enough for instance to forget the amount of Saturday or after-hours work that is required and this needs to be mentioned in the advertisement and at the interview. Subject to the local labour laws, a probationary period, which will enable both sides to review and determine the suitability of the appointment, should be mentioned here.

2.1.2 Collecting information

If a well-designed job description form is invaluable, the method of completion is equally important. While a job description form can be completed simply by the present postholder or by the line manager, perhaps the most effective way is to talk it through together. In this way communication (see Chapter 4) at all levels is improved. A line manager completing a job description form should do the following:

1 If post is already filled, ask present postholder to complete in pencil.
2 Discuss fully, asking questions to get full details.
3 Agree the final version and have typed.
4 Retain one copy and send a copy to postholder or to new occupant.
5 Revise annually or on change of duties or incumbent.

This is the simplest way of establishing the duties of a job, but if this is felt not to be precise enough then the occupant can be asked to keep a running diary over say two months to illustrate the range of duties undertaken. One school established the exact nature of the tasks undertaken by secretaries at registration time by getting the staff to agree to a video being made of the whole process. This proved an invaluable input to training and to job definition. If all else fails there are firms of specialized job analysts who can be asked to come in and examine jobs in fine detail, but most schools will find a well-discussed job description form is the most effective method.

2.1.3 Defining the qualities required

The job description form stands as a guide to tasks and performance. It should also lead the manager to define the qualities of the person needed to fill the post. It is to this aspect that we shall now turn. Some companies incorporate the person specification, as it is called, into the same form as the job description, while others prefer to have it separate. The person specification only needs to be written when the jobholder changes, while the job description will need to be regularly updated.

There is no set format for a person specification form but many companies follow the Alec Rodger 7-point plan which covers the following points:

1 *Physical* i.e. age, health, fitness
2 *Attainments* i.e. education, experience
3 *Intelligence* i.e. what qualities required
4 *Aptitudes* i.e. writing skills, mechanical etc.
5 *Interests* i.e. literature, travel, sport etc.
6 *Disposition* i.e. cheerful, calm, self-reliant etc.
7 *Circumstances* i.e. weekend working, travel, car driving etc.

Against each of these points essential and desirable features are marked. Other organizations, and this would probably include language schools, find this too much information and go for something simpler, as illustrated in Figure 2.2 opposite.

Here the emphasis is on experience and qualifications, though it is important to note that the skills requested as essential should arise naturally from the job description. The temptation is to overemphasize the essential quality of certain qualifications. It is, for instance, salutary to consider carefully whether the Director of Studies really does need an MA in Linguistics rather than an RSA Diploma plus considerable experience.

Once the job description and the person specification arising from it are completed, recruitment for the post can begin in earnest.

2.1.4 Advertising a post

Many posts in schools are advertised internally before outside recruitment is initiated, and that may be a matter of agreed policy within the school. This is undoubtedly preferable to the inefficient – and unfair – advertising of the post by word of mouth. Moreover, an advertisement can help future recruitment by enhancing the school's image whilst the mere fact of advertising a post, rather than appointing on the basis of friendship and length of service, can signal to the staff a more open management style.

Whether recruitment is to be internal or external, the intention is to produce a reasonable field of candidates suitable for the job and motivated to accept it. Consideration of the following features may help when drawing up an advertisement.

CONTENT	STYLE	LANGUAGE
A description of the job	Factual	Simple
Qualifications needed	Unambiguous	Clear
Experience required	Attractive	
Location	Eye-catching	
Fringe benefits		
Salary		

The initial consideration should be the content of the advertisement and here the job description is invaluable. It is also worth trying to think yourself into the mind of the prospective candidates. What do they already know about the school and the job? What else will they want to know before applying? In some countries and in some situations where there is a certain delicacy about discussing money the remuneration to be offered may have to be left to the interview stage. Ideally the pay should be in the advertisement since it is a

PERSON SPECIFICATION FORM

1. Name of last jobholder:

Reason for vacancy:

N.B. Are you satisfied the post is still required?

2. Skills, qualifications and experience.

In line with the company's Equal Opportunities Policy, skills, qualifications and experience required should be those genuinely needed to do the job. Please refer to the Job Description form when completing this section.

2.1 *Skills*

Essential: *Desirable:*

2.2 *Qualifications*

Essential: *Desirable:*

2.3 *Experience*

Essential: *Desirable:*

3. Other factors

Required:

Would disqualify:

4. Training

4.1 *What training will be given on the job?*

4.2 *What other training is recommended?*

Signed:

Position:

Figure 2.2 A *person specification form*

waste of everybody's time to have applications based on a lack of information. Indeed because it is increasingly being realized that selection is a two-way process, many organizations are now inviting candidates to phone for further details or to visit informally.

When specifying the qualifications and experience required, the person specification should be drawn upon to indicate what is desirable and what essential. Great care should be taken too that no discrimination, however implicit, is contained in the advertisement. While not all countries have the codes against discrimination on grounds of race, colour, sex or disability that Britain does, the sensibilities of the country must be considered when advertisements are being framed.

In deciding where to place the advertisement, not only the cost but also the readership of the newspaper or magazine will need to be taken into account. It may also be that the readership varies for particular days of the week. In addition, it is worth remembering that if you advertise too regularly it will suggest that the school cannot keep its staff. Better to wait and advertise several posts at once or stress that such vacancies are due to expansion or due to promotion of the previous holder, both of which suggest that a career may be enhanced by working in the school.

2.1.5 Selecting on paper

Opinion is divided as to whether it is better to have a standard application form or to ask for a short curriculum vitae or statement of suitability for the post. In some countries it is necessary to state the length of the curriculum vitae required since there is a tradition of everything being included, down to the last minor course attended. An application form assures standard information on each candidate and can allow for individual differences by an open-ended question, perhaps on the reasons for applying for the job, at the end of the form.

Faced with a number of applicants, all of whom seem on the surface to be equally well qualified, it is tempting to interview everybody. In fact the costs, with often more than one interviewer involved, are such that it is rarely economic or practical to interview more than four to six people. A rigorous paper sift will normally ensure that the numbers interviewed are not excessive. The occasional exception may occur if, for instance, you are introducing the process of open advertising and clear selection procedures into an organization. Interviewing all applicants will demonstrate commitment to the new procedures.

A paper selection, like an interview, has to be made against the job description and the person specification derived from it. A form like the following can be of help in whittling down a large field.

SHORTLISTING MATRIX List in these columns the skills, qualifications and experience thought to be essential (E) and desirable (D)					
Names of candidates	E Experience of financial management	E Postgraduate qualification in EFL	D Knowledge of computer applications in ELT and management	D Experience of writing materials for adult students	Comments
B. Smith	✓	✓	✗	✓	Not available till January
T. Jones	✗	✓	✓	✓	

Figure 2.3 A shortlisting form

2.2 Selection interviewing

At this final stage, given the cost and the average 45 minutes spent on each candidate, it makes sense to interview no more than a maximum of six people.

Everybody at some stage has done some interviewing and nearly everybody considers that they are reasonable at it. There are two principal reasons for this feeling. One is that interviewing a candidate puts the interviewer in a flattering position of power, and the other is that there are no objective standards for assessing the effectiveness or otherwise of the choice made.

The procedure can be made more objective by bearing in mind throughout that the purpose of the selection interview is to collect information, not feelings, about the applicant. This information is necessary in order to match what the candidates have to offer with what the job requires, as defined in the job description and person specification forms. Considering the importance of the interview, for the candidate as well as for the school, should also help to give recruiters the necessary detachment.

The first of many decisions to be made is whether to have a single person or a group interviewing. There are occasions when individually interviewing candidates can be effective. This applies particularly when some kind of preliminary screening is necessary or when for various reasons, which might well include cost, a panel cannot be justified. Panel interviews, though they are more expensive and can be cumbersome to arrange, do help to eliminate individual bias and do appear to the candidate to be fairer. Moreover, such a panel can represent all shades of consumer interest and ensure that questions cover all relevant topics and not just a limited range. And yet to have too many people on the panel forces the candidate to give a lecture. In practice, three interviewers seems to be a good number, with one person acting quite clearly as the chairperson. Such a system also enables new interviewers to learn the skills of interviewing in a more sheltered environment than that of a one-to-one situation.

Whatever system is adopted, the planning is almost as important as the actual interview.

2.2.1 Preparation

A few days in advance of the interview the panel should have been sent:

1 The job description.
2 The person specification.
3 Conditions of service.
4 Applications.
5 If possible, references (though these can be taken up later).

For the members of the panel, the documents received can be daunting and too detailed for use at the interview. They will need to make notes and even write specific questions. Some organizations assist this process by issuing a form to enable interview notes to be made in advance and used as a working document at interview. One example is given on the facing page.

It is not only the interviewers who need to be prepared. The candidates should have been sent details of the post, including conditions of service, at the time they expressed interest. When it is decided that somebody is to be interviewed, the time and place of interview will be sent; and in addition further information about the school may be included.

By having magazines and brochures available for waiting candidates to read, schools can not only help momentarily distract attention from the tension of the situation, but also provide further information on job and organization. Any travel expenses to be reimbursed should be sorted out at this stage.

The room where the interview is to be held should receive as much attention as a classroom being prepared for groupwork. Normally a table is useful since, though the atmosphere is more relaxed if everybody sits in

POST NAME OF APPLICANT:

Person Specification	Work Experience	Questions	Notes
Essential:			
	Education		
Desirable:			
	Interest		

Conclusion and overall rating	Accept ☐☐☐☐ Reject	Summary of reasons

Figure 2.4 An interview sheet

armchairs, it can be difficult to make notes. The chairs and tables should be set in close proximity – not in eyeball to eyeball contact but not so far away that each side has to shout to be heard. If there is a clock in the room then the table should be set so that it can be seen easily. If not, it is easier to put a watch on the table than attempt to peer at one's wrist while interviewing.

Minor points that may need to be attended to are ashtrays if smoking is allowed, paper for the panel to make notes and water for everyone. Needless to say, all telephone calls to the interview room should be stopped and a 'Do Not Disturb' notice put on the door.

2.2.2 Chairing

The chairperson's role is crucial. A chairperson not only has to guide and control the panel, and plan an approach to the form of questioning and the making of assessments, but must also welcome and set the candidates at ease. Hence a chairperson has to be designated in advance.

Before starting the interview the chairperson will want to discuss with other panel members the qualities to be looked for, distinguishing between essential and desirable as in the person specification, and making sure the procedures are clear to everyone.

There are different ways of organizing a panel interview:

A FREE FOR ALL
Each member of the panel asks questions on any subject.
May be repetitive and confusing for candidate.
Works for a panel that knows each other well.
AREA DISTRIBUTION
Each panel member agrees to take a subject area.
Having asked questions the interviewer passes back to chairperson.

The latter format is the most common and has the advantage of systematically covering all areas, but it can be boring for members once their turn has come and gone. Naturally, such boredom should not reveal itself in the faces of those not questioning. One variation that an alert chairperson can try is for each member to take one subject area but to stop occasionally to allow others to ask questions in the same area.

Whatever system is used the chairperson is usually the link between questioners. In this way he or she is responsible for ensuring timing is adhered to, the pace is lively and that candidates are at ease.

The way the introductions are made can be an important factor in reducing tension. The candidate should be introduced to each person on the panel indicating not only their names but also their role within the organization. Indeed this information can often be sent to the candidates with the letter inviting them for interview or it can be available in the waiting area. Ideally the members of the panel should give a welcoming response.

Pace in interviewing is as important as in teaching and it is very much the chairperson's role to control this. A leisurely calming introduction with the emphasis on the candidate talking is often necessary to get the candidates to unwind. The more probing questions can come later. However, a loquacious, over-confident candidate may need to be firmly controlled. The tone is set by the chairperson who can from the very beginning control the pace of the interview.

At the end of the interview it is the chairperson who has to ask the candidates if there is anything they want to ask or to add. At that stage too the chairperson will indicate when the result of the interview might be available and how it might be communicated. And, after the candidate leaves, there is the leading of the summing-up.

2.2.3 The stages of an interview

Any interview can be seen as progressing through several stages, though in a good interview the flow is such that the changes of emphasis are not overtly marked. The stages are:

1 Introduction of interviewers and settling down remarks.
2 Explaining the form of the interview.
3 Questioning to obtain information.
4 Inviting questions from the candidate.
5 Conclusion.

The timing on such stages is, of course, approximate but it would be reasonable to expect that in a 45 minute interview at least 30 minutes would be concerned with questioning, which is why this area is covered in detail below.

THE INTRODUCTION

Here the chairperson will introduce him- or herself and the members of the panel. It is worth deciding in advance whether to shake hands or not, to avoid that embarrassed fumbling that gets the interview off to a bad start. It is also helpful at this introductory stage to have some bland general remarks to settle the candidate down, provided of course these do not go on too long. This might be called 'British Rail' chat since so often it consists of questions like 'How did you get here?' 'How was the journey?' etc.

EXPLANATION

The length of time the interview is expected to last should be clearly explained and the form of the interview should be outlined. Candidates need to know that they will have a chance to ask questions at a certain stage.

QUESTIONING See 2.2.4 below.

INVITING QUESTIONS FROM THE CANDIDATE

The candidate must be encouraged to ask questions so it is important to leave time for this. It is also helpful to ask at this stage if the candidate feels that there is any relevant area that has not been covered. This prevents the candidates from complaining afterwards that there was no chance to tell the panel about experience which was directly relevant to the job.

THE CONCLUSION

It is important to make sure that the candidates know when and how they will hear the results of the interview and this should compose the bulk of this section. Unsuccessful as well as successful candidates will be informed.

2.2.4 Questioning techniques

The aims of the interview are:

1 to enable an exchange of information to take place
2 to assess the candidates' qualities in relation to the job
3 to enable candidates to feel they have been given a fair chance.

These objectives are more likely to be achieved if the interviewers appreciate that their role is in the main to listen creatively and critically: *creatively* in interpreting what is said and *critically* in weighing it against the person specification.

The questions asked should therefore elicit evidence from the candidates' past experience as to whether they are suitable for the job. The checklist opposite shows how questions may be funnelled by the interviewer from general to specific.

Naturally the direction of the questioning depends upon sensitivity in listening and ability to follow up clues that are offered, but certain general points, summarized below, do lead to good questioning techniques.

1 Open questions like *Who?*, *What?*, *Why?*, *How?* allow a freer response on the candidates' part.
2 Clarifying questions such as *I'm not clear about that. Could you explain in a little more detail?* are important for checking understanding and help probe.
3 Extending questions like *Could you tell me a bit more about that?* and *Could you expand on that?* serve a similar function.

1. Focus on the past rather than the future.

AVOID hypothetical questions like :

What would you do if the teachers went on strike ?

2. Start with general, open questions

USE Wh or general questions like :

Tell me about your work in the Kennet School of English

3. Then use funnelling techniques

MOVE from general to particular e.g.

Tell me about your work.......Describe.......Please outline....

Can you give me an example of..............?

Why..............?

When..............?

What..............?

Who is 'we'..............?

How..............?

FUNNELLING
from assumption to
evidence

Figure 2.5 Checklist for questioning techniques

4 Linking questions like *You mentioned timetabling. What experience have you had of that?* show the interviewer has been listening and they also enable the questioner to move the interview in a new direction.

In contrast the following types of questions, unless followed by an open question like 'Why?', do not reveal much about the candidate and tend to close the interview down.

1 Closed questions like *Did you have responsibility for training teachers?* allow only a *yes* or *no* answer. If followed by an open question they might be used occasionally to establish the facts.
2 Leading questions such as *Are you confident you can do this job?* give a very clear indication of the answer expected so are of little value.
3 Double-barrelled questions like *What was your main aim in that job and how did you achieve it?* can be confusing, and astute candidates will only answer the part of the question they feel like answering.
4 Listing alternatives such as *Which is the most effective form of methodology; structuralist, pragmatic or communicative?* prompts a required answer and again limits communication.

However it has to be remembered that interviews are not just a series of questions and answers but, like ordinary conversation, rely upon paralinguistic gestures to facilitate interaction. If you watch experienced interviewers on video-recordings, it is noticeable that they sit with a look of alert interest and they also nod, say 'um', 'ah', or 'Yes' or use gestures to indicate their involvement and to encourage the speaker to continue. Occasionally a pause for silence may help to draw more from the candidate or a paraphrase of what was said may evoke more comment. Such a summary may not only indicate careful listening but also mark a move into a new subject.

At times the interviewer may have to be quite firm in order to ensure the interview is not taken over by a candidate who wants to steer the interview in his or her chosen direction. Interviewers should be clearly but unobtrusively in command throughout. In addition to covering prepared subject areas, interviewers should listen carefully to store topics that might be pursued at a later stage. Above all the information gleaned during the interview must be set against the criteria for the job.

There is a danger that if one quality is revealed, the interviewer will assume that others must be there too. This is the so-called halo effect. Thus the hard work and intelligence shown by candidates do not automatically mean they are adept at handling human relations – evidence is needed. Just as prejudice or bias needs to be watched for when interviewing, so the reception of one unfavourable piece of information should not mean a condemnation on all counts. Indeed some interviewers recommend looking for 'contrary evidence' at this stage. That is, if all the evidence from the interview suggests a lack of initiative ask questions like 'Can you give me an example of when you had to do something without guidance?' This may reveal a different side of the interviewee and if it does not, the interviewer's impression is confirmed as accurate.

2.2.5 Assessment

The over-riding consideration throughout the interview is the search for the qualities required, but evidence collected is easily forgotten, particularly if a number of candidates are interviewed. For this reason as soon as a candidate leaves the room it is essential to write notes and a summary of conclusions. One example of the kind of assessment sheet that might be used for recording is given in Figure 2.6 overleaf, though many prefer a composite question and recording sheet of the kind shown in Figure 2.4 on page 45.

2.2.6 Supplementing interviews

Some large organizations like to supplement interviews with a personality, intelligence or aptitude test and there are a large number on the market to choose from. If they are used it is probably better not to look at the results until *after* conclusions have been reached at the interview. In that way such tests act as confirmations and checks.

Even if commercially-prepared tests of this type would not be considered by most schools, practical tasks can be used, for instance to test whether a fluent bi-lingual secretary can type efficiently. One large school after a series of accidents and needlessly complicated journeys instituted a driving and navigational test for drivers previously appointed only after an interview.

2.3 The induction of new employees

Having selected the successful candidate, written a letter to offer the appointment and received acceptance then, before the arrival of the new employee, it is a good idea to think of what kind of training will be needed. On pages 64 and 65 of Chapter 3 there is a training profile and a discussion on training that indicates some of the areas that a school might wish to consider for a specific training programme. However, the concern at this stage is to give an introduction not so much to the job as to the school and the procedures used, which will enable the newcomer to be an effective member of staff as quickly as possible. What areas then need to be covered?

In terms of motivation the Principal will wish to spend some time with each new member of staff since this sets the tone for the rest of the induction procedure. A walk round the school and an introduction to as many staff as possible will undoubtedly be followed by a visit to the Personnel Department for registration, letter of appointment, salary and bank details etc.

Name	Post applied for:

Summary:

Strengths	Weaknesses

CONCLUSION: Overall rating: Accept Reject

Summary of reasons:

Signature:

Figure 2.6 An assessment sheet

It is then worth considering whether a mentor needs to be appointed to see the employee unobtrusively through the first week. Many organizations find this good practice and many too have a staff induction manual of some kind wherein the following sorts of topics can be covered:

1 Welcome letter from the Principal.
2 Brief history of the institution.
3 Statutes of the institution if applicable.
4 Organizational structure.
5 Staff names and positions held.
6 Departments' areas of responsibility.
7 Working conditions.
8 Details on holidays, sick-leave, maternity leave etc.
9 Recreational and welfare facilities available.
10 Staff appraisal system.
11 Details of any probationary period.
12 Where to find details of administrative procedures.
13 Where to turn for further advice.
14 Trade union representation.
15 Equal opportunity policy.

The details given will vary from organization to organization and many schools will not feel anything complicated is needed. All new employees do, however, benefit from a readily available body of knowledge about the school and its procedures which they can keep for reference, perhaps through a 'Welcome File' or staff induction manual of the type above.

Conclusion

Whatever method is used in selection, a good school needs to be clear about the nature of the job and the qualities needed to succeed in the post. It is also important that the selection process is carried out as professionally as possible in order to ensure that nearly round pegs are found for round holes. The match cannot always be perfect but it could be more skilfully and thoroughly undertaken than in many institutions at present. A selected candidate, even with a good knowledge of what the job entails, will need induction to ensure maximum effectiveness as quickly as possible in the school. It is this induction process that serves as the starting point for the training and development of staff which is considered in detail in the next chapter.

Follow-up activities

1 Interview one of the people in the school whose job you feel you know least and complete a job description form as if you were looking for a replacement.
2 Look carefully at current job descriptions in the school to see how far they cover the points made in this chapter and consider what improvements can be made.
3 Compare the two job description forms below in terms of their coverage of points you feel are essential.

Figure 2.7 Job description form A

BUILDING SOCIETY

JOB DESCRIPTION REF:

JOB TITLE: JOB HOLDER:

REPORTS TO (TITLE): JOB DESCRIPTION ADVISER:

OFFICE/DEPT: DATE:

1. JOB PURPOSE: (State concisely your job's overall objective)

2. DIMENSIONS: (List (a) Annual income/expenditure amounts directly controlled or indirectly influenced by your job (b) Numbers/categories of total subordinates (c) Any other key statistics relevant to your job)

3. ORGANIZATION CHART: (Show, by job title, your immediate superior, other jobs reporting to the same superior and any staff reporting directly to you. Below the title of each direct subordinate, add a brief statement of job content)

4. PRINCIPAL ACCOUNTABILITIES: (State concisely – in numbered statements and in the form described in the Guide Notes – the principal *end results* expected of your job)

5. JOB CONTEXT: (Describe briefly (a) Role of your Department/Section within the Society and the local environment (b) Relations with other areas of the Society and externally)

6. JOB CONTENT: (Describe briefly – in correspondingly numbered statements – *how* you fulfill each of the Principal Accountabilities of Section 4)

7. RELATIONSHIPS: (List by title those jobs inside or outside the Society with which you have significant working relationships and indicate briefly their nature and purpose)

8. PROBLEM SOLVING: (Describe briefly the most challenging aspects of your job and indicate by example the most complex problems *you* have to solve)

9. DECISION MAKING: (Indicate by example (a) Decisions you can make without reference (b) Your recommendations which are usually accepted (c) Procedures to be followed)

10. JOB KNOWLEDGE, SKILLS & EXPERIENCE: (Identify the acquired expertise needed to perform your job at fully-acceptable level)

11. ADDITIONAL INFORMATION/JOB CHALLENGES: (Note any other significant features of job not already covered. Also summarize key features and greatest challenges of job – now and for the future)

JOB DESCRIPTION AGREED & SIGNED BY:

JOB HOLDER: DATE:

SUPERIOR: DATE:

Figure 2.8 Job description form B

JOB DESCRIPTION	Job Title	Location
Key areas & standards	Department	Date

1 OVERALL PURPOSE

2 POSITION IN ORGANIZATION
Draw an organization chart showing who the job holder reports directly to, what colleagues he has and which people report *directly* to him.

3 Other regular functional contacts:–
(Who do you liaise with *frequently?*)

4 DIMENSIONS OF THE JOB
Your total responsibilities. How many people, value of buildings and machinery, turnover, value added in manufacture, cost budget, etc.

5 LIMITS OF AUTHORITY
To recruit, dismiss, spend money, allocate.

6 KNOWLEDGE & QUALIFICATIONS
State the special knowledge, qualifications and personal attributes that are necessary. If the job is to be done in an acceptable manner:–

a) *essential*

b) *desirable*

7 KEY AREAS
State the broad Key (result) Areas of the job in which you must spend the majority of your time if you are going successfully to achieve your Overall Purpose (i.e. Budgets; Communication and Liaison; Planning & Innovation; Staff Development; Use of Staff, Materials, Equipment; Quality and Costs).

KEY AREA No.	KEY (RESULT) AREAS Simply name the area and write a few words of explanation of what you mean by, for instance: "Communication & Liaison".	STANDARDS OF PERFORMANCE What things will *you do* and *how often* will you do them in order to create the conditions that exist when the job is being done to an *acceptable* level (not ideal). (Usually begins: "When I . . . . . .")

8 MEMBERSHIP OF COMMITTEES
(and other special duties)

9 IMPORTANT CONTACTS OUTSIDE COMPANY

10 SPECIAL ADDITIONAL BACKGROUND NOTES
Highlight here any background or extra information that an Evaluation Committee should consider when evaluating the job.

SIGNED: ....
Immediate Superior Job Holder

4 In order to help their managers write about what they call 'Principal Accountabilities', one company gives the format:

ACTION VERB – OBJECT OF ACTION – END RESULT

and appends the following list of action verbs.

Accumulate
Achieve
Advise
Analyse
Appraise
Approve
Ascertain
Assess
Assist
Authorize

Budget

Check
Compile
Complete
Conduct
Consult
Contact
Contribute
Control
Co-ordinate
Counsel

Design
Determine
Develop

Follow-up
Forecast
Formulate
Fulfil
Furnish

Gather
Give

Help
Hire

Identify
Implement
Improve
Inform
Interview
Inspect
Issue

Keep

Limit

Maintain
Meet
Motivate

Participate

Receive
Recruit
Recommend
Reject
Report
Represent
Review
Research

Safeguard
Search
Secure
See
Seek
Select
Sell
Serve
Service
Set
Specify
Standardize
Store
Structure
Study
Submit
Supply
Survey

Take
Train

Examine this list to see what has been omitted that you might have expected to be in. What are the advantages and disadvantages of such an approach?

5 Take a job description for somebody currently employed in the school and write a person specification as in Figure 2.2, indicating the essential and desirable qualities.

6 How far is the person specification form used here of value to your school? What changes would you like to see made?

7 Look at the last advertisement placed on behalf of the school and try to assess its effectiveness.

8 The two lists below relate to the form and the content of advertisements for jobs. Add any points omitted and then rank in order of importance those points you have and discuss with others.

FORM	CONTENT
Attractive	Financial rewards
Clear	Job description
Brief	Qualifications needed
Detailed	Experience required
Informative	Organizational structure
Accurate	Holidays
Appealing	Pension

9 Examine on video some interviews (if possible record each other) looking particularly at:

1 Funnelling techniques.
2 Open v. closed questions.
3 Non-linguistic gestures.
4 Rapport.
5 Pace.

10 Prepare an observation sheet or checklist for those observing interviewers and interviewees.

11 List pupils you know under 'halo' and 'horns' effect and examine your reasons for placing them in each category.

12 Note down the procedures gone through by your school whenever a vacancy occurs and alongside each note down the person responsible. Can any improvements be made?

13 Using a volunteer, interview in a panel for a suitable post and video. Consider the procedures and techniques afterwards bearing in mind the interviewee's comments on the panel's performance and the above areas of investigation.

14 What should be included in an induction manual for your school? Using the checklist on page 53 note down the headings that should be covered.

15 You need to recruit a new Assistant Director of Studies to look after the teacher-training work at the school. Try to define carefully the essential and desirable qualities for this post and then role-play interviews from interested teachers.

16 The list below indicates how an interview may be broken into separate components. Do you agree with the divisions? After discussion you may care to role-play the micro skills of (a) introduction (b) eliciting (c) concluding the interview.

a) Introduction	1 Put candidates at ease. 2 Outline structure of the interview. 3 Clarify purpose of the interview.
b) Elicitation	4 Obtain information. 5 Clarify. 6 Summarize.
c) Conclusion	7 Give information (terms and conditions). 8 Handle questions. 9 Outline what happens next. 10 Close the interview.

17 Drawing upon your experience either as interviewer or interviewee, consider in terms of the following areas what helps or hinders interviews.
a) Preparation (including room).
b) Non-linguistic gestures.
c) Questioning.
d) Listening.

3 STAFF DEVELOPMENT

Aims

The aims of this chapter are:

1 to consider the role of training in staff development.
2 to examine career planning in schools.
3 to outline types of performance appraisal and career counselling.
4 to examine procedures in the case of discipline and dismissal.

Introduction

Successful organizations are learning organizations, and the potential to learn is present in all who work therein. Staff development is a way of ensuring that people learn and develop and that the organization can grow and respond to a changing environment. Even if people decide to reject the opportunities for professional and personal growth that staff development makes available, they need to know that such possibilities are there. For management, the problem may lie in communicating the opportunities, motivating people to respond and ensuring that the knowledge learnt can be applied within the school.

English language teaching organizations are not alone in having often given little time and money to developing training and career opportunities, the effects of which can be seen in the apparently random way in which teachers are promoted. If salary scales exist, the criteria for moving through the scale may not be clear and can be a source of contention between staff associations and management. Unfortunately, the same situation may also apply to other members of the organization – secretaries, receptionists and technicians. Yet if all staff are able to feel that they can progress within the organization, that criteria for promotion are established and that there is a concern with their development, then morale within the organization should improve.

That means that everyone – Principals, Directors of Studies, teachers and administrative staff – should see that one of their major responsibilities is the growth and development of all people within the organization. In order to achieve this, it will be necessary to have regular reviews of achievements, difficulties and career aspirations. Such discussions should keep in mind training possibilities to enable individuals to develop new skills.

All of these points will be considered in this chapter beginning with the question of training.

3.1 Training

Broadly speaking, any organization will have training needs among staff, as follows:

1 Staff newly appointed from outside the organization.
2 Newly promoted staff.
3 Existing staff.
4 Anybody facing change including those returning to work after a long absence.

The following table indicates the different types of training for each of the above categories of staff and the main sources of information providing a guide to training needs.

Figure 3.1 Training needs

<table>
<tr><th>Staff category</th><th>Type of training</th><th>Source of information</th></tr>
<tr><td>New staff</td><td>Induction training</td><td rowspan="2">Job description and person specification</td></tr>
<tr><td>Newly promoted</td><td>Skills training</td></tr>
<tr><td>Existing staff</td><td>Continuous development</td><td>Self-assessment and changing needs of the organization</td></tr>
<tr><td>Those facing change</td><td>Training for specific needs</td><td>Environment including new methods and equipment</td></tr>
</table>

3.1.1 Induction

When new staff join a school, careful thought should be given to training. Although, as suggested in Chapter 2, an induction manual may be used as part of the initial training for newly recruited staff, it is a good idea to augment the handbook with a personal explanation of salaries, welfare, safety, staff associations, and conditions of employment generally. In fact, the initial induction period can be crucial in setting the tone of the relationship between the individual and the organization, so personal as well as printed sources of information are important.

In addition to any formal induction training many schools have a probationary period. During this time the new staff member may well be guided and informed by a mentor – somebody who knows the routines, materials and customs of the school well.

Where a school has run its own pre-service course it is a good idea to maintain the contact established between tutors and probationers during the initial period of teaching. In one large European school this is done by all probationary teachers being called together centrally for one morning every two weeks during their first term. They then have a chance to discuss common problems with each other and the tutors, who can also at that stage add to the initial training programme. During the second term such meetings are less frequent, and less necessary. At the end of the probationary year in that school, the Assistant Director of Studies makes a decision on whether the probationary period has been successfully completed by each individual after talking to fellow tutors and the school Principal.

The strengths of such a system lie in its continuation of both local and central support, thus ensuring that probationary teachers are not left floundering. Furthermore, weaknesses can be identified and dealt with and if probationers are found to be unsuited to teaching they can be advised of this before they or the organization have made an irrevocable commitment. In this way both the individual and the organization can benefit and teaching standards can be maintained – an important consideration for the success of any school.

Unfortunately, even when a school has a similar period of probation for non-academic staff, it rarely considers their training in as much detail as it does for teachers. Yet schools rely on the marketing skills, counselling abilities and behind-the-scenes expertise of such staff and an effective induction programme can be of great benefit to this important section of the organization. Not least among its benefits can be a reduction in staff turnover.

For all new staff, whether academic or administrative, a job description (Chapter 2) is a valuable part of the induction process. It is important that new staff carefully study their job description, discuss it with their line manager, reach an understanding of what the job involves and what training may be necessary.

3.1.2 Newly promoted staff

To design a training programme for newly promoted staff, reference can be made to several sources of information, including the job description, the person specification (Chapter 2) and consultation with the person leaving the job. In addition, the new incumbent may have a very clear idea of their own areas of training need, and the annual assessment should add further details.

Using the details of the job a training profile can be built up for each post in the organization. An example created for a newly appointed Assistant Principal in a branch of a large Cultura in Latin America is shown on page 64 and illustrates the detail involved in writing such a profile.

Figure 3.2 Training profile for Assistant Principal posts

AREA	TIMING	TRAINING AND PURPOSE
1. Branch accounts	Immediate	On-the-job experience in RECEPTION covering daily statistics, control of accounts, despatch to administration, typing accounts, fees, discounts, petty cash, balancing accounts.
2. Statistics	End of first month of term	To learn system of preparation of school general statistics.
3. Students' records	Beginning and end of term	Trainee to join secretaries in checking class registers against card, registering results, removing non-payers, keeping card up to date.
4. Publicity and public relations	From first day	To ensure courses and events are well publicized in the branch and branch is well represented outside. Visit Cultural Dept. Identify responsible secretaries or do advertising personally. Check noticeboards every week.
5. Entrance testing	From first day	To know procedures and reliability of entrance tests. Talk to Principal and DOS. Timetable and plan use of teachers.
6. Probationers	From beginning	1. Prepare classes with probationers. 2. Arrange observation visits. 3. Arrange tutors. 4. Advice on books, lesson planning, resources and students. 5. Vary personal teaching levels each term as well. 6. Jointly observe classes with teachers and DOS. 7. Team teach.
7. Teachers	After first term	1. Individual discussions with teachers on academic and discipline problems. 2. Discussions with Principal.

By attempting to detail the purposes of the training, the Principal can ensure that it is closely related to the job description and individual needs. In addition, the thought and discussion which accompany drawing up such training profiles and the individual training plans subsequently derived assist management and promote communication. It is also important to consider the timing of such training, otherwise it can be concentrated into the initial few months on the new job rather than being a process of continual development.

Any training profile should be carefully worked out and should indicate the steps to be gone through before the job holder is considered to be fully trained. But it should not be seen as a rigid prescription that cannot be changed, especially in the light of evaluation of the training experience.

The training profile is itself one way of assessing training needs. However, such profiles are very detailed. A less detailed approach is to examine those critical incidents that are vital for the success of the job. The list of questions given in the first of the Follow-up activities at the end of this chapter could therefore serve as an alternative way of creating a training profile for an Assistant Principal.

This post illustrates the many management problems faced by teachers when they are promoted. Often teachers are appointed to managerial positions on the grounds that 'a good teacher must be a good manager'. Although, in a broad sense, this is true, Aitken and Handy (1986) point out that being a good classroom manager does not necessarily enable the teacher to grasp the implications of, for example, dealing with adults rather than children for the first time, or of relating to other teachers in a management role, or of dealing with parents as a marketing agent and educational counsellor. Some training in these new roles is important, both before and after appointment, to enable the good classroom manager to become a good educational manager.

Formal training sessions also need to be organized for non-teaching staff whose needs can be revealed through discussion and meetings. It was through such a discussion that one school came to see the value of video as a training medium for secretaries as well as teachers. With the agreement of all concerned, a video recording was made of two secretaries counselling different groups of parents on the most suitable course for their children. The playback and subsequent discussion with all the secretaries in the school revealed some alarming gaps in the flow of academic information to the secretaries, while the over-familiarity of secretaries with their job had led to some awkward mannerisms in dealing with clients. As a result, a jointly agreed training course was set up.

These examples illustrate how important it is for Principals to give careful consideration to training, as summarized in the diagram on the following page.

Figure 3.3 Summary of training needs

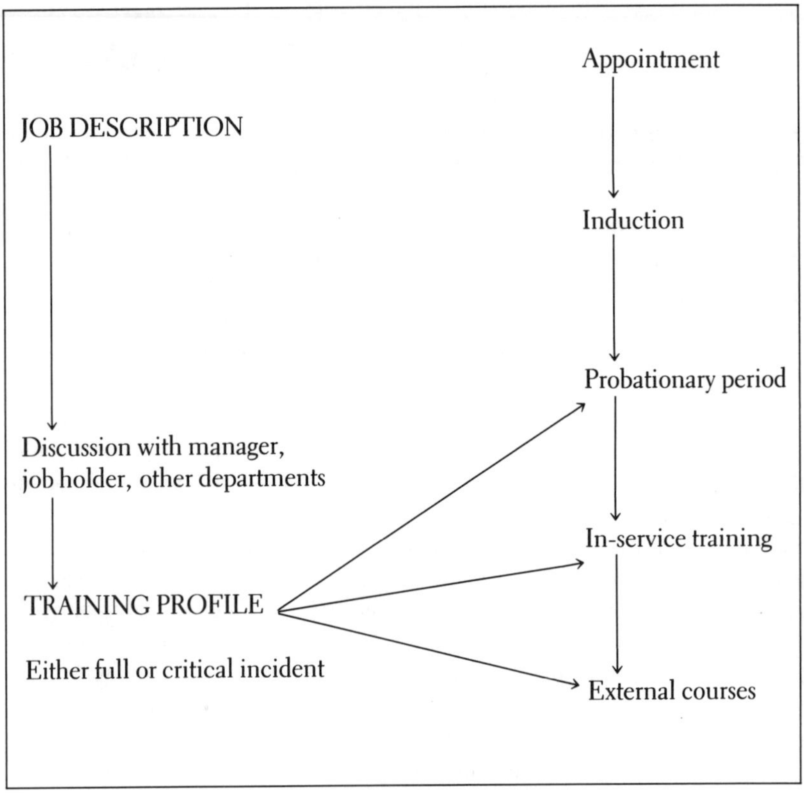

Someone has to be responsible for arranging the training, and this person should have overall responsibility for ensuring that training profiles are drawn up, that on-the-spot training is provided and that information about outside courses is available, since not all training will be provided in-house. In most schools, the Principal can take on this role, or it can be delegated to another senior member of staff. Large organizations may have a Training Manager or Training Officer who is responsible for the training budget, monitoring standards and even for organizing a department to provide training.

3.1.3 Existing staff and changing environments

The best source of information on training will usually be the teachers themselves, especially those who, through membership of a teachers' association, are aware of the possibilities that are available outside the organization. Another important source of information will be performance reviews, discussed below. Such reviews provide a good opportunity for establishing individual training priorities.

A training budget should be established, especially if outside rather than in-house courses are to form a substantial part of the training programme. In the commercial world it is recommended that 2% of the annual turnover be devoted to training. In the case of a school, much of this sum would be spent on external courses and on sending staff to conferences. In dealing with outside training, the procedure below could be followed by the Principal:

1 Establish funds available in budget.
2 Collect information on courses.
3 Identify appropriate courses or conferences for the organization.
4 Select those staff members deserving or needing training.
5 Calculate the approximate cost, including fares and subsistence.
6 Estimate the number of staff to be sent.
7 Ensure fair distribution of those selected between academic and non-academic staff.
8 Hold some money in reserve for the unexpected.
9 Collect individual feedback on courses and conferences. Hold this on file for reference next year.

The above checklist omits, deliberately, two essential steps that need a little more consideration. Firstly, how are outside training opportunities to be advertised and, secondly, how are staff to be selected? If the school really wishes to develop a learning culture, there is much to be said for making sure that everybody is fully informed about the possibilities there are for outside training. It is also important that selection procedures are just and equitable.

In addition to training which is closely related to specific job descriptions and roles, there is another form of training which is concerned with the whole person, as seen in the recent growth of interest in Teacher Development. Such concern can contribute significantly to the growth of harmonious and fulfilling relationships between individual teachers, students and management. And, it hardly needs to be said that what is true for teachers will also be true for all members of the organization, administrative as well as academic.

3.2 Performance reviews

> Performance review is the core of good management if done well. Managers need to be challenged to face up to the outcomes for their department if they continually allow work pressure to get in the way of performance and career discussions with their subordinates. (P. Long)

Such a statement is regularly made regarding industrial concerns, is increasingly being adopted by the Civil Service, but to date has made little impact on schools. It is easy to see why a Principal of a small school who is in everyday contact with his staff and relies on them for continuity and support may be reluctant to undertake performance reviews. However this reluctance may be based on a false assumption of what they are and a failure to recognize the benefits they may bring to both staff and school.

3.2.1 Reasons for reviews

From the individual's point of view a performance review enables him or her to get to know clearly what the job consists of and what standards are expected. It is a chance for encouragement or help, the latter perhaps, as has been seen, in terms of training, changed procedures, or even an altered job description, to ensure a greater use of potential. At such a review factors in the job that appear to be hindering performance can be identified and talked through with the Principal or Director of Studies. The manager concerned should see a performance review as a way of encouraging staff and giving feedback on the work undertaken. That in turn should lead the manager to a clearer understanding of what is involved and, through discussion, how the individual has tackled the job. Equally, sensitively handled by both sides, it should give teachers and non-academic staff the chance to indicate where poor management is inhibiting performance.

Finding ways to improve performance should lead to a consideration of suitable training or even to a reorganization of the tasks undertaken in that particular job. It should also provide more informed decisions on promotion and career development, or on rare occasions provide evidence for disciplinary action. Sometimes it will lead to management reorganization.

Many Principals accept all the above arguments and then point out that reviews take place regularly when members of staff pop in for a coffee or a chat. Such ongoing discussions on the job, the problems experienced and possible solutions are important and are to be encouraged. However something more formal and more regular is being proposed here for all the staff, with clear objectives established and records maintained for future reference. Ideally, such formal reviews would take place every six months, but it is more realistic to envisage them being on a yearly basis.

3.2.2 The form of reviews

Performance reviews usually fall into three types – comparative, absolute, and results-orientated.

COMPARATIVE REVIEWS

In this form of review the performance of the employees relative to each other is measured. Thus the teachers on the establishment could be put in order from strongest to weakest. Another version of this is to decide on a number of performance levels, each of which will contain a pre-defined percentage of the staff. Hence it might be decided the distribution, possibly linked to salary reviews, should be as follows:-

Most successful 10%
Above average 20%
Average 40%
Below average 20%
Least successful 10%

The weakness of this form of assessment is that it is very subjective. One Principal's top teacher could be another's worst. Just as important is the fact that it is very difficult to give individual feedback and encourage development with such a system. The post holder also plays little part in this review except perhaps to argue afterwards that he or she is better than another higher in the ranking order.

ABSOLUTE METHODS

These try to evaluate the performance of an individual by reference to objectively defined standards of performance and not by comparison with others. Hence in a narrative version of this method of evaluation the appraiser describes the individual's strengths, weaknesses and potential as well as making suggestions for improvement.

Another commonly used version of this is the trait or skill rating scale as seen on pages 70 and 71.

Figure 3.4 Profile of teacher qualities

A. *Qualities relating to lesson preparation and presentation*

1	Lesson objectives, subject matter and activities are appropriate, given course aims and learner needs	10	9	8	7	6	5	4	3	2	1	0	Objectives, subject matter and/or activities are unsuitable for achievement of course aims
2	Structure of lessons facilitates what is to be learned	10	9	8	7	6	5	4	3	2	1	0	Lessons lack overall organization and plan
3	Activities display originality, imaginativeness and resourcefulness	10	9	8	7	6	5	4	3	2	1	0	Activities are dull and unimaginative
4	Materials introduced as teaching aids are appropriate for the activities	10	9	8	7	6	5	4	3	2	1	0	Such materials are inappropriate or else non-existent even though necessary
5	Teaching techniques are appropriate to the learning tasks	10	9	8	7	6	5	4	3	2	1	0	Suitable interaction strategies are not introduced or else are used inappropriately
6	Teacher sets high standards and requires that each student gives his/her personal best	10	9	8	7	6	5	4	3	2	1	0	Teacher *either* accepts low standards of work (and conduct) from students *or* sets unrealistically high ones
7	Teacher is responsive to feedback and adjusts content and pace of lessons to student requirements	10	9	8	7	6	5	4	3	2	1	0	Teacher *either* adheres rigidly to predetermined plans irrespective of how students are responding *or* allows lesson objectives to be destroyed by intrusion of irrelevant matters
8	Teacher maintains suitable class control	10	9	8	7	6	5	4	3	2	1	0	Teacher *either* loses class control *or* assumes an authoritarian role
9	Teacher adopts a positive attitude to what is being taught	10	9	8	7	6	5	4	3	2	1	0	Teacher *either* appears uninterested in what is being taught *or* feigns an over-lively, insincere enthusiasm
10	Teacher has a friendly and encouraging manner towards all of his/her students	10	9	8	7	6	5	4	3	2	1	0	Teacher displays *either* a discouraging *or* an over-effusive attitude to some or all of his/her students

B. *Qualities relating to general characteristics of a teacher*

11	Teacher is aware of recent developments in ELT theory and practice, and of their significance	10	9	8	7	6	5	4	3	2	1	0	Teacher is uninformed, misinformed or confused about such developments
12	Teacher is willing to consider new ideas and try out fresh approaches and techniques	10	9	8	7	6	5	4	3	2	1	0	Teacher is *either* opinionated, unwilling to take advice, suspicious of new ideas; *or* has impetuous but short-lived enthusiasms
13	Teacher is capable of evaluating his/her own teaching strategies and making appropriate changes and modifications	10	9	8	7	6	5	4	3	2	1	0	Teacher is incapable of self-evaluation
14	Teacher possesses a breadth of outlook and range of interests which informs his/her teaching with a general richness	10	9	8	7	6	5	4	3	2	1	0	Teacher is limited and confined in outlook so that his/her teaching is generally impoverished
15	Teacher makes every effort to do what he/she knows is expected of him/her professionally	10	9	8	7	6	5	4	3	2	1	0	Teacher cannot be relied upon to do what he/she is expected to
16	Teacher is reasonably self-confident and assured	10	9	8	7	6	5	4	3	2	1	0	Teacher is *either* insecure, diffident, lacking in confidence *or* is over-confident
17	Teacher displays sound judgement and good sense	10	9	8	7	6	5	4	3	2	1	0	Teacher lacks sound judgement and good sense or is erratic in them
18	Teacher is always in sufficient control of his/her feelings in professional situations	10	9	8	7	6	5	4	3	2	1	0	Teacher often loses control of him/herself so that professional performance is affected
19	Teacher has good relations with his/her colleagues	10	9	8	7	6	5	4	3	2	1	0	Teacher is difficult to get on with and may sometimes disturb harmonious staff relations within school
20	Teacher is both willing and competent to help in general ways towards success of school	10	9	8	7	6	5	4	3	2	1	0	Teacher is unwilling to help even when feasible and/or is not competent to help

The difficulties of using such apparently absolute scales are easily seen in the above form. Staff tend to compare themselves in terms of the total number of points gained and despite the appearance of being objective, it is in fact very subjective. It is also a document that encourages a Principal to decide and mark rather than discuss, and thus does little to help the individual concerned.

RESULTS ORIENTATED METHODS

These methods concentrate on specific accomplishments achieved as a result of job performance rather than on behaviour. Thus job performance is viewed as a series of expected results which can be compared to actual performance results. The problem with teaching is that targets are not very easily set. One attempt to overcome this difficulty and yet still remain within the results-orientated framework is shown below and other examples can be seen in the activities section.

Figure 3.5 Yearly review

Procedures for completing the yearly review form

1. The Principal and teacher will together discuss the work done during the year bearing in mind the following points. This is not intended to be an exhaustive list merely a guideline and other areas may well be touched on.

TEACHING:

Choice of activities
Lesson planning
Timing
Creativity/productivity
Achievement of aims
Command of English
Clearness
Resources used
Classroom language
Flexibility
Student assessment

NB Much of the information for discussion under these points will come from reports on lessons seen.

ORGANIZATIONAL SKILLS:

Classroom management
Record maintenance
Organization

PERSONAL QUALITIES:

Rapport
Drive
Willingness to improve
Reliability
Awareness
Potential
Punctuality

TEACHER'S COMMENTS:

Ambitions
Areas of dissatisfaction
Areas of interest
Suggestions

2. After this discussion the Principal and teacher will together fill in the Yearly Review form and both will sign.

2.1 Some principals will wish to do this by writing comments in pencil and altering according to teacher's comments. Others may wish to compose in conjuction with teachers.

2.2 *The most important point on the Yearly Review form is the mutually agreed plan of action which may include courses to be undertaken or points to be reviewed again at a later date.*

3. One copy of the Yearly Review form will be sent to ADOS for Teacher Records, and one will be kept by the Principals. Teachers will have the agreed plan of action written down for future reference.

Yearly Review	Principal	
Name of teacher	Branch	
Date of admission	Levels taught	
Present Grade	Average number of hours	
Date of last promotion	Computer no.	Date

Qualifications (Please note only alterations since last form)		
Strengths in teaching performance		
Weaknesses in teaching performance		
Any other comment by Principal		
Any other comment by teacher		
Plan of Action 1. 2. 3. 4.		
Teacher's signature	Principal's signature	Date

The reasoning behind this approach, which is the most commonly used, is that shared goal setting will gain individual commitment and that managers will also support and provide resources to jointly agreed plans. However a great deal of time and effort is involved in implementing such an approach effectively. Moreover, a detailed job analysis is helpful to establish key areas and job priorities, and it is difficult sometimes to define these in clear reasonable terms.

3.2.3 Procedures for performance reviews

Whatever form of performance review is undertaken, commitment is demanded on the part of both managers and the staff being reviewed. It is important that before attending performance reviews individuals think about what has been achieved in the year and what targets might be set for the future. To help this process, many firms issue a form on the following lines prior to the performance review.

Figure 3.6 Preparation for review

Staff performance, appraisal & development programme

Preparation for review

To ....

From ....

This confirms our arrangements to hold your next appraisal interview
on .... at .... in ....

The purpose of the appraisal is to review your current work performance as an aid to effective working in the coming period and to assist in your further development.

The aim of the interview is to:–

Provide an appraisal of your performance in your job

Determine your training needs

Consider your ambitions

Give you an opportunity to discuss any problems or suggestions you may have that affect your work

In order to obtain maximum benefit from our discussion, it is important you prepare for this meeting because the more you are able to participate the more we will both benefit from it.

The importance of the meeting formally is that we can discuss together your work, agree what can be done to improve your performance in your job and make plans for the development of your career.

I would like you, before the interview, to consider how you would answer the questions listed overleaf. It may help you to make notes to remind you at the interview – they will be for your reference only and you may retain this form afterwards.

1. Have you a clear understanding of the purpose of your job and what is expected of you?

2. How well do you think you have done the job during the period under review?

3. What do you think can be done to help you to improve your performance and prepare you for future advancement:–

(a) by yourself?

(b) by your supervisor/manager?

4. What do you think are your particular strengths and weaknesses?

Are your strengths being utilized to the full in your present job?

Do your weaknesses affect your performance? If they do, what can be done to rectify them?

5. What are your ambitions?

Do you want to develop in your present work or are you interested in work elsewhere in the Company?

6. What are your personal targets for the coming year?

Space for notes:

Figure 3.6 Preparation for review

This makes clear where the interview might go and provides a framework for discussion. Others prefer a less formal approach and ask the individual to arrive at the interview having thought carefully about their achievements and failures in the past year.

Principals or Directors of Studies will also need to prepare for the interview. It is helpful to look at the results achieved since the last review and to define the possible outcomes of the current interview. These should be seen against the overall objectives of the school, and the training framework being established. Consideration must also be given to the management style and whether this has given rise to any difficulties. A checklist of the following type might be usefully run through both before and at the interview:

1. Does each of the main duties contribute to the purpose of the job?
2. Are the levels of performance to be achieved clearly established?
3. Do these duties and levels of performance fit into the overall objectives of the school?
4. Are all the tasks in the school covered by all the duties defined by job holders?
5. Are staff spending too much time on certain activities?
6. Are the resources provided adequate to help staff achieve the necessary results?
7. Do staff know all the resources available?
8. Can any duties be regrouped to ensure a more effective or more balanced workload?
9. Are any duties unnecessary?
10. Is this person capable of carrying out this task to the level of performance required?
    If not, what can I do about it?
    If yes, how can I stretch their ability more?

3.2.4 Performance interviews

Creating the right atmosphere in which the interviewee feels at ease and able to participate freely is crucial. A sympathetic manner is important and time must be allowed for settling down and 'breaking the ice'. Initially it may help to summarize the purpose of the interview so that everyone is clear as to what can be expected. The job description or developments since the previous performance review can be a good starting point for the discussion. This might include comment on what action was agreed last time, any training received and the way the job has evolved over the year. As always it is the use of open questions that ensures this is a two-way discussion. At this stage it should be possible to agree the important points to be discussed in greater depth.

The main part of a performance review might well be summarized by the acronym SWOP:

S Strengths W Weaknesses O Opportunities P Problems

STRENGTHS

Full use should be made of this opportunity for both parties to comment favourably on what has been achieved during the year. The staff member being reviewed should be encouraged to describe and comment on strengths and successes. A useful question to open this session may be 'What has given you most satisfaction in your work this year?' The reply can then be built on.

WEAKNESSES

Great care needs to be taken here that after an opening question like 'What sort of difficulties did you face with the new course?' an unending catalogue of woes is not produced. Reasons for weaknesses need to be explored and positive actions to improve matters should be agreed by both assessor and assessee. Options available might include training, altering duties, adopting a different management style or even a change of job.

OPPORTUNITIES

What changes or events are likely to occur in the school during the next six months or year that can be used to develop the potential of the member of staff? What are the ambitions of the person concerned? How far do these integrate with organizational priorities? Would a teacher for instance, be interested in attending a Teacher Development weekend and then leading a training session in the school on return?

PROBLEMS

Look first at those problems that have been satisfactorily overcome and then talk through any that remain. It may well be that this section has been covered under 'strengths' and 'weaknesses' but a return to the subjects at this stage may not come amiss as they can serve to reinforce the lessons and objectives agreed earlier in the discussion.

By the end of the interview it should be possible to define objectives for the next six months or year. The formal definition of an objective is 'a statement of something to be achieved to a pre-determined level of quantity/quality within a specified time'. The qualifications are important since without due care objectives may well be only a vague declaration of intent. 'To improve performance of the receptionists' signifies little whereas 'Within six months to have reviewed the duties of both receptionists' is exact and time-bound.

Objectives when agreed by the job holder and the reviewer should be written down and held on file. A copy should be sent to the job holder.

In general the performance review needs the following interlocking skills and the jigsaw is not always easy to complete.

Figure 3.7 Performance review skills

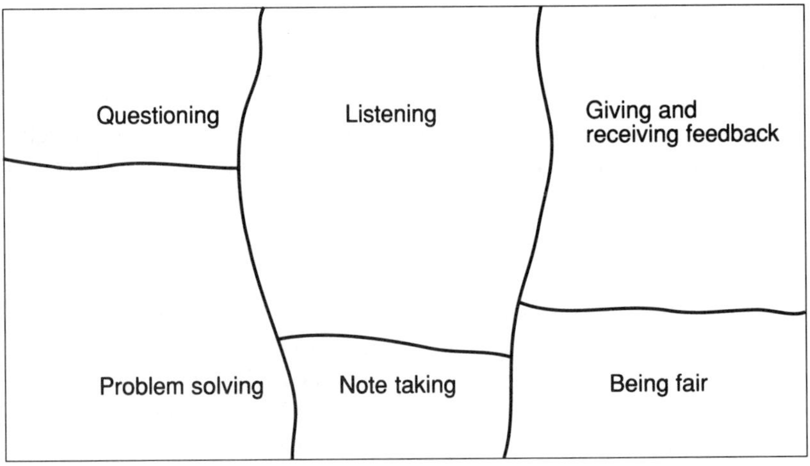

In this interview the positive should be emphasized wherever possible whilst at the same time self-criticism is encouraged. The interviewee should do most of the talking, though it may be necessary to draw to the interviewee's attention the fact that certain aspects of performance do not reach expected standards. This should be done clearly to avoid ambiguity about what is being said, sensitively and with plenty of opportunity for the other point of view to be expressed. It is worth remembering that performance often depends on areas of responsibility and the failure of a job holder to achieve something may in part be due to the poor management of the person conducting the review.

As is implied above, plenty of time has to be allowed for such interviews to be effective and for all areas of performance to be explored. In addition, and this is a point that has been stressed with reference to selection interviewing, such discussions are more fruitful if they are collaborative. This can be suggested by the room layout as much as anything else. For instance, many people find that chairs set at 45 degrees to a small table encourage discussion more than talking across a large desk.

Many organizations have performance review forms which are filled in and signed by the reporting manager. Space is left, as illustrated in Figure 3.5, for the assessee to comment. In addition, there is often a countersigner who will give a written comment on performance and will broadly ensure that the original review was fair and in line with agreed reporting standards. In schools where Principals and Directors of Studies are in everyday contact with staff and where the management team is often small, such countersignatories might be considered unnecessary. Larger colleges however may choose to adopt the idea.

The reporting circle therefore looks like this:

Figure 3.8 The reporting circle

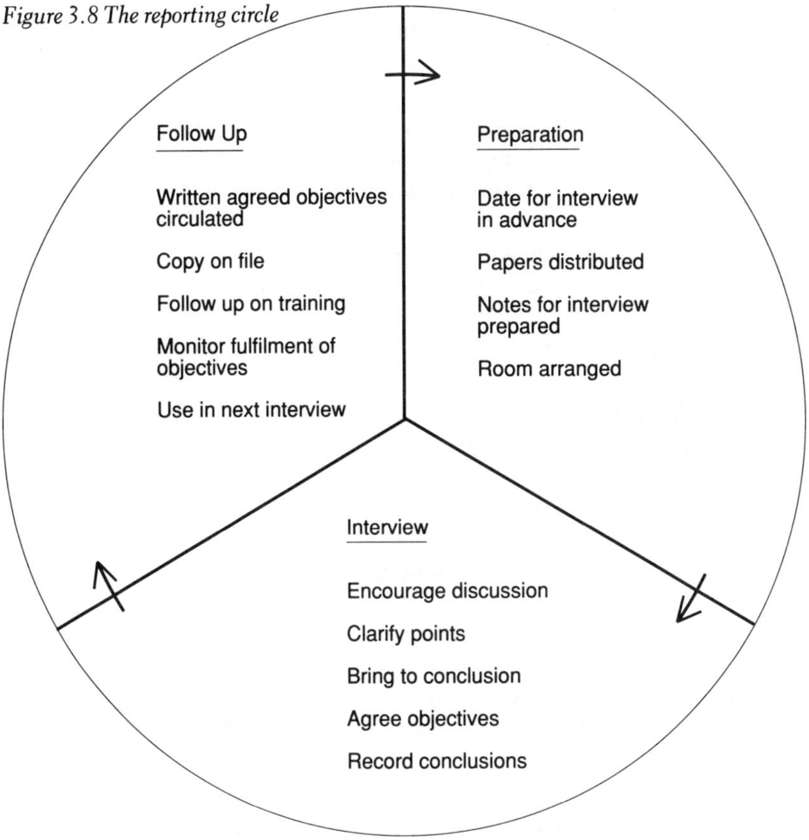

Whilst this performance review system is important, it should not be seen as an annual exercise. Good management practices need to be maintained at all times. Excellence requires praise whenever it occurs and in the same way weakness may need to be pointed out and help given when needed rather than waiting for a formal performance review to take place. Good Principals will always consider the effects of their and the management team's style and decisions on the staff. Finally, if an employee is allowed to under-perform regularly, the problem lies in the management.

3.2.5 Lesson observation

Lesson observation is considered here only in the context of performance reviews since for teachers performance in the classroom is of paramount importance. Lesson observation is therefore one of the major inputs for any performance review for a teacher but quite often such observation is not easily accepted, particularly if it is being introduced at a time of change or economic stringency.

The reasons for having lesson observation may include the following:

1 To encourage high standards of teaching by ensuring
  – materials are interesting, appropriate for the level and effectively used
  – aids are used appropriately
  – classrooms are well equipped, clean, attractive and comfortable.
2 To assist teaching performance in the classroom by
  – creating a relaxed but professional relationship between observer and observed that will
    a lead to the free exchange of ideas on materials and methods
    b enable plans to be formulated for the career development of the teacher
  – assessing the effectiveness of teacher training and planning future courses.
3 To assess the standards attained by students by
  – observing classroom performance.

But to state these aims is not to gain acceptance. Like many of the management strategies being suggested, it is necessary for all teachers and academic managers to be involved from the outset in discussing, for example:

1 The reasons for lesson observation.
2 The form it should take.
3 The frequency of such observation.
4 Checklists on what might occur before, during and after observation.

Best of all is when the aim of each observation is defined not by the observer but by the teacher and relates to an area of improvement the teacher wishes to work on. That kind of cooperation depends on good, clear communication and an acceptance from both teachers and academic managers of the reasons for and the difficulties likely to occur from lesson observation and performance appraisal. Inevitably, many of the suggestions made above for the conduct of performance review interviews will apply to discussions both before and after a lesson has been observed.

3.3 Career planning

Although individuals undertake training in order to be more fulfilled, and more aware of their skills and how to use them, such training also needs to be seen in terms of career progression both from the school's and the individual's point of view. In an earlier chapter it was suggested that the manager should 'maintain and develop resources', and one of the major resources, as well as being the major cost, in any school is the staff. Hence the need for staff development through training.

Any such training provided or paid for when staff attend outside agencies must be recorded. Since training in specific areas may be crucial at certain stages in a school's development it is vital that an ongoing record is maintained. The individual also will want such a record kept for future references that may be requested and so that, for example, criteria for promotion can be set against training undertaken. Computerization of personnel records in larger schools may simplify matters.

One major reason for keeping such information may be to select on qualifications or experience for promotion to a higher grade.

3.3.1 Scales

The problems with salary scales revolve around the elements to be taken into account. Should promotion be related to performance, length of time in the job, qualifications or experience?

At a micro level when the scales for academic staff are considered, such questions as the following will arise:

1 How does the hourly rate between grades compare?
2 Should an experienced teacher be earning more than a newly appointed Assistant Principal? If so, what incentive is there for a teacher to apply for promotion?
3 Is the difference between each scale worthwhile?
4 Should the differences between scales be published? e.g. 'There will be a 20% difference between Scale A and Scale B and a 30% difference between B and C'.
5 Are there too many scales? Each school must decide on the right number but it is worth noting that any attempt to lessen the number of scales can be an expensive business since payments cannot normally be reduced and scales will therefore have to be confluted upwards.
6 Will supervisory or text writing duties count for promotion in grades?
7 Above all, are the criteria for promotion known?

Each school will have different requirements as to the number of grades and the differential. What will be common is the need for accepted criteria to be seen to be fairly applied.

3.3.2 Criteria for promotion

One approach, widely used in schools, is to base promotion on a combination of the following factors:

1 Length of time working in school.
2 Qualifications.
3 Performance in school based on classroom observation and other factors.

The first two elements may well make for a better teacher or receptionist, but there is an increasing emphasis on performance being judged and considered when promotion is decided upon. This is a contentious subject and there will be many points of view, but below is illustrated for discussion purposes a possible set of performance criteria for promotion within three scales in a school where the majority of the teachers are hourly employed and non-native speakers of English:

Figure 3.9 Performance-orientated scale for promotion

SCALE A: Satisfactory completion of the probationary year as defined by the college Principal. Teacher's own level of English at Proficiency or above. Has the ability to teach competently in at least two levels as defined below.

SCALE B: By virtue of previous knowledge and regular attendance on courses of teacher development has sufficient knowledge of the language methodology and culture to teach at three or more levels. In addition the teacher offers at least 16 hours a week service.

SCALE C: Has the ability to take on a large number of academic responsibilities of a more supervisory nature such as giving assistance to probationary teachers, preparing materials, or pre-service or in-service teacher training. Offers at least 16 hours a week to the school.

Eight levels of teaching (i.e. Junior Basic, Teenager Basic and Intermediate etc.) are envisaged in the school as below:

	Basic	Intermediate	FCE	Post FCE	Proficiency
Junior					
Teenager					
Adult					

Notice that where a school has a large number of part-time staff, boosting the number of hours required to be worked may well cut administrative costs and create a more stable staff. In addition, there may be occasions when the offer of one-off bonuses, paid for the acquisition of additional qualifications, may promote interest in such study.

The above example is only one example of performance-orientated criteria for teachers' promotion. Whatever criteria are selected for promotion, staff should be involved in establishing the parameters and should be informed of their existence. In addition opportunities should be offered for discussion with management as to why promotion has or has not been awarded.

3.3.3 Establishing scales

As was indicated earlier, scales need to have a good percentage differential between them if promotion with increased responsibility is to be attractive to staff. Indeed setting scales at the right levels is generally one of the most taxing problems faced by Principals. This is especially so where there is high staff mobility or an inflationary economy. Unfortunately 'What can we afford?' often has to give way to or at least be influenced by 'What is the going market rate?' The market rate as perceived by staff may not be the complete picture though, and the other factors the Principal may need to take into account might include:

holidays
number of weeks paid in the year
additional payments – for working after certain hours
substitution
Saturday work
training courses
cultural events

Given these caveats, an informal outside marker system can be established by consultation with other comparable schools, provided that all can agree that the release of such information on salaries paid is of general benefit. In Britain schools often refer to the scales for teachers in state schools or colleges of further education, but in many countries these may offer too low a base for comparison. Advertisements serve to indicate the going rate while local management consultancy firms may produce marker comparisons. The last two may be particularly useful when setting rates for non-academic staff.

Getting the scales right and ensuring that promotion criteria are known are only part of management responsibility. Attention needs to be given to performance appraisal as has been seen and career counselling may be necessary as a result of considering all these factors.

3.4 Career counselling

A good manager will be encouraging his staff to think about promotion even if this leads to a greater staff turnover than would be ideal. Many individuals, too, will want to discuss their career aspirations with the Principal or appropriate academic manager. A caring organization concerned to extract the full potential of its employees will therefore try to ensure that career counselling happens on a regular basis. Although much of this will be done on an informal basis there must also be a place for regular, more formal reviews and discussion on promotion aspects.

It can be seen from the performance review forms used in the activities at the end of this chapter that some employers use the performance review to assess the suitability of the employee for promotion. To a large extent this seems logical but discussion on promotion should not obscure the main purpose of the review – to set performance goals for the coming year. Given the often limited promotion possibilities within schools, Principals may well choose to put performance and career reviews together.

3.5 Discipline

Performance reviews have been considered so far in the light of setting objectives for the coming period and in relation to promotion and salary scales. On occasions the standard of performance may be such that disciplinary measures are called for. The term 'discipline' usually conjures up the idea of punishment, and yet discipline is concerned with improvement, with instruction and training. It is for this reason that it has to be considered in the context of performance reviews since some form of disciplinary action may be necessary when a gap opens up between required conduct or performance in a job and the actual behaviour.

Poor performance should not be left until the annual performance review. It needs to be addressed as soon as possible. Often an informal interview is sufficient to clear up the difficulty but if the problem persists it may be necessary to go to a formal disciplinary procedure, which is why it is worth all establishments setting up a disciplinary code agreed between staff, management and unions. Unfortunately a tactic frequently employed is to transfer a person who is performing inadequately from one job to another and this helps neither the individual nor the organization. Indeed it often stores up further problems. Both informal and formal approaches to discipline are considered below.

3.5.1 Informal disciplinary interviews

Such interviews are really concerned with the gap between expected and actual performance and how this might be eliminated. Hence before the interview the Principal will need to:

1 Check the facts relating to the person's performance (e.g. job descriptions, sickness and absence records, correspondence, evidence from other staff if appropriate).
2 Check the facts relating to the school (e.g. rules and procedures, job description, training given, meetings when regulations are discussed).

With the help of this information the interview can be tackled and really falls into three parts as follows:

1 INTRODUCTION – ESTABLISH THE GAP

1 State the problem clearly.
2 Be specific.
3 Discuss relevant regulations.
4 Both come to an agreement on the gap.

2 EXPLORE THE GAP

At this stage the manager conducting the interview should be asking open questions and listening attentively to the answers. The areas likely to be covered are:
1 What were the problems encountered?
2 Why did they arise?
3 How can help be given to overcome the difficulties?

3 CONCLUSION – ELIMINATE THE GAP

At this stage it should be possible to:
1 Restate the problem areas.
2 Agree targets together with the assistance to be given.
3 Fix a review date.
4 Jointly make a plan.

After the interview the Principal should record clearly the agreed action noting particularly the review date and training to be given. A copy should be sent to the staff member concerned. Thereafter, performance should be monitored against the agreed targets so that by the end of the review period there should be clear evidence of improvement.

3.5.2 Formal disciplinary interviews

Most disciplinary problems end at this stage. The required improvement in performance takes place and everything returns to normal. However, sometimes further and more formal disciplinary action is called for, and then it is necessary to have a code which has been agreed on by the school in consultation with the staff association. Written standards, clearly established and notified to all staff are the basis of discipline in an organization.

'Fair, reasonable and just' are the watchwords in such cases, and procedures for discipline and dismissal should be written down, in accordance with local labour law and circulated amongst members of staff. If a staff association exists then such procedures will ideally have been discussed and agreed upon at one of the regular meetings of the management-staff committee. If all this seems bureaucratic for small schools, it is worth noting that staff morale can be undermined by what appears to be a series of arbitrary discipline cases or dismissals. In the long term the school may suffer heavy fines and/or industrial action unless procedures are established.

The grounds for starting disciplinary cases will vary depending on the labour laws of the country and these should be carefully checked before any action is taken. In Britain formal discipline cases can be broadly divided into the following categories:

Inefficiency – Incompetence
Continual absence without certification
Misconduct – Breaking the regulations of the organization
Unreasonable refusal to carry out legitimate instructions
Neglect of duty
Violence
Criminal activity (if relevant to job)

The last two categories are often labelled gross misconduct and can, unlike the other categories, result, in certain circumstances, in immediate dismissal.

The procedures for tackling disciplinary cases are likely to include the following steps.

Figure 3.10 Disciplinary procedures

Informal oral warning in interview

STOP

Interview + formal written warning

STOP

A trial period

STOP

Perhaps a new line manager

STOP

Dismissal interview

Appeals procedure

The importance of an honest and reliable written record of performance may seem obvious but is often neglected. It is not always easy, but managers do need to be honest in their performance appraisals if they are to avoid future difficulties.

Written records of disciplinary interviews, except in the informal cases, need to be kept on file in case there are appeals and to allow for a judgement to be made on reasonable evidence. There may be a case for destroying such records after 2–3 years since the aim of disciplinary proceedings is to reform not to permanently brand a member of staff as incompetent or troublesome.

3.6 Dismissal

Sadly not all disciplinary cases are resolved successfully and even an exemplary manager may occasionally have to dismiss a poor teacher or an incompetent non-academic member of staff.

There may also be times when a contraction in trade means that staff have to be asked to leave who would not normally be considered as discipline cases. It is just as important that the criteria for redundancy as for discipline are clear, widely known and closely adhered to. In some cases early retirement may be an option to explore.

Any individual dismissals or reductions in staff numbers are of interest to the staff associations, and Principals will need to ensure they are kept fully informed on what is happening.

When considering the actual dismissal interview the words of Macbeth come most readily to mind 'If it were done when 'tis done, then 'twere well it were done quickly'. Presumably all the options will have been explored, reasons for actions understood and advice offered. At this stage open questions are for once not the order of the day. By being brief, calm and to the point a great deal of anger and distress for everybody may be prevented. Equally the choice of the time of day and even day of the week for such interviews may lessen or heighten the emotions involved.

Witnesses may be necessary for both sides including representatives from staff associations. The attention of the employee should at this stage be drawn to the appeals mechanism if one exists. Much will depend on the ethos of the country, but there are sound reasons for the establishment of such an appeals mechanism. Appeals are usually heard either by the board of governors of the school or a specially selected sub-committee.

Once again written records must be carefully preserved and steps taken to adhere to local labour laws.

Conclusion

From training to dismissal is not a route that most employers follow, but, as was stated earlier, school management is concerned with practical results – academic, financial and cultural – in the context of the school. Ideally training, career planning and performance reviews will lead to staff development and promotion, either internally or externally. Sometimes, however, the management of a school is a more difficult process than many would believe it to be at the time of their promotion. The morale and productivity of the school may call for a firmness of decision-making, together with a clarity of communication with all concerned, that is difficult to hold in balance. It is that vital communication aspect that will be explored in the next chapter.

Follow-up activities

1 The following are fairly typical events at a school:
   1 A teacher telephones to say that she will be absent. Her class starts in an hour.
   2 Statistics need to be sent urgently to the administrator and there is a mistake somewhere.
   3 Your new OHP screen has been delivered but is the wrong size.
   4 A teacher wants to see you and change her classes. She is in a hurry because she has to pick up her children from school.
   5 Phone call from Accounts Dept. They want your secretary to find a copy of a receipt immediately. They are insistent and your secretary is getting very upset.
   6 The lock on the back door of the school is not working properly. The caretaker tells you it can't be repaired today and the door will be left open tonight.
   7 A student wants to talk to you in private. She won't say why but has obviously been crying.
   8 There's a difference in your daily intake between receipts and cash. You must deposit the money in the bank by 2 p.m. Your head secretary is annoyed.
   9 A group of students want to see you to complain about a teacher.
   10 Your secretary must send details of substitutions and extra hours worked by the teachers to Personnel Dept., and you have to check all the details before signing the paper.
   11 An irate father has arrived to complain about a teacher.

   Add any other typical problems you can add from your own experience and then, imagining you are the Principal, arrange the above in order of priority to be dealt with.

   What does this suggest about the training of the management team in a large school?

2 Try to create a training profile for two non-academic members of staff.
3 Examine the training recommendations contained in your job description. With colleagues in similar jobs try to build up a profile of training divided in to a) necessary and b) desirable.

4 List the external courses and seminars attended by staff members last year and compare with the number to be sent this year. Look carefully too at the advertising of such scholarships and the criteria for acceptance. What could be done to improve matters?

5 A teacher who may be coming to work at your school is being shown around. Make a checklist of points he/she might want to consider under the following headings:

Surroundings
Academic
People
Administration
Pupils
A/V aids
Other

What does this suggest might be included in the training plans of a school Principal?

6 Consider the scales established in your school for non-academic members of staff. How could they be improved? Are comparisons possible with outside organizations?

7 What are the percentage differences between each of the teacher scales in your school? What is the percentage of teachers on each scale? Do the numbers suggest any revision is necessary?

8 In Figure 3.9 an example is given of a performance-orientated scale. Discuss the advantages and disadvantages of such a form compared to your school's criteria for promotion.

9 Use the following brief questionnaire as a basis for group discussion.

How often is staff performance reported on?
How often do career interviews take place?
Which of the following are agreed each year?

Job title
Main purpose of job
Main duties
The way a performance is evaluated
Resources held

Is it assessed whether the objectives have been achieved?

10 How far should personal qualities such as the following be assessed in a performance review?

1 Acceptance of responsibility
2 Judgement
3 Ability to produce constructive ideas
4 Drive and determination
5 Reliability

6 Adaptability
7 Perseverance

Are there others you would add?

11 Below is a list of certain aspects of performance. Which of these appear, or should appear, on the form used in your school?

Work activity
planning
output
quality

Working relationships
staff
parents
children

Management
of staff
of self
of resources

Knowledge/Skills
application of knowledge
application of skills
professional development

Communication
oral
written

12 How far do the following statements help you to understand the main purpose of a job?

1 Clerical support in the reception area.
2 To ensure students are placed in suitable accommodation.
3 Overall responsibility for all aspects of technical resources.
4 To provide an effective and official service to the public within the constraints laid down by the Principal.
5 Teach students at all levels.

Note down five to ten sentences that express the main purposes of your job and compare with each other.

13 Note down five examples of non-verbal signals you would not like to see used in a performance review.

14 Examine the following quotations made by employees after performance interviews. What remedial action is necessary?

1 *I was really annoyed to be 20 minutes late. His secretary had given me the wrong time.*
2 *Towards the end of the interview she looked at her watch.*
3 *We had to change rooms halfway through because a class arrived.*
4 *He couldn't remember what we'd agreed last time.*
5 *When I mentioned teaching at that level she said there were plenty of others before me in that particular queue.*
6 *Well it was all right but she seemed rather remote and impersonal behind her desk.*

7 *He rarely stopped talking and jumped from one subject to another.*
8 *She seemed to have expected me to prepare some notes.*
9 *I'm not quite sure what happens next.*

15 Comment on the strengths and weaknesses of the performance review form below.

Figure 3.11 Performance review form

SECTION 1 – MAJOR APPRAISAL

1. Is there an up-to-date Job Description?
   If 'No' what action will be taken?

2. What have been the main achievements since the last appraisal?

3. What has been done less than satisfactorily during the period? Were there any factors that hindered the achievement of satisfactory results?

4. If difficulties were experienced, what action points have been agreed for the coming year to enable objectives to be achieved and performance to improve
   a) by the employee

   b) by the supervisor/company

SECTION 1 – CONTINUED

5. Does the employee have aspirations beyond the present position?
   If 'Yes', are these realistic in the light of past and present performance?

   What, if any, action is required to help the employee develop further skills and knowledge relevant to the present post and what career development action is necessary to prepare him/her for possible future appointments?

6. Overall performance rating

	OUTSTANDING	Superior work of an exceptionally high standard.
	VERY GOOD	Work is highly satisfactory. Regularly displays initiative and strives for improvements.
	GOOD	Work is very competently handled. Major tasks satisfactorily completed.
	AT STANDARD	Performance satisfactorily meets normal Company requirements.
	BELOW STANDARD	Work sometimes fails to meet acceptable standards. Has some notable weaknesses.
	TOO EARLY TO ASSESS	Employee is new to this post or the Company. Full review planned at next appraisal.

7. Comments of countersigning second level manager

Signature ....

8. Comments of employee

Signature .... Supervisor's signature ....
Date ....

SECTION 2 RECORD OF MAJOR JOB OBJECTIVES FOR PERIOD .... TO		
Major objectives	Key milestones including expected results	Results achieved

Figure 3.11 Performance review form

16 Examine the procedures established in your school for discipline cases. How might they be improved?

17 *Discipline case study*
Read the briefs below, decide on roles and names and then give a disciplinary interview. It may be helpful for one or two people to act as observers and/or for a video recording to be made.

Principal's brief
Your chief receptionist has spoken to you informally about one of the receptionists on several occasions since her timekeeping is notoriously bad and her attitude to her work is casual. During the past few weeks this lateness seems to have increased, particularly after lunch, and on three occasions in the last two weeks the lunch break has been extended from one hour to two hours without permission. As a result important work has not been finished that should have been and others in the office have complained about having to do extra.

Receptionist's brief
Over the last year your interest in your job has lessened, partly because you feel the chief receptionist is always giving you the mindless tasks when you feel capable of tackling bigger things. Besides, you had been working in the school for two years before the chief receptionist came. Above all though what has taken your attention away from work has been your mother who lives by herself not far from the school and who is becoming increasingly frail. You have been going round to her house every lunch hour to cook a meal for her and recently you've also had to do quite a lot of the housework because the helper she had in the house has left.

18 Prepare a description of a disciplinary case omitting the outcome. If a real case is likely to cause embarrassment in the group then try to make one up. Then role-play the person being disciplined with somebody else taking the part of interviewer. Again it may be useful to have one or two people observing and/or a video recording. What should the observers be looking for? Discuss the techniques afterwards in the light of points made in this chapter.

19 What are the labour laws in your country relating to dismissals? Should any more be done to ensure that they are widely known in the school?

20 Who has the power to dismiss staff in the school? At what levels? What compensation might need to be paid? To whom can an appeal be made? Consider also what grounds there are for dismissal from the institution and how far you agree with these.

4 COMMUNICATION IN SCHOOLS

Aims

The aims of this chapter are:

1 to outline and examine the various types of everyday communication in schools.
2 to look at the procedures for dealing with individual and group grievances.
3 to consider health and safety needs in schools.
4 to examine why staff associations might be established and how they work with management.

Introduction

To operate effectively every organization depends upon a four-way flow of information. Downwards communication enables decisions taken by managers to be put into effect by staff and ensures that this is done in a consistent and coordinated fashion. Handled properly, it may stimulate a greater commitment from staff and hence a better service to students. Upward communication may equally enhance everybody's sense of participation in the school while providing management with the necessary information for decision-making. It can also act as a valuable safety valve and facilitate downward communication. Lateral communication operates in a third dimension and this may help to bind groups together as well as divide them. Finally, outward communication links the school with the external world.

Previous chapters have indicated that procedures for conducting performance reviews, for instance, or establishing job descriptions need to be set up but it is clear that the manner in which such tasks are undertaken may in itself repay attention. Thus, a performance review conducted by an aggressive manager may not only adversely affect performance but also hinder communication with staff at all levels. Management style then is an important element in the creation and execution of procedures. Underlying the suggestions that follow in the chapter for handling meetings, establishing agenda and dealing with staff associations and individual grievances is the strong feeling that the process is often as important as the product. It may be, for instance, that an imperfect job description form that has been fully talked through with teachers and non-academic staff is more likely to be successful than a more exact, but imposed, form.

4.1 Oral communication

Schools, like most organizations, make use of varied forms of oral communication. The figure below attempts to summarize and indicate the direction of the message.

Figure 4.1 Oral communication

FORM	DIRECTION			
	Up	Down	Lateral	To Public
Grapevine	×	×	×	×
One-to-one	×	×	×	×
Staff meetings	×	×		
Departmental meetings	×	×		
Interdepartmental	×	×		
Informal groups	×	×	×	
Telephone	×	×	×	

4.1.1 The grapevine

This is usually seen by managers as constituting the greatest problem in ensuring good communication, but it can also be viewed as symptomatic of the quality of the communications strategy operating in the school. Rumours are bound to occur but if members of staff are continually worried and in small groups discussing problems, real or imaginary, then something must be wrong with the other forms of communication that are being used. Equally it must be remembered that students and parents, the paying customers, become aware of rumours and a school may need to act quickly and clearly to dispel misinformation. This is usually achieved by written communication direct to adult students or parents, since the oral message in such situations can be, unwittingly but greatly, distorted.

4.1.2 Meetings

Schools are not generally as plagued with meetings as commercial organizations since a large percentage of the staff is at any one time in the classroom. However, the reluctance of Principals to hold meetings and of staff to attend them may be based on a fundamental misapprehension of what meetings might achieve and how they might be organized. Like most management tools a meeting needs to be thought through beforehand and the questions listed on the next page may prove a useful initial stimulus to this process:

Why have a meeting?
Who should attend?
What needs to be prepared?
What needs to be done as a follow-up?

The first question may appear simplistic but there is a tendency for meetings to become established practice, just handed on from one Principal to the next. The cry of 'We always meet on Fridays at 10' begs the question of whether there are other means of achieving the same ends. Valid reasons for holding meetings might be:

decision-making
communication
negotiation
ideas generation
team building
consultation

The form of the meeting may vary with the purpose. Thus the generation of ideas might be better achieved by a small group brainstorming prior to an official meeting rather than in a large meeting.

Indeed preparation for a meeting is vital and one necessary aspect of this is the collection of information and its circulation along with the agenda well in advance of the meeting. Such preparation time will assist informed discussion, though as not all participants will have read the papers in advance a brief oral summary may be necessary. What form should an agenda take? Compare the following:

Figure 4.2 Agendas A and B

A	B
Could we please meet on Friday 21st August at 9.30 in Room 5 to discuss:	Meeting 28/8 9.30 Room 5 AGENDA
1 Food – should we sell at school?	1 Parking.
2 Fire drill – reports on practice.	2 Discounts.
3 F.C.E. – pass rate and reasons for.	3 Teacher training course.
4 New materials for Upper Intermediate – already circulated.	4 Video.
5 A.O.B.	5 Drama competition.

The inclusion of Any Other Business (A.O.B.) provides the chance for upwards communication on matters of concern, though ideally all participants will have been asked beforehand for items for the agenda and A.O.B. should consist only of minor addenda. If major issues are raised at this stage then they should be carried over to the next meeting to allow for sufficient discussion time. Secondly, short subject references as in Agenda B are acceptable providing everybody understands what is being referred to, but occasionally it may be necessary as in Agenda A to supplement these with a few notes. Finally it is wise not to expect to cover too many points in a meeting; ten items are probably the maximum to aim at when discussion is involved.

Of course the number of points covered depends to a large extent on the preparation done by the chairperson. This will include:

1 Appointing a secretary – preferably somebody who will not become too passionately involved in the questions under discussion.
2 Preparing the room. As is so often the case communication is aided by a circle or horseshoe formation.
3 Managing the agenda. It is usually better to consider easy items at the beginning of the meeting including any action to be taken as a result of the minutes of the last meeting, to discuss difficult items in the middle, and to place non-controversial items at the end.
4 Mentally allocating time to each item on the agenda. Meetings cost money and should not be allowed to go on for too long. It is wise to think about the agenda beforehand, considering the following questions:

What are the objectives of the meeting?
What are the essential points to be covered?
What information and experience do members bring?
What are the conclusions likely to be on each item and what follow-up will be suggested?

4.1.3 The management of meetings

Chairing a meeting means ensuring that each point on the agenda is fully discussed and that all participants have the chance to speak, though not excessively. The strain on the chairperson who not only has to ensure orderly discussion but also monitor the time available is immense. It helps to start promptly, even if not everybody is present and to make this regular practice in order to educate latecomers. Speakers should be listened to carefully, should be stopped from going on too long and should take turns in speaking. In addition, and just as important, is what is happening to the non-speakers and this greatly increases the difficulty of the chairperson's job. The astute chairperson, though, knows the name and likely role of each participant. Effectively the following are key questions throughout the meeting:

What is the speaker implying as well as saying?
What is the speaker feeling?
What are the others feeling?

As the last question suggests, the chairperson is not only concentrating on the agenda but also identifying members who are silently expressing anger, dissent, boredom, confusion etc. It takes a sensitive touch to know when it is right to allow these feelings to be expressed and when they should be disregarded. When conflict arises, as it inevitably will, the chairperson should, as always, remain neutral and listen. If this is not possible then it is worth considering handing over the chair, if only temporarily.

In cases of conflict it is helpful to insist on views being aired. Some people find it advantageous to have a whiteboard or flipchart available in cases of conflict so that advantages and disadvantages can be listed. Discussion of personalities should be avoided and statements should be backed by facts. Try to summarize the arguments with impartiality and then conclude the discussion. Avoid repeating the same points again in detail, but the conclusions reached should be emphasized and noted.

Figure 4.3 A checklist for chairing

1 Prepare thoroughly.
2 Arrive in good time.
3 Consider the room layout.
4 Get to know newcomers before meeting.
5 Get administrative and routine matters out of the way early.
6 Stifle any secondary meetings.
7 Bring newcomers into the discussion early on.
8 Listen carefully.
9 Stop people who wander from the point or anticipate later items.
10 Ensure all views get a fair hearing.
11 Don't forget coffee and tea at the appropriate points.
12 Summarize occasionally, particularly in long or complicated discussions.
13 Try for a consensus when you feel it might be possible. If it is not then summarize differences clearly.
14 Be polite no matter how provoked.
15 Do not be afraid of firmly closing discussion at the appropriate time.

If things are too controversial or the discussion is obviously not getting anywhere, then it may be worth postponing the discussion to the next meeting so that a different strategy may be adopted. Firmness but openness accompanied by sensitivity to speaker and listeners are the aims of the good chairperson. In order to achieve these, the chairperson must listen to, permit and follow the discussion whilst never allowing subjects to be run together nor permitting two or three subsidiary discussions to take place at the same time.

Much of this control will come by means of eye contact. A contribution can be elicited, another ignored and another cut short simply by looking in the right direction. Other points to be borne in mind are the need for good manners at all times, the value of humour to defuse a tense situation and the observance of time constraints.

And if this seems too daunting a prospect do not forget there is much to be said for rotating the chairing of meetings, provided that all those members of staff chosen have the ability to learn the art of running a meeting.

4.1.4 Minutes

The chosen secretary will have kept accurate notes of the meeting which will be typed up and distributed as soon as possible to all staffrooms or even to all individual members of staff. Many Principals like to check these minutes before distribution to ensure that they constitute an accurate record and contain no references likely to provoke dissension.

One other way of disseminating the conclusions of meetings is that of *team briefing* or, as it is sometimes called, 'the cascade effect'. Very common in industry, this is basically an oral briefing on the results of the meeting given by each level of management. Thus, after a discussion among several school Principals who are part of a chain of schools, each Principal might brief his or her senior teachers who would in turn talk to the teachers. The difficulty with this method is that the message can sometimes become distorted, and so if it is used, a copy of the minutes of the meeting displayed prominently in the staffroom may be a useful adjunct.

Action notes, as in the following example, are a useful alternative to full minutes, particularly where smaller, less formal meetings are concerned.

Figure 4.4 Action notes

Meeting of 17th May

ACTION

1 DOS to draw up a list of teachers able to teach on summer course by end of June.
2 DOS to check examination scripts prepared for mock FCE.
3 Ass. Principal to arrange lunch for marking panel on 6th June.
4 Administrator to report back to June meeting on bathroom costs.
5 Principal to check fire drill notices clearly displayed.

The references in this section have been to staff meetings but many of the points made apply with equal validity to departmental and interdepartmental meetings.

4.2 Written communication

Written communication, like oral communication, takes on a variety of forms.

Figure 4.5 Written communication

FORM	DIRECTION			
	Up	Down	Lateral	To Public
Official memos	×	×		
Letters	×	×	×	×
Newsletters	×	×		×
Noticeboards	×	×	×	×
Booklets		×		×
Suggestions book	×			
Questionnaires	×	×	×	×
Administrative manual		×		
Electronic (fax, telex, electronic mail etc.)	×	×	×	×

4.2.1 Memos and letters

All schools have headed notepaper for letters but not all systematize the official exchanges between members of the institution. Notes from Bursar and Principal, for example, must be filed thereafter so need a coded reference. It may be that formal memorandum pads with reference numbers are useful and labour-saving devices, not merely the mark of a bureaucracy.

4.2.2 Newsletters

Some large schools find that a newsletter written once a term by the Principal to all members of staff or by the Director of Studies to all academic staff, is a useful way of making everybody feel they are in touch. This does enable managers to pass on main points of information, but it is a channel for purely downward communication and some schools therefore prefer to have something more akin to a staff magazine where everybody has the chance to express their ideas. Such a publication needs a good editor if it is to provide a regular review of important issues, convey information and not degenerate into a forum for individual complaints.

4.2.3 Noticeboards

These often seem to be the most neglected aspect of a school but, as any teacher who has attended a school for interview knows, they often reveal more than any letter or brochure. Equally they are revealing to parents and students keen to discover whether the school is suitable for them. The majority of noticeboards convey messages from managers to staff or staff to students, but many schools have successfully instituted student noticeboards where students can advertise books or articles for sale, and display notices of parties, theatre tickets etc.

Whatever form of noticeboard the school has there is a very good case for appointing one person, preferably somebody with visual flair, to work alongside the Principal to review noticeboards once a week in order to discard out-of-date notices and display everything to best advantage. Such a person could also be the point of contact for those wishing to display notices if more formal control is thought to be necessary.

4.2.4 Booklets and manuals

Mention has already been made in a previous chapter of the importance of a booklet for new students and perhaps of an induction booklet for staff. Consider also the way practices are codified so that everybody knows the procedures involved. Again it may appear bureaucratic, but there is much to be said for an administrative handbook. It may be nothing more than a looseleaf file but on it can be kept all the up-to-date, relevant instructions on how to deal with such matters as repairs, registration, leave, sickness, estimates, salary scales etc.

Suitably indexed and kept regularly up-to-date, an administrative handbook can cut out much of the agonized indecision and baffled communication that accompanies re-inventing procedures which are in existence but have not been communicated.

4.2.5 Suggestions books and questionnaires

Both these can be effective ways of ensuring that managers learn what is working successfully and what changes need to be made. Suggestions books, one for students and another for staff, can prove a source of useful ideas, particularly if a prize is awarded for the best suggestion, though it is important to inform all who cooperate of any action taken. Comments therein can provide a useful safety valve and pointers to problems previously not recognized.

Many schools prefer to use regular questionnaires to sample opinions. The difficulty here is that designing a questionnaire is not as easy as it may appear. You need to have thought through carefully whether you are going to question all pupils or just some of them and what you are going to do with the answers. The latter observation is based on the experience of a school which sent out a long questionnaire to all of its students and then found its staff swamped with paper as they sifted the responses. By the end of the day, or rather weeks, little usable information had been established from the exercise.

The following may be a useful checklist when writing questionnaires:

1 Decide what information you seek.
2 Decide what type of questions to use.
3 Prepare first draft.
4 Examine and revise the questions, i.e. get others to comment.
5 Pretest the questions on a limited sample.
6 Edit the questionnaire and issue clear instructions for use.
7 Give time limit for collection.
8 Establish date for release of results.

Questionnaires can be of two main types. A structured questionnaire will ask precise questions, often with multiple-choice or yes/no responses required, e.g.

Were you satisfied with the teaching on your course?
Completely/partly/not at all.

In contrast, an unstructured questionnaire consists of a number of open questions admitting a variety of responses, e.g.

What did you think of the teaching on your course?

Each type has associated advantages and disadvantages.

Figure 4.6 Structured and unstructured questionnaires

	Advantages	Disadvantages
STRUCTURED QUESTIONNAIRE	1 Precise conclusions can be drawn. 2 Analysis is quick and easy. 3 Little risk of bias.	1 Inflexibility. 2 Conclusions may be precise and quantified, but trivial and irrelevant. 3 Much depends on the skill of the questionnaire design.
UNSTRUCTURED QUESTIONNAIRE	1 Flexibility. 2 Varied and rich answers.	1 Time consuming to analyse. 2 The analysis of answers is difficult and may be biased.

4.2.6 New technology

The great developments in information technology over the last decade are only slowly reaching language schools. The presence of computers in the

Resources Centre, which helps to sell courses to customers, is not always paralleled by word processors in the office or the provision of electronic mail, fax or telex facilities to improve customer communication. The management of information is a tool that school Principals will increasingly need as their management role expands and computerization can help to achieve this.

Thus, classroom occupancy rates, drop-out rates, age profiles, examination results, names and numbers of late payers, and branch profitability rates over the years are just some of the areas of information that may need to be examined. Manpower planning, a concern of the larger industries, is not likely to affect most Principals to any great degree. However there is a need for staff records of such things as salaries, holidays, sickness, addresses, next of kin and qualifications, and it may well be that one of the numerous personnel software systems now available will not only provide such basic data but also give more sophisticated information if required.

4.3 Welfare

This represents the area where there is a need to communicate most efficiently with staff and students and where considerable distress and indeed danger can be caused if communication breaks down. It is estimated that over 15 million working days are lost each year in Britain because of failures in the areas of Health and Safety. On average there are 1600 incidents a day with 2 deaths a year; and that is in a country which has a reasonably detailed set of laws governing Health and Safety at work. In other countries the record is worse.

It is usually suggested that schools are inherently less likely to have such problems than factories or offices, since the amount of dangerous equipment around is less. Whilst that may be true schools also have a greater number of untrained and often vigorously exuberant people passing through than any other industry. This imposes a considerable burden of responsibility on Principals and, through delegation, on teachers and staff generally.

Each Principal will need to be aware of the Health and Safety regulations of the country and ensure that the school complies with these at all times. Unfortunately the regulations are not always as exact as they might be and external inspection to ensure compliance may not be as regular as desired. Hence it may be worthwhile for the staff to consider the following hazards and the possible questions that might be asked.

4.3.1 Fire

This is perhaps one of the most obvious hazards in a school and yet given the rapid changeover of students, some of whom may be in the school for only two evenings a week, and staff who are often themselves part-time, it is the most difficult for which to prepare people.

Most schools display notices in classrooms giving instructions on what to do in the event of fire but few ensure that these are uniformly introduced to students at the beginning of each term. Fewer still hold fire drills, though, given the changeover of students, these should perhaps be held once a term. A possible checklist for a Principal might be:

1 Are there instructions in each classroom and corridor as to what to do in the event of fire and can all students understand them?
2 Are there fire extinguishers? Are they regularly serviced? Do staff need training on how to use them?
3 Is the school acting in accordance with the fire regulations of the country?
4 Are all fire exits clearly marked and kept free of obstruction?
5 Are practice drills held regularly?
6 Do administrative staff as well as teachers and students know what to do?
7 Is the telephone number of the local fire station clearly displayed?

4.3.2 Security incidents

It may seem excessively cautious to stress this hazard, but many schools teaching English overseas are seen as representatives of the British government and become easy targets when political problems occur. Looking for bombs in wastepaper bins as the Principal and Director of Studies of one school in South America had to do on one occasion is only funny in retrospect. At the time it can cause distress amongst students and anger in parents and staff.

Clear procedures are necessary. They will vary from country to country but it may be helpful to consider the following points:

1 Has general contact been made with the local police force to find out the appropriate section to call and the telephone number to use?
2 Is this name and telephone number available to all those people who might need it?
3 If evacuation of students is necessary, how will it be carried out?
4 Who will search the building?
5 When will students be readmitted?

It is a difficult decision to cancel classes and evacuate buildings when the threatening calls could be a hoax, and it may not always be necessary, but fuss and disruption can be kept to a minimum with clear, well-established procedures.

4.3.3 Medical and first aid

With up to 5000 students coming in and out of a school in a week, accidents are likely to occur. Yet it is often very difficult to find a first aid box and somebody who can not only open it but also use the materials inside. It is essential that at least one person in a school at any one time is trained in first aid, that a first aid box is readily available and that in the event of a serious accident someone is available to take the injured person to hospital.

In most countries, hospital treatment is not free and one should avoid the risk of being turned away with an injured student for lack of insurance cover. Hence an arrangement may well have to be made with a local hospital. Finally, a full report of the accident must be made to the Principal who may need to set up an investigation to discover how and why the accident happened. Below is a list of prompt questions with an example of a report form:

What caused the accident?
Who was involved in the accident?
When did the accident occur?
Where did the accident occur?
Why did it happen?
Could the accident have been prevented?
What should be done to prevent it happening again?

Figure 4.7 Accident report form

ACCIDENT BOOK

1 About the person who had the accident	2 About you, the person filling in this book	3 About the accident
▼ Give full name ▼ Give the home address ▼ Give the occupation	▼ Please sign the book and date it ▼ If you did not have the accident write your address and occupation	▼ When it happened ▼ Where it happened
Name Address Postcode Occupation	Your signature Date / / Address Occupation	Date Time / / In what room or place did the accident happen?

4 About the accident – what happened
How did the accident happen?

4.3.4 Safety checks

A regular monthly check of the school premises should be operated. The areas in school and office that should be inspected are indicated in the safety checklist on the opposite page.

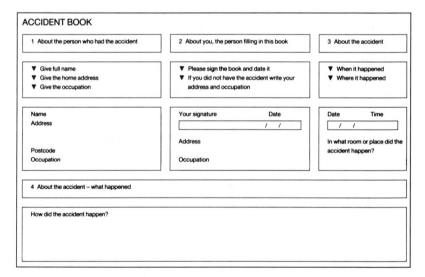

Figure 4.8 School safety checklist

Place		**Action taken**	**Reported to**
Access			
Emergency Exits	Free of obstructions?	Yes/No	
Doorways			
Lifts	Do emergency buttons work?	Yes/No	
	Regular inspections?	Yes/No	
Toilets	Cleanliness	Yes/No	
	Towels	Yes/No	
	Paper	Yes/No	
	W.C. functions/taps work?	Yes/No	
Canteen	Clean		
	Seating facilities		
	Cooking hazards		
Classroom and Offices	Noise from outside		
	Temperature adequate?		
	Lighting Suitable?		
	Cleanliness		
	Chairs and desks OK?		
	Equipment in good repair?		
	Electrical plugs/sockets:		
	Safe/Regularly maintained?		
	Electrical Wires also?		
	Smoking/Non-smoking signs?		
	Filing cabinets safely positioned?		
Outside	Parking-system working?		
	Hazards for visitors?		

4.4 Counselling

It is not intended that counselling in its professional sense could or should take place in schools. The term is used more in accordance with the definition given by Michael Megranahan (1989)

> Counselling is therefore a process which enables problems to be identified and clarified and to facilitate the exploration of potential solutions or ways in which the problem can be managed more effectively by drawing on the individual's inner resources.

If we look first at the situations in a school where this process is occurring then we get a picture like this:

Figure 4.9 Counselling

Teacher – Student Teacher – Parent Teacher – Teacher Receptionist – Student Receptionist – Parent Principal – Student Principal – Parent Principal – Teacher etc.

Students talk to teachers about their study problems: teachers communicate with each other not only about academic matters but about personal problems, and senior academic staff need to suggest and receive suggestions on methods and books. There is a whole network of people in the school *helping each other to solve their problems*. Many people manage this function quite naturally, without reflection, but it is of value to look at what helps and what hinders such conversations. The important thing is to look out for the warning signs such as irritability, tiredness, lack of confidence, poor work standards, absences etc. that suggest a counselling conversation is needed. Having made the decision to hold such a conversation the following points may be of use:

Helps	*Hinders*
Listening carefully	Talking down
Reassuring	Being dismissive
Plenty of time	Concerned about time
Sympathy	Anxious to talk about own problems

Warmth	Interfering
Concrete solutions	Vagueness
Physical proximity	Physical distance
Smiles	
Coffee, tea etc.	

Open rather than closed questions are essential when such discussions are taking place. They are particularly needed at the beginning of the interview when the problem is being discussed and identified.

Figure 4.10 Stages of a counselling interview

IDENTIFY PROBLEM ↓	Gain acceptance that there is a problem. Indicate your helping role. Ask open questions. Listen carefully.
EXPLORE THE PROBLEM ↓	Listen. Ask open questions. Test understanding – 'So are you saying that . . .' Begin to summarize – 'So you mean . . .', 'I get the impression . . .'
PREPARE AN ACTION PLAN ↓	Try to bring out suggestions for a solution from the other person. Translate ideas into details. Set goals and times for achievement.

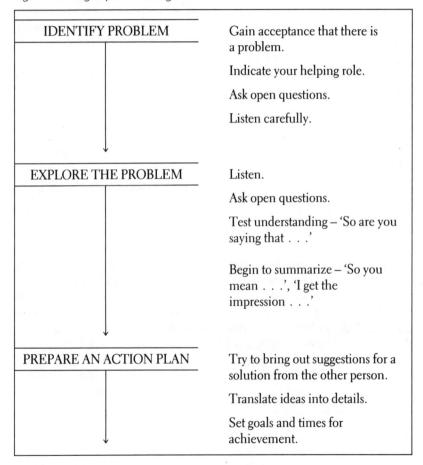

Although notes may be taken during the discussion the process should not be obtrusive since it is important that the speaker feels he or she is being listened to rather than written about. The point at which writing is particularly important is when the action plan is being prepared. It may not always be possible to reach this stage in a single interview but by the end of the discussion a plan of action with a definite timescale should have been agreed. The difficulty, of course, lies in drawing the conclusions from the speaker rather than imposing them, and this is where delicacy of questioning helps. 'What do you suggest you might do to help your daughter,' carefully built on, is likely to produce longer lasting solutions than 'I suggest . . .' early in the conversation, because the person with the problem has to accept not only the existence of the problem but also contribute to its solution.

4.5 Conflict management

No matter how good the welfare in the school and how much care is taken over communication, situations will inevitably arise where communication starts to break down, and conflict, not necessarily always between managers and staff but quite often between individuals, occurs.

The formal definitions given below represent points on a scale of increasing dissatisfaction:

> DISSATISFACTION – anything that disturbs an employee whether or not the unrest is expressed in words.
> COMPLAINT – a spoken or written dissatisfaction brought to the attention of the supervisor.
> GRIEVANCE – a complaint formally presented to a management representative or union official.
> Pigors and Myers
> (1977, p. 229)

It is important to be on the watch for the signs of problems. It is for this reason that many management books extol the virtues of 'walking the floor'.

Often dissatisfaction, and hence conflict, arises because people have an imperfect grasp of school practices or procedures are not clearly defined. Sometimes dissatisfaction may arise from weak management, unbeknown to the Principal, or poor working conditions. Frequently it is caused by a clash of personality. Ignoring the conflict or grievance will not cause it to disappear but will merely drive it underground only for it to emerge again in another form. Often such neglect breeds distrust and leads to the formation of polarized groups.

4.5.1 Complaints

Conflict then, whatever the cause, has to be managed. Moreover it is not necessarily unhealthy and, properly managed, can be creative. It can also indicate to staff and managers the areas where communication needs to be improved. It is better to deal with complaints at the informal stage, and thereby prevent the initiation of formal grievance procedures.

At the informal stage of dealing with conflicts a series of steps should be taken:

STEP 1: Interview as soon as possible

Be aware of problems.
Take them seriously no matter how trivial they may seem since they are important for the people involved. Listen carefully to discover what the real grievance is.
Probe problem areas.
Discuss the grievance or conflict.
Make notes.
Do not rush into a hasty decision.

STEP 2: Consider

Talk to all others concerned.
Identify constraints.
Check records.
Check facts.
Is it a case for disciplinary action?

STEP 3: Return to interview

Discuss points considered.
Agree possible solutions together.
Write these down with agreed deadlines.
Communicate results of interview to all directly concerned in the conflict.

The pause in the interviewing procedures will enable the manager to obtain a more balanced view of the problem. This is important to avoid a temporary solution being put forward at the first interview which falls apart shortly after. Even an individual grievance can provide a collective spin-off in that the other members of the group can benefit from a well-handled grievance case. In addition, it is important to remember that even though individuals may not receive the outcome sought, they will experience some degree of satisfaction if they feel they have been treated with respect. Thus a good manager, not afraid to manage conflicts, can use them to further the well-being of the school.

4.5.2 Formal grievance procedures

In most schools the Principal will be able to resolve conflict by quick action along the lines described above. However, larger schools might wish to have documented and published procedures that will enable individual members of staff to have discussions first with line managers and then, if that fails, with the Principal possibly with a union representative in attendance.

The principle that is normally applied in grievance procedures is that there should be the possibility of an appeal up the line of management. Thus, for example, a teacher who has a complaint against an Assistant Director of Studies should try first to resolve matters directly with that person. If that fails, then an appeal can be made to the Director of Studies, and finally, to the Principal. Time limits should be defined for a decision at each stage of the appeal so that the grievance is resolved within a reasonable time.

Such procedures should be agreed with staff associations and then publicized widely, perhaps in the administrative handbook mentioned earlier, so that all members of staff are aware of how any grievance will be handled.

4.6 Staff associations

A number of benefits to staff and management can follow from the presence of a staff association in the school. Not least is the existence of a set of procedures by which individual problems can be brought to the attention of managers by staff association representatives. They, in their turn, may take the opportunity offered by a particular occasion to raise points of more general import.

Moreover, some of the tension inherent in conflict situations is automatically reduced if it is widely known that a considered, stable set of procedures is to be followed. Hence, the establishment of such procedures will constitute a priority for associations and management.

Associations can grow naturally out of small working parties or committees set up to consider conditions in the school. Such committees, usually composed of equal numbers of managers and staff, can provide a valuable testing ground for the future development not only of formal associations but also for procedures that might be adopted subsequently in the more formal context of management meetings with union representatives.

4.6.1 Composition of associations

Both leaders of associations and managers will need, for different reasons, to consider the following two questions before discussions begin:

Is this association formally and legally recognized in accordance with the civil laws of the country?

What percentage of the members of staff does it represent?

Vague or incorrect legal status can damage the interest of members, while the percentage composition of the association will force Principals to consider how they communicate with the individuals who have not joined the association. This becomes more and more difficult the higher the percentage of members of staff who are not members of the association. Another concern, again for management and unions, must be the groups which are represented. In many schools it is common for teachers to have their association, but perhaps less common for non-teaching staff. It may be that two associations, one for academic and another for non-academic staff, will best represent the interests of the two groups, though the existence of separate associations could lead to rivalry over salaries and therefore a joint association may be preferred. Local circumstances, including the existence of established unions, will probably dictate what type of association prevails.

4.6.2 Meetings with associations

If there are advantages to all in the existence of associations, it follows that it is important to have agreed procedures and common attitudes to negotiation. Thus the group that meets should be representative and therefore with some power, equally composed of managers and staff but probably with the Principal as chairperson. It should not be an unwieldly size – six to ten people seems to be an ideal number for this kind of committee; above that number it is difficult to reach a consensus and move through the business reasonably quickly.

It helps to have regular meetings, not just when there is a crisis, and at such meetings the agenda, although probably published by management, will have been agreed in advance by both sides. Similarly, it is important to have agreed the minutes before their distribution. Some schools like the minutes to be agreed between the leaders at the close of each meeting, others circulate a draft for comment, while yet another practice is for each side to take it in turns in preparing and circulating minutes.

In normal circumstances such minutes will probably be sent to all staff rooms or offices for staff to read. But it may well be that in larger organizations heads of department or school principals will need to be briefed in advance since morale can suffer if staff know the results of meetings and even pose questions arising from them before the managers have been informed. It is therefore worth the time and effort to ensure that some telephoning is done immediately after a meeting to inform relevant staff, just as distributing the agenda in advance ensures maximum information flow before the meeting.

These stages are summarized below:

Date and time of meeting agreed.
Agenda agreed and distributed.
Agenda circulated to managers.
Each side has a pre-meeting if necessary.

MEETING

Minutes agreed at the end of the meeting where possible.
Information passed by phone or in person.
Minutes distributed.

The agenda for such meetings will regularly concentrate on such items as salaries, staffing, jobs etc. but there is much to be said for staff association involvement in and discussion of academic matters, though managers may need to ensure in this case that academic staff are fully consulted.

4.7 Negotiating

No matter how regular the meetings and how good the communication, occasions will arise when detailed negotiation is required. Pay is the obvious, but not exclusive, area of bargaining.

The following guidelines may be of value to anyone involved in negotiating. It is worth adding that some organizations using similar approaches have arranged joint training for management and unions to ensure discussions operate on the basis of common assumptions.

Figure 4.11 Negotiating

STAGE 1 *Pre-meeting*		Agree agenda Analyse problems Plan strategy Construct ideal realistic fallback solutions
STAGE 2	Prepare room	
STAGE 3 *The negotiation*	Communicate Influence	

4.7.1 Analysing and planning

The first thing to be decided is *what the negotiation is about* and this may be, on reflection, something other than the apparent issue. Thus an apparent disagreement about the number of teachers to be made redundant because of falling rolls may in fact mask the real problem of *how* decisions on dismissal are being made. An issue presented as one item on the agenda may, on analysis, be seen to subsume several points of dispute. Hence to take our example:

a) number of teachers to be dismissed b) who decides c) when
d) compensation.

There may also be other objectives not directly related to the points at issue, such as generally maintaining good relations, that need to be borne in mind.

Having established what the negotiations are about, the negotiator may find the following checklist useful:

Which of the issues are important to you?
What are the priorities?
What is unimportant or can be traded?
What are the perceived issues?
What points will be raised?
What are the other side's objectives?
What strategies will be adopted?

At this point it is as well to consider what the other side might lose or gain by accepting or rejecting likely proposals. Burdened by the endless possibilities raised it may come as a relief to turn to a more concrete final step. The acronym NIRF comes in useful at this stage:

Note down
Ideal
Realistic
Fallback
positions

The aim is to ensure the possibility of movement in any negotiation that may take place. Pursuing the example above we get, from the management point of view:

Figure 4.12 Planning for a negotiation

	Ideal	Realistic	Fallback
Number of teachers leaving	40	25	20
Date of departure	August	December	February
Compensation	1 month salary	6 weeks	2 months

Hoping that the other side has equally given itself room for manoeuvre, you are ready to meet.

4.7.2 Pre- negotiation

A settlement is easier to achieve in a constructive atmosphere of mutual respect and therefore attention to detail that can signify this is important. It might encompass the following:

a) A polite invitation made well in advance of the meeting.

b) A respect for formalities such as handshakes, introductions, style of address and punctuality.
c) Attention to the layout of the room with comparable seating for both sides.
d) The provision of courtesy items such as water, ashtrays etc.

4.7.3 Opening phase – information getting and gathering

Once the formalities are over, and the subject for discussion has been announced, each side can be expected to make an opening statement. Listening and questioning are important when the other side presents its case e.g.

Listen carefully.
Ask a lot of questions, but make them reasonable and pertinent.
Ask for explanations.
Check out your understanding.
Sound out their priorities.

In presenting a case avoid provocative remarks like labelling one offer as 'fair and just' and another as 'unreasonable'.

Phrase positively – 'We are here to agree . . .'.
Sound confident.
Put forward your ideal position.
Do not dilute reasons for arguments/requests.
But indicate that you may be willing to negotiate.

4.7.4 The middle phase – influencing and moving

The main aim of this stage is to reinforce constructiveness and movement towards your position. A good negotiator will do this by trying to change the other party's expectations, and will emphasize the advantages of accepting the proposals and the disadvantages of rejecting them.

However, movement must be made if there is to be a negotiated settlement and one of the most important points to be reached in this stage is that of hypothetical proposals:

IF YOU . . ., THEN WE . . .

IF WE . . ., THEN, AS I UNDERSTAND IT, YOU WILL . . .

In this way possibilities are sounded out, ideas are floated, tentative proposals are made and finally areas of mutual accommodation should become apparent.

Figure 4.13 Negotiating – the middle phase

TRY

1 Emphasizing common ground.
2 Matching concession for concession to give a climate of movement and cooperation.
3 Pointing out advantages and disadvantages clearly.
4 Suggesting an alternative to avoid driving the other side into a corner when you reject proposals.
5 Formulating hypothetical situations – 'If we . . ., then you . . .'.
6 Bargaining for something in return for a concession.
7 Linking issues together and building on earlier proposals.
8 Referring to third parties only if things are really difficult e.g. 'The Management Committee/the membership will really need to be consulted before . . .' does not help.
9 Using adjournments to overcome deadlock.
to cool down.
to change stance.
to appraise the position.
to rest.

4.7.5 The closing phase

It may be that a settlement is not possible and the meeting will agree to register disagreement. However, if all the possibilities enumerated above have been explored, the closing stage may be over quite quickly.

It is essential, however, to *summarize and record* what has been agreed before the meeting breaks up to minimize subsequent disputes and misunderstandings.

4.7.6 Communicating the results

The association will want to inform its members of the results of the meeting as soon as possible but it is equally important for managers to be kept in touch with developments. In addition, the non-association staff who might well be affected by the resolution or otherwise of a conflict should not be forgotten. Indeed, the agreed conclusions should be circulated promptly to all staff members to prevent the spread of rumours.

4.8 Dealing with industrial action

Occasionally conflicts are not resolved through negotiation and industrial action of some kind may result. There are no hard and fast rules for handling these situations but the following considerations may repay attention.

Above all, staff and managers must be kept informed of what is happening. Some will not have faced a situation like this before and will need the firm support, help, information and strengthening resolve of the Principal. This is especially true in the case of a newly-appointed academic manager who may feel a conflict of interest with former colleagues.

It is not only internal communication that becomes important at this stage and it may well be a good idea to have a single spokesperson, kept fully briefed, to deal with all the outside media. Because of the need to communicate effectively with all concerned, arrangements should be made for the regular issue of newssheets or letters, whose contents should be as factual and unprovocative as possible.

Mass meetings, while superficially attractive to both managers and union leaders, frequently prove disastrous occasions where individuals can rouse the body of the meeting in the most unexpected manner. Oral briefings are therefore perhaps best handled down the line of management or through association representatives.

Whilst firmness and resolution are necessary, for leaders the overriding aim must be a speedy return to the negotiating table since it is there that ultimately a solution must be found. All communication should have that end in mind.

Conclusion

Schools are concerned with outward communication to the student, but the numerous ways in which information flows through the organizational structure to produce either understanding and action or mistrust and inefficiency will always bear closer examination. In fact, the major part of effective management consists in ensuring that communication is taking place, formally through arranged meetings and informally through the whole network of links discussed earlier. Together these create good multilateral communication in sharp contrast to the 'top-down' variety of more bureaucratic organizations. It is not an easy task and one made worse in many schools by the fact that many members of staff are employed part-time and therefore cannot always be seen face to face. This intensifies the need to explore and reinforce all the channels of communication described in this chapter.

Follow-up activities

1 Imagine that you are the managing director of a group of schools. One is failing badly and you decide to close it. Note down the people you would have to inform once a decision had been made and compare your list with the list made by others. In pairs or groups place these people in the order in which you think they should be informed and indicate, as you do so, the conflicts that are likely to occur.

2 What advice would you offer to those who run meetings in your school on how they might be improved?

3 Compare
   a) The forms of agenda for a meeting illustrated in Figure 4.2 with those you use.
   b) The minutes of your meetings with the action notes outlined in Figure 4.4.

4 Try to remember what noticeboards are present in your school. Who uses them and for what purpose? Are there sufficient? Draw up a checklist for a person to oversee the noticeboards on a regular basis.

5 Below are some of the areas for which you might wish to have management information. Add as many points as you can and then set them out in order of priority.

   average classroom occupancy rate
   occupations of students
   average age
   examination results
   drop-out rates
   teacher qualifications
   classes taught by each teacher over a number of years
   exam successes of each teacher
   scholarship holders

6 Try to list those elements you feel should be in an administrative handbook for a school.

7 Attempt to draw up a questionnaire on a limited area but one that is of concern within the school e.g. catering facilities. Who should be sampled? Can the questions be more tightly phrased?

8 Look at the mini-questionnaire on the next page. What comments would you make?

Figure 4.14 Textbook questionnaire

Textbook Questionnaire

Name: Class:

Age: Textbook used:

Do you like the book?

Please give reasons:

Reading passages	Interesting/Not interesting	
	Easy/Too difficult	
Pictures	Helpful/Not useful	
Comprehension questions		Varied/Monotonous
		Difficult/Easy
Grammar		Good/Average/Poor
		Sufficient/Insufficient
Oral work		Good/Average/Poor
Written work		Good/Average/Poor

Any other comments?

Please complete and send to the General Office by 1st November.

9 'The reactions of employees to any event will be favourable only if it matches or exceeds their expectations' and 'Where an announcement or award will fall short of expectations, there are only two alternatives to avoid trouble: improve the content of the announcement until it does match expectations, or take time to reduce expectations to the level of the subsequent announcement.' (D. Drennan)

What are the implications of these two remarks for Principals of language schools?

10 Attempt to improve the fire instructions given below and then compare your finished version with those in use in your school. In addition, note down the places where you think such notices should be displayed.

Figure 4.15 Fire instructions

FIRE

In the event of fire follow the instructions below:

1 Do not attempt to put out the fire but immediately ring the fire alarm.
2 Get the secretary to ring the fire brigade for assistance.
3 Lead the pupils in single file down the back staircase to the square opposite. Walk, do not run.
4 Check that all pupils are with you.
5 Report to the Principal who will inform you when you can return to the school.

11 How useful is the model accident report form in Figure 4.7 for reporting accidents in your school? What changes would you wish to make?
12 Using the model form in Figure 4.8, prepare your own safety checklist.
13 Look at the record for accidents in the school over the past year. What types predominate? What does this suggest your first aid box should contain?
14 *Counselling*

X is aged 39, is single and has taught at this school for the last two years, mainly at the intermediate level. Although not an inspiring teacher he has got by up to now without too many problems, relying on 'chalk and talk' rather than the use of audio-visual aids. His approach pays lip-service only to the communicative approach and relies heavily on the textbook. Homework is rarely set and marked, and some students have complained.

X is a 'loner' and does not get on with other teachers in the staff room though some of them have attempted to talk to him about the use made of certain books. Nor does he attend the occasional staff party. His isolation is made worse by personal hygiene problems.

In recent weeks he has caused difficulties for the Principal by being frequently absent through sickness. Last week a friend telephoned to say X would be absent for two days with flu but X has just reappeared saying that he is suffering from nervous exhaustion.

Use the above outline, or one based on your own experience and in pairs role-play the interview between the Principal and X to discuss the problems.

15 List the common cause of grievances in your school and alongside each, note down what action has been effective in dealing with the problem.

16 *Grievance handling*

Although smoking is allowed in the staff room smokers and non-smokers have in the past tended to congregate in different parts of the room. However, one teacher, recently arrived from another school, persists in smoking in all areas and has thereby greatly annoyed the non-smoking staff, one of whom has come to see you.

Role-play that interview in pairs and add any subsequent interview you feel may be necessary.

17 Drawing on your own experience outline a case study of a person and the grievance he or she had as in the example above. If real life cases might pose problems then invent. Role-play the interviews.

18 *A simulation for negotiation practice*

Two years ago the Head School opened in what was hoped would be temporary accommodation. Student numbers have since expanded rapidly. Throughout this time it has been widely known that the proprietor was looking for new premises. Unfortunately he had no success and a third year with the same facilities is about to begin. A delegation drawn from teaching and administrative staff went to management a year ago to complain particularly about the number of toilets available for their use and the fact that these were being shared with students.

In addition, the staff resented the fact that in the washroom the hand-towel machines were often out of order and the towels dirty. An architect was invited in to suggest where a new staff cloakroom might be built and his report, as all know, arrived six months ago and has since not been acted upon. Management has done nothing because the proposed new cloakroom would cut down on classroom space thereby reducing the number of students and hence profits, and perhaps delaying a move to new premises.

Two other problems surfaced at the meeting last year but though both sides are conscious of their seriousness nothing has been done. The first is the problem of noise in the classrooms. The Head School is situated on a busy main road and when the windows are open teachers find it difficult to make themselves heard. On the other hand, closed windows mean the ventilation is poor and teachers and students complain. The architect suggested that the cost of remedial measures would be fairly prohibitive so again no action has been taken.

Finally, being a converted house the school has room for only 3 or 4 cars on the drive and the Principal and Deputy Principal have reserved two places for themselves. The majority of staff members therefore have to leave their cars on one of the side streets off the busy main road, where one or two have been vandalized. The alternative is a public car park, which closes at 6 p.m. and is fairly expensive. A month before the start of the new term the staff have requested a meeting with management to discuss the situation.

Divide into two teams to represent management and staff. Allocate roles within teams e.g. chairperson, lead speaker, expert, hawk, dove, observer.

Spend time preparing, during which you should identify the issues. Consider your ideal, realistic and fallback positions. Think through your priorities and the opposition's likely demands, reactions and bargaining power. Work out your opening moves, style and tone. After preparation time go into a negotiation.

5 ORGANIZING RESOURCES AND INFORMATION

Aims

The aims of this chapter are:

1 To review the importance of time management and to apply time management procedures to self management.
2 to describe procedures for timetabling.
3 to describe office systems and procedures.
4 to review the choice of office hardware.

5.1 Management time

It has been said that one of the greatest scarcities in contemporary society is not one of physical resources, but one of time. Since the days of the scientific management movement, time and motion have been the subjects of investigation aimed at improving the use of this non-replaceable resource and various methods have been developed for controlling, budgeting and saving time. It is to some of these that we shall now turn.

5.1.1 Managing your own time

Before considering how to manage other people's time, managers need to consider how best to manage their own because most of the same considerations apply. Before managing our time, we need to find out what we are actually doing with it. This means keeping a record of activities over a period – say a full working week, less being of little value. A time log will be organized by time slots – 30 minute sections provide a good basis – and other categories will include the activities carried out in each time slot, the time taken and the people involved.

Day ____________ Date ____________

Time	What happened?	Duration	People	Comments
0900 0930				
0930 1000				
1000 1030				
etc.				

Having kept a time record over a working week, the next thing is to analyse the material. The following headings have been suggested (Pedlar, Burgoyne & Boydell, 1986).

A OUTCOME

How successful were the various activities?
Have you any habitual failures?

B TYPE OF WORK

Things you must do.
Things you should do.
Things you would like to do.

In reviewing the type of work that you have done, consider how much of this work has been done because it is easy or because you like doing it compared with those activities which were most difficult. It is possible to spend too much time on less important activities because they are routine or easily accomplished and thus avoid doing those things which are vital, but which may be difficult or challenging. It's easy to give the impression of getting on with business, yet without in fact dealing with the most significant aspects of one's work.

Then consider the proportion of your time which goes on *managerial work*, that is, planning, organizing and motivating, and *professional skills*, that is, exercising your existing professional skills which for ELT managers usually means teaching.

It is very easy for teachers who have become language school managers to hanker after practising the professional skills which made them good teachers but which may be less relevant to the management job they are now doing.

C WHERE DOES THE WORK COME FROM?

It is important to know where work comes from because identifying the sources of the work which you do will help to show whether delegation is working effectively. Thus, if very little work is coming from the boss, but lots is originating from subordinates, the boss may not be delegating enough while subordinates are too dependent upon you. Similarly, if you find that you yourself are the source of very little of the work which you are doing, you may be setting yourself too few tasks and targets. In other words, you are reacting to others rather than controlling your own work goals and workload. Finally, the source of work may be from elsewhere, such as outside the organization. Again, this may indicate a need for greater delegation or for improved means of gatekeeping by your secretary or other members of the organization who have regular contacts with the world outside the school.

D DELEGATION

Given the importance of delegation, it is necessary to consider the following questions:

Could this task have been delegated?
If so, to whom could it have been delegated?
If not, why not?

If a task could have been delegated but wasn't, you should consider very carefully why it wasn't. Is it a sign of wanting to retain too much control? Is it because you feel the need to be indispensable? Or is it based on a reluctance to delegate because other staff are felt not to be up to it? If the last, some thought should be given to giving the staff concerned the training necessary for them to take on the work concerned.

Once you have analysed the way you spend your time, you have to make some decisions about how to reorganize it. In other words, it is necessary to establish a sense of priorities. The first thing to do is to sort things out into those which can be reduced or delegated, and those which should be given higher priority and greater time or commitment. Here it is useful to categorize work into those things which *must* be done, those things which *should* be done, and those things which you would *like* to do (which may not, as noted earlier, necessarily be the things which must be done). It is the things which must be done that have to be given top priority.

Having identified priorities, you should then work out an action plan in the form of an agenda organized as follows:

	Action	To be completed by
1		
2		
3		
etc.		

Carrying out the action plan will have to be monitored, again using a time log.

Keeping a weekly and daily agenda is both useful discipline and a way of exercising control over one's time and commitments. To some extent, this is a very personal thing, but there are some general principles which usually prove helpful.

1 Establish goals for the week and for the day.
2 Prioritize activities according to this list of goals and according to the priorities just discussed.
3 Set deadlines and make realistic time estimates. Most of us *under*estimate. So, add about twenty per cent of the first estimate of the time needed for each task.
4 Don't try to do too much at once.
5 Learn to say 'no' to others as well as to yourself.
6 Don't get bogged down in minutiae.
7 Delegate.
8 Don't put off unpleasant things. Make firm commitments, stick to them – and feel better for having got the unpleasant things out of the way.
9 Use a gatekeeper, such as a receptionist or secretary, to filter phone calls and visitors.
10 Reserve a block of time each day when you will not be interrupted and make sure that this is sacrosanct. It is during this time that you should be able to get on, uninterruptedly, with 'must do' work. It is also a time when thinking and planning can be done. It's impossible to think strategically when coping with here and now things.
11 Don't spent too much time in conversations and meetings, and learn to use the time more efficiently and effectively. In particular, if you have a regular meeting with a colleague, cancel it if you have nothing to discuss. Also, if you are chairing a meeting, set time limits, have a well-organized agenda and stick to it. Don't allow yourself and other people to keep getting off the point.

12 Avoid being overwhelmed by incoming paper. Ways of doing this are to use a gatekeeper – usually your secretary – to sort incoming material into categories: action now, action later, information. Also, review circulation lists – maybe you don't need to be on lists for some information – and generally encourage succinctness and clarity in others, while practising the same virtues yourself.

13 Avoid writing too many letters or memos. The telephone can be used more, though it's a good idea to place a note on file of the substance of a phone call as it's easy to forget what might have been agreed when returning to the same subject at a later date. Succinct handwritten responses on memos can also save time. The FAX has also made it possible to transmit and receive written material quickly without the need to have it typed up and posted.

14 Deal with paperwork sooner rather than later. It is a good idea to have a regular time of the day, such as the first half hour or so, to deal with urgent correspondence, while leaving a later point at the end of the day for less pressing matters. It's also a good idea to aim to clear at least 90 per cent of the paper on your desk each day.

15 Have a day file. Your secretary or you yourself should operate a system whereby items are put in a file organized chronologically so that things are filed under a bring-up date, that is, a date when an item is to be attended to. An accordion file, with divisions numbered 1 to 31, will suffice. Check the file daily for that day's items.

16 Have an efficient filing and retrieval system. This is a matter which will be dealt with in more detail in a later section.

17 Don't spend too much time on travelling. Use the phone if you can; or delegate, and, for yourself or others, use the quickest means of transport for the journey concerned. Parsimony on fares may be a false economy.

5.1.2 Managing other people's time

Not surprisingly, many of the guidelines given for managing one's own time can also be applied to managing other people's time. Partly this can be done by example, and partly by setting up systems and procedures which make the best use of other people's time. As with your own, other people's time should be prioritized in terms of organizational goals, both short- and long-term, and in terms of cost and opportunity.

Assigning people to tasks will depend on the organization's action plan for the period concerned, as well as on people's job descriptions and on the individual goals which have been agreed in an annual appraisal. These goals should be in line with organizational goals as well as being realistic. No individual should be encouraged to work towards goals which cannot possibly be achieved within the time scale concerned.

The planning of people's time commitments will, within a school, be in great measure determined by the time scale according to which the school operates. Most schools will have an overall annual plan, with peaks and troughs of activity, the summer often being a busy time for schools in Britain, while the autumn is the peak period for enrolments in many schools on the Continent and in Latin America. Within this annual plan, there will be cycles of longer or short duration, depending on whether the school's courses are organized on a monthly or termly basis.

The demands on staff time will depend, then, on the length of the planning cycle and on the nature of their job and responsibilities. Priorities will need to be established, both for the whole organization and for individuals, following similar principles to those outlined earlier. If, for instance, time is to be made available for course development and materials production, people will either be assigned or will assume such responsibilities as part of their agreed work. Reaching such agreement will be the subject of individual as well as group discussion. Once agreement has been reached, an action plan for the period concerned will be set and deadlines agreed.

What the manager will need to consider carefully is not overloading staff, either administrative or teaching, with work. It is useful, therefore, to maintain a plan of people's commitments and responsibilities. One way of doing this is to have a year planner on which individual's names and duties are indicated. This is especially useful when there are a number of projects taking place simultaneously, with varying deadlines, and involving many different staff. When, inevitably, new requirements have to be met, such a planner will enable you to see very quickly who is likely to be available to take on the new work. It may also indicate the need for employing extra staff for the work concerned.

5.2 Timetabling

Within schools, the most important way of managing time is, of course, through the timetable and it is the organization of this which can give most headaches to the Director of Studies. Basically, timetable planning involves reconciling the following factors:

courses to be taught
number of students or class hours to be covered
number of teacher hours available
space
cost

Simply put, the larger the classes, the lower the unit cost because fewer teachers will be required. There are, however, a number of important constraints on simply going for low cost on such a basis and in most language schools, there will be an agreed limit on class size which will be related to the kind and quality of service which the school sets out to provide. Similarly, the size and amount of teaching space – whether classrooms, language laboratories or self-access centres – will be a further limiting factor. Finally, there will always be a trade-off to be made between having enough of the things which cost money – teachers and space – and the financial constraints under which the organization must operate.

What follows is a step-by-step timetable planning sequence. Variations on this sequence will occur, depending on the size and complexity of the organization concerned.

1 **Courses to be taught** The total number of different courses and their duration is the first factor to consider. Each course will require its own timetable, staffing, classroom and resources.
2 **Course components** Before any timetabling can occur, it is essential to have agreement on the course components which have to be taught. To some extent this will depend on tradition or on commitments already made. A general English course will usually have such components as General Language Improvement, a skills component and, possibly, some options or projects. The balance among these components will vary, but in general, two thirds of a programme will be devoted to core courses, with another third to options.
3 **Session length** It is usual to work with a standard session length. This may be highly variable, ranging from as little as 40 minutes to as much as two or even three hours. On the one hand, teachers may be given virtually no latitude in the way in which sessions can be used; on the other, they may be given complete freedom as to how they make use of session time. From the timetabling point of view, it is necessary to establish and keep to standard timetable sessions so as to avoid overlapping use of facilities and resources or timetable clashes for teachers moving from one class to another.
4 **Teacher hours** Teachers are normally employed to teach a specified number of hours per week. If the number of teaching hours is out of synchronization with the number of class hours requiring cover, it will be necessary to consider such options as merging classes for certain activities, splitting course components between two or more teachers, or employing extra teachers.
5 **Teachers' responsibilities** A good school will build in allowances for other activities so that staff may be given remission from teaching for a specified number of hours per week in order to get on with materials and test production, administration of various kinds, such as running a study centre or library, organizing examinations, acting as union representative or organizing research and development. It will be necessary to consider such allowances when accounting for teacher hours.
6 **Teachers' areas of expertise** Teachers usually have particular skills or areas of expertise which also have to be considered when timetabling. Thus, Teacher A may be the Literature person, while Teacher B is the Media

Studies expert, and so on. This will be another factor to keep in mind when timetabling.

7 **Teachers' preferences** In any organization, it is well known, though not always overtly expressed, that a certain teacher prefers teaching certain kinds of groups rather than others; or that certain teachers do or do not work happily together; or that the domestic circumstances of a particular teacher require absences at certain times; and so on. Much of this sort of information is privileged knowledge which an Academic Manager will have acquired over years of experience. It is not information which can usually be committed to print, still less keyed into a computer program. Yet, it is the kind of information which the timetable planner has to keep in mind when assigning teachers to classes.

8 **Vacations** In a school which works all the year round, it is inevitable that there will almost always be someone on holiday, unless there is a period set aside during the year when the school is completely closed and all staff are required to take their vacations at that time. If staff take their vacations at various times through the year, account will have to be taken of this in timetable planning.

9 **Room availability** How many rooms are available and for how long? Ideally, there should be one classroom per group, but there will be some rooms, such as a library, language laboratory, computer room and self-access room or learning centre, which must be shared. Timetabling will have to take account of such shared space so as to avoid clashes. This will mean planning a complementary room timetable to fit in with the teaching timetables for each course.

10 **Cost** Teachers' pay represents a major cost for all schools and staffing levels will be determined by staffing policy, which in turn will be related to financial as well as professional and pedagogic factors. It is inefficient to overstaff and thus have underemployed teachers. However, teachers must be given sufficient time for preparation and marking, not to mention space between teaching sessions. Expecting teachers to work uninterruptedly throughout the day is bad for them and bad for the students. Even so, a balance will have to be made between being very fully staffed and going over budget on staff costs. Similarly, if room space is being rented, care will have to be taken to ensure, firstly, that its use is maximized, and secondly, that unnecessary space is not booked.

Once information in the above areas has been gathered, a master chart will be drawn up along the lines of the example overleaf.

Teachers' Names	Course components A	B	D	Responsibilities	Other	Total
BM	3	9	6	5	0	23
KH	6	6	3	5	3	23
LD	9	6	3	0	5	23
etc.						
Total hours	50	55	30	35	25	230

From this it should be possible to see if there is a shortfall in the number of teachers' hours required for course components because, ideally, the total at the foot of each column should match the total number of hours' cover required. Meanwhile, the total number of hours in the right-hand column for each teacher should match the number of hours' work for which they have been contracted. If there is a mismatch, in either total, adjustments will have to be made.

Once the totals given above have been worked out and reconciled, the master timetable will be planned. This will indicate the daily timetable for each class and each slot will be filled by a teacher's initials. Such a master timetable should reveal if there are clashes when one teacher is scheduled for two different classes at the same time. Adjustments will then have to be made.

The master teaching timetable will then have to be mapped against the room timetable. In fact, the scheduling of certain sessions in shared rooms should already have been taken account of in planning the master timetable. For instance, if there is only one language laboratory and all classes are going to use it at least once a week, the total number of language laboratory hours will be worked out and then matched against the total number of classes potentially available. If it were the case that there was a preference for all classes to have their language laboratory sessions at a similar point in their daily timetable, the laboratory sessions could be scheduled according to the number and time of timetabled slots available at that time.

The master timetable will by now have a session-by-session display for all courses, showing each component, with teacher's initials in each slot, plus the room location for the slot concerned. It should be possible, therefore, to see exactly who is teaching whom and where at any time. From this master timetable, specific timetables for teachers, courses, rooms and equipment, such as video, can, if required, be drawn up.

Computerization of timetabling can be a great timesaver, and proprietary software is available for this purpose. However, it is as well to remember that computers cannot make decisions and no program has yet been devised which can take account of all the complex personnel and personal variables which only the Academic Manager or Director of Studies can cope with. So, even with a good computer program, timetabling policy decisions will have to be made by the person responsible for timetabling, while the slog of identifying double bookings and overlaps and printing out class, individual and other timetables, can be accomplished very quickly once the relevant information has been entered into the computer.

5.3 The office system

The work of the Director of Studies in planning timetables is an example of the meeting point of professional, managerial and administrative responsibilities. The Academic Manager has a primary responsibility for the academic management of the school, and will normally report to the Principal. Also reporting to the Principal, and carrying out the administrative functions of the school will be the administration, which usually consists of someone who is responsible for the registration of students and someone who looks after the finances. In a small school, the registration and financial functions might be in the hands of one person, but in a school which has an enrolment of fifty or more students, the work load will generally require a splitting of administrative functions between two people with designated responsibilities in these two areas.

The efficient organization and running of the office system is crucial for a number of reasons. To begin with, it is often through the office that clients and students make their initial contact with the school, as will various service providers. Any sloppiness or inefficiency in the office will provide a lasting bad impression.

Secondly, the operation of all the routines which underpin successful teaching will be the province of the school administration. Students have to be registered, fees collected and banked, invoices raised and receipts issued, materials and services ordered and paid for, examination entries arranged and paid for, accommodation organized and allocated, landladies paid, catering provided, and so on. It is the school administration which performs all of these tasks.

Who, then, is who in the organization as a whole and in the administration in particular? The following diagram shows the organizational structure of the Bell School at Bowthorpe Hall, Norwich, in September 1988. From this, it is possible to obtain a clear overview of the organization of the school and to see how the administration is organized and what its relationship is to the teaching side of the organization. Another similar diagram, with the names of the people occupying each position within the structure, would show precisely where individuals fit into the scheme. Clearly, no two schools will be exactly the same, but the roles and functions depicted in the Bowthorpe Hall diagram will have to be performed by members of staff in most schools, even if one person may occupy more than one role, as will be common in a smaller organization.

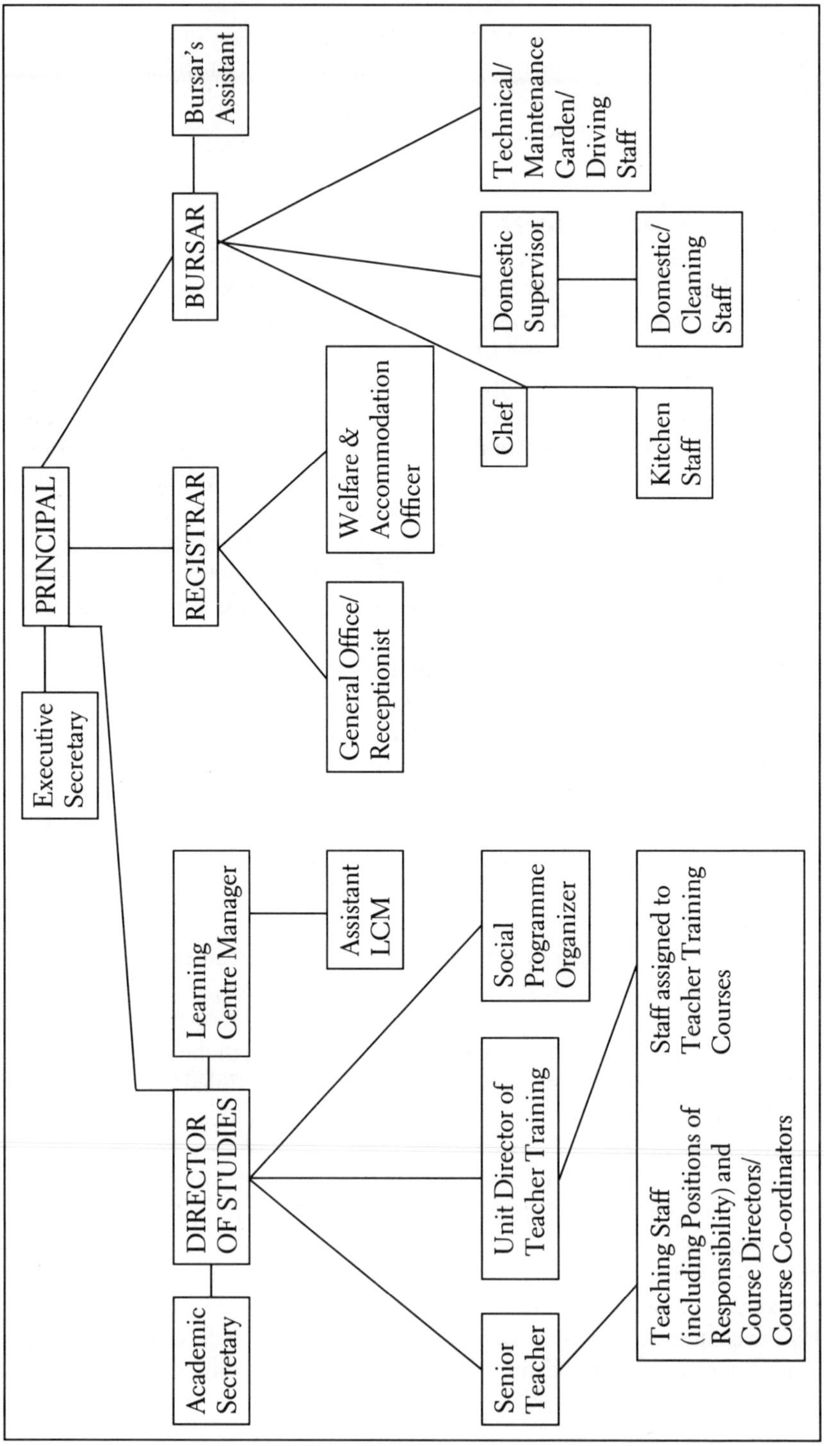

Figure 5.1 Organizational structure of the Bell School, Bowthorpe Hall, Norwich

5.3.1 The Registrar

This is the person who is responsible for recording the admission of all students and for maintaining student records. In addition, the Registrar may also be responsible for the administration of student welfare and accommodation.

The Registrar's department will normally deal with examination entries, for which a system is needed so as to make accessible the following information:

examination
date of examination
fee payment

A cross-checking system will be needed between the person responsible – usually a teacher – for examination administration and the Registrar's department so that entries are arranged and payments collected, recorded and made to the board along with the entries.

5.3.2 The Bursar

The Bursar is responsible for receipts, payments and banking. Ordering goods and services will go through the Bursar's department and routines and systems will be needed to ensure that payments are made when necessary and to avoid double payment. Orders will tend to originate with the teaching, office or domestic staff, and the systems which are set up should be designed with simplicity and avoiding confusion in mind. If a system is too cumbersome, people will tend to by-pass it.

Ordering will normally be sanctioned by the budget-holder for the item concerned. Once the purchase has been agreed – and possibly a mandate for the purchase signed – the person responsible for placing the order will do so. It will normally be the case that the order will go through the Bursar's section so that permission for the purchase is noted and the order is recorded. When the order is filled, a bill or invoice will be submitted by the supplier. If the order has been sent direct to the person with whom the order originated, the Bursar will have to be informed that the order has been filled so that payment can be made on receipt of the bill. If, however, the order comes to the Bursar's department, its receipt can be noted and the order handed over to the originator. The amount of the purchase can then be debited against the appropriate budget heading so that a cumulative total of expenditure and balance remaining is maintained for monitoring and accounting purposes.

TYPICAL PROCEDURE

1 Check order with budget-holder.
2 Validate order.

3 Place order with supplier.
4 Inform Bursar's department.
5 Receive order.
6 Confirm receipt with Bursar's department.
7 Bursar arranges payment.
8 Payment entered on financial record.
9 Receipt received and filed.

Among the services which come under the Bursar's section will be insurance for buildings, contents and third party liability. It is especially important in an organization providing a service to its clients that third party liability is covered, since the school is liable for injuries received on the premises or as part of a function organized by the school. If the school provides catering, whether the service is contracted out or owned by the school, the school could find itself liable for illnesses attributable to food supplied by the school's catering establishment. Finally, cover is needed for passengers and their possessions while travelling in school transport. In all of these matters, if there is any uncertainty, advice should be sought either from an appropriate trade association, such as ARELS/FELCO in Britain, or from an insurance consultant.

5.3.3 Welfare, accommodation and social

The people responsible for these will either come within the Registrar's or the Bursar's sections. In some cases, the Social Organizer will be part of the academic section and will report to the Academic Manager. In all cases, liaison with the academic section is important, especially where student welfare is concerned.

The setting up and management of an accommodation register can be a major job, especially in a school which regularly arranges for the placement of dozens of students throughout the year. The person in charge of accommodation will have to set up and maintain a record system which will include such details of the hosts as:

name
address
telephone number
number in family
public transport facilities, e.g. bus route
pets
smoking/non-smoking
male/female guests
availability
other

The 'other' heading covers a multitude of items, such as whether the host concerned prefers guests from certain countries, what the ambience of the home is like, and so on. If such information is entered on a computer database, there is a requirement that it should be accessible to the individual concerned, so for this reason confidential information may best be entered on paper records.

In addition to information on each host, it will be necessary to have some kind of timetable showing availability and current use so as to avoid double booking. It will also be necessary to up-date the register, both by removing the records of hosts no longer on the register and by adding new ones.

Recruiting new hosts may involve advertising, either in the local press or by means of a leaflet drop in selected areas of the town. Prospective hosts will then have to be visited to check on the quality and accessibility of the accommodation, the personality of the host and the facilities which are offered. In any case, it is important for the person managing the accommodation register to establish a personal contact with the host because judgements will have to be made when assigning guests so as to ensure that there will be a congenial match between the known characteristics and requirements of both guest and host.

5.3.4 Accountant or Bursar's assistant

In a large organization, the Bursar's staff will include an accountant or an assistant who will deal with accounts and payments, including salaries and wages and VAT (Value Added Tax) payments.

Routines for claiming and paying salaries and wages will vary. Hourly paid part-time staff may be required to fill in a time sheet, particularly if their teaching hours fluctuate. Responsibility for administering this may lie with the Academic Manager. Full-time staff will not normally complete time sheets and any changes in their circumstances will be dealt with by exception.

The salaries and wages section will be responsible for calculating and paying such items as national insurance and superannuation or pension contributions. In addition, this section will also be responsible for the deduction of PAYE (Pay As You Earn income tax). In Britain, any exceptions to the deduction of PAYE must be negotiated with the local Inland Revenue tax inspector. In general, the Inland Revenue is very reluctant to waive this obligation, and when staff are being employed who claim Schedule D tax status, this must be verified because the employer is liable for any defaults on PAYE payments. In other countries, such as Japan, it may be common for expatriate staff to be hired on a self-employed basis and the restrictions which are common in Britain will not apply. Whatever the prevailing requirements, it is a legal requirement that the employer conforms to them.

Another function of the Bursar's section will be maintaining inventories, that is, lists of equipment, furniture and hardware. Inventories are normally required for insurance and auditing purposes and it is usual to review the inventories annually and to write-off faulty or obsolete equipment. There is no doubt that checking inventories is a tedious business, but it represents good housekeeping as it is important to have an up-to-date check on the status of equipment and furniture.

Finally, conformity to copyright legislation will normally involve subscription to a copyright agency to whom payments are made for photocopying copyright material. It will be necessary to set up and maintain a record of the source and quantity of such material so that regular returns can be made to the agency along with payment. In countries which are signatories to international copyright agreements, it is illegal to copy copyright material – print, audio, video or computer software – without the copyright owner's permission and, if required, payment.

5.3.5 Domestic and maintenance

The staff responsible for such things as catering, cleaning, maintenance and driving will usually be part of the Bursar's section, and they will receive orders from and report back to the Bursar or the Bursar's deputy. Such staff may include the following:

catering manager or chef	caretaker
kitchen staff	handyman
domestic supervisor	driver
cleaning staff	gardener
maintenance co-ordinator	

In a small organization, several of these functions may be carried out by one person. For instance, the roles of maintenance co-ordinator, handyman, driver and gardener may be combined.

The person responsible for co-ordinating each area – catering, cleaning, maintenance, transport – will normally control a budget for their area and they will be accountable to the Bursar or the accountant for expenditure. This means that appropriate sub-systems for ordering and payment will have to be maintained. Obviously, the same systems and procedures will normally be used throughout the organization so as to help co-ordination. For instance, cleaning staff would ask the supervisor and budget-holder to order materials. The supervisor would then place the order through the Bursar's section so that records and payments are controlled in the usual way.

5.3.6 General office staff

The general office staff will include the telephonist/receptionist and secretaries and typists. They will normally report to the Bursar or the Bursar's deputy. It is important that routines and systems are established and maintained for the distribution of secretarial and typing work, particularly as it is usually through the general office staff that daily contact between administration and teaching sections is maintained. Teaching staff who require typing or photocopying to be done will have to work with the office staff, and it is important that everyone understands what procedures are to be used for requesting that such work be done. It is also important that the system should be simple to operate.

A simple system is to have an in-tray for typing. Staff put work in the in-tray and the work is then distributed to typists according to their responsibilities and workload. When the work is ready, it is then put in the staff member's pigeonhole or basket for collection. Periods required for the completion of routine work would be agreed as a matter of course. Thus, work delivered one day might be returned the next. However, the time required for work of exceptional length or complexity would have to be negotiated separately, while a regular, heavy influx of work, such as might occur in the run-up to examinations, would require an extended lead-in time to permit completion by agreed deadlines.

It is bad practice constantly to work in a state of impending crisis because of inadequate planning of lead times and deadlines. Thus, the Academic Manager and teaching staff need to work in collaboration with the office supervisor, typing and clerical staff to agree on such matters. It is a good idea to have a bring-up scheme whereby people are reminded of the need to have work ready to meet deadlines, such as the beginning of term or an examination period.

5.4 Records

As will be clear from the preceding sections, not to mention the preceding chapters, the administration of a language school will both produce and require a substantial range of records, some of which, such as accounts, will be a legal requirement, while some will be needed for the smooth and convenient running of the organization. Different countries will have different requirements so it is impossible to have a universal list of records, although the list below, which is categorized under different headings, will be a useful guide:

Financial
Allocations and budgets
Commitments
Expenditure
Reconciliations
Receipts
Money owed

VAT returns
Payroll
PAYE/National Insurance

Accommodation payments

Targets by term and year
Register of recurrent payments

Book orders
Stationery orders
Equipment orders
Inventory of equipment
Stocklist of books
Stocklist of audio, video and computer software

Building
Certification of
  fire safety
  insurance
  VAT registration or exemption
  catering, e.g. licence to sell alcoholic liquor

Registration
Target enrolments
Actual past enrolments
Registers
Re-registration rates
Class break-down by level
Waiting lists
Timetable
Reconciliation statements

Marketing
Student population in school by age, sex, profession, funding
Competitors' prices
Competitors' salaries
Promotion – when, where, how?
Agents: names and addresses, agreements and arrangements with
Student questionnaires and follow-up
Lists of actual and potential clients
Brochures, past and present

Staff
Contracts
Personnel files with references and qualifications
Appraisal records
Timetables
Overtime
Sick leave
Vacation leave
Non-school work, e.g. textbook writing, consultancies
Substitution list of teachers
Job descriptions

Students
Academic record
Names and addresses
Profession
Whether sponsored and name of sponsor
Record of payments
Teachers' recommendation for next term or for another course
Age

Courses
Levels
Syllabuses
Course objectives
Books
Catalogue of materials
Exam results: internal and external (e.g. Cambridge)
Planning, setting-up and running procedures
Reports on previous courses

General
Filing guide
Addresses (bookshops, service providers, etc.)
Legal affairs, e.g. employment regulations, health and safety
Standard letters

5.4.1 Student records

Student records will have to be maintained in such a way that there is easy access to information for whatever purposes it is needed. In a school with a large, regular turnover, such records may only be needed for the duration of the course, although it is a good idea to maintain records of past students in an archive for future reference in case they return.

A typical student record and card will contain the following information:

family name
first name
nationality
language
date of birth
home address
sponsor
profession
test results
educational background
professional background
previous English studies
future intentions
summary of courses taken
public examinations taken
level achieved

In addition to the above, there may be comments by teachers.

5.4.2 Filing systems

The maintenance of such an extensive system of records as outlined above will require careful organization. In general, records will be kept by the staff whose responsibility includes the area concerned. Thus, financial information will be kept in the Bursar's or Bursar's assistant's files, while course information will be the Academic Manager's responsibility. Inevitably some information will be needed by more than one person, in which case duplicates can be stored in different filing systems.

The systematic classification and filing of material is crucial for efficient retrieval purposes. Much depends on the way in which the administration is organized and how responsibilities are allocated and work carried out. There is little point in setting up categories in a filing system, however logically conceived, if they don't reflect the actual work of the people who will make use of the system.

Like any classification scheme, there will be general categories, sub-divided into more specific ones, as in the list of records given above. An example may make this clear. Material on courses will need to be classified into past, present and future courses.

Courses
- Past
  - syllabuses
  - class lists
  - reports
- Present
  - syllabuses
  - class lists
  - timetables
  - materials
  - social programme
- Future
  - syllabuses
  - staffing projections
  - costings
- Planning, setting-up and running procedures

Because information on courses will also involve such matters as student accommodation and travel, some information will be split between two or more parts of the administration. Thus, enrolment, payment, joining and accommodation arrangements will be filed in that part of the Bursar's section which deals with such matters. If members of the teaching staff require such information, they will then have to refer to the appropriate member of the administrative staff.

Obviously, there will have to be a system for cross-checking and keeping each other informed. For instance, the Academic Manager will need to know how enrolments are proceeding for forthcoming courses because staffing and resourcing the course will depend on student numbers. The need for cross-checking, plus the desirability of avoiding duplication of effort, makes the use of a computer-based system very appealing. A good system will make it possible to enter much of the information outlined in the previous sections only once or twice at most. This will reduce the possibilities of error while at the same time making it possible for different members of the administration to call up information as and when they need it.

5.4.3 Correspondence

Letterhead paper, with details of the school's address, telephone, fax and telex numbers is usually taken for granted. What is less often considered is a house style for regular types of correspondence, and indeed form letters of this type will usually be kept on the word processor for adaptation as circumstances require. If all correspondence goes through the general office, a scheme for filing and retrieving copies of the correspondence is essential. To make it possible to retrieve correspondence originating from different members of staff, a simple code may suffice. A typical code is to have the initials of the originator in upper case and those of the secretary in lower case, thus: RVW/ah. All correspondence for RVW will be filed under his name, either chronologically or under sub-categories according to topic or geographical area. Another code is to file according to topic or geographical area and to use appropriate initials for the file name, e.g. FRA would indicate correspondence with France. A numbering system can then follow the initial letters for each item on file.

All secretaries should maintain a day-file in which a copy of all typing is filed chronologically. Such a day-file can be referred to when other means of tracking down an item have been unsuccessful.

Now that it is increasingly common for individual staff members to have the use of word processors, more and more correspondence will by-pass the central office and go straight from the originator to the recipient. Although this may reduce turn round time on correspondence, the danger is that information which should be centrally filed will no longer be located in this way, with individual files accumulating in a haphazard fashion throughout the organization. The dangers inherent in such dispersal are obvious. This means that a system of copying to relevant central files must be maintained so that staff needing to get access to such correspondence are able to do so. Probably the simplest way of achieving this is to have individually-produced correspondence photocopied by someone in the central office before it is posted. A copy will be returned to the originator for his or her file, while another copy will be placed in the appropriate central file. Similarly, replies will be copied to both individual and central files.

5.4.4 Registration procedures

Students will usually come to a school under one of two circumstances. Either they will be recruited individually by word of mouth or publicity; or they will come as part of a group recruited by an agent or sent by a client. In either case, the students will have to be registered because, of course, the school requires a record of students for both financial and pedagogical purposes. There will be variations on registration depending on whether the school runs full-time residential courses or a part-time programme.

FULL-TIME RESIDENTIAL COURSES

1 Potential student writes for information on courses.
2 Information sent. Information includes general and specific material on courses, dates, costs, accommodation requirements and options.
3 Course enrolment form is returned by student, together with pre-payment. This may be either a deposit or the full fee.
4 Accommodation arrangements are made. Student's details are added to list for the course concerned.

5 Acknowledgement sent to student, together with joining instructions: how to reach the school, name and address of accommodation, time and date of first session.
6 Student arrives at school and checks with Bursar's department to pay balance of fees or confirms presence with appropriate member of staff.
7 Final class lists prepared and copied to Academic Manager. Arrangements put in hand for paying accommodation provider.

PART-TIME COURSES

If students are to enrol at the beginning of the term or semester, enrolment will be a major exercise involving teaching as well as administrative staff. Procedures will need to be simple to operate and as time-efficient as possible. The information required will set the basic procedure.

1 Identity of student
2 Course required
3 Payment

To avoid logjams, it will probably be best to have students complete most of the registration form in advance. A room or rooms could be made available for this purpose. Students will then take their completed form to a desk for checking, registration and computation of fees. If fees are to be paid in advance, the fee may then be paid or the student can proceed to a second desk to make payment. The receipt provided may then be required as evidence of payment when students arrive for their first class.

To assist in the efficient running of the process, registration desks may be organized alphabetically. This will help break up the mass of enroling students into sub-groups, provided that the alphabetical grouping reflects the tendency prevailing in the local situation. If, for instance, there are few family names in the Q to Z section of the alphabet, there will be little point in devoting one desk to it.

As students enrol, registration forms can be collected up and sorted into appropriate categories according to the level and course for which they have enrolled. It may be very important to maintain an on-going list of courses if numbers have to be restricted so that registrations for a given level of course can be halted if there is a danger of it being oversubscribed. Alternatively, decisions to set up and run an extra class or classes for a popular programme will have to be made as the true picture emerges during the enrolment process.

5.5 Office hardware

With the growth of information technology, the options open to the manager for office hardware have become enormous, as indicated by the list below. The electronic office has arrived.

- Typewriters
  - manual
  - electric
  - electronic with memory
- Word processors
  - word processing software
  - desk top publishing (DTP) software
- Printers
  - dot matrix
  - daisy wheel
  - laser
  - ink jet
- Photocopiers
- Off-set lithograph
- Computers
  - individual
  - centralized network
  - work stations
- Modems
- Telephone
  - individual
  - network
  - answering machines
- Fax
- Telex
- Electronic Mail

The choice of hardware and accompanying software should be determined by the present and future needs of the office organization. The availability of cheap and powerful computers has now put very sophisticated information management systems within the reach of all but the most shoe-string organizations, but therein lies the danger. It is very easy to install a computerized office system without considering firstly whether it is really necessary and secondly, what the system will most efficiently be used for. It is also common to underestimate its training needs and its organizational effects.

It is common for an organization to 'go into' computers on a small scale as a toe-in-the-water exercise. Or, possibly, there is a computer enthusiast on the staff who persuades people that it would be a good idea to turn over some part of the office system to a computer. A machine and software for word processing or enrolment information may be purchased and the innovation introduced. If, as is likely, the innovation is successful, new uses for the system will soon be found and, quite possibly, the original system is rapidly outgrown. This is where the crunch can come. If records have been entered on a now obsolescent system, introducing a new generation system may require the transfer of data from the old to the new, with all that this implies in terms of time and work.

Rather than move into computer-based systems by accident or default, it is best to take advice from a consultant – as well as from other institutions – because the time and money spent taking such advice will save not only time and money in the future. It will also save stress and strain if an inadequate or inappropriate system is chosen in the first place and has to be replaced subsequently. An independent consultant who is not tied to any particular hardware manufacturer will spend some time interviewing administrative staff and working out a specification of the existing administrative system and predicted needs. Such a specification will form the basis for selecting appropriate hardware and software for a computer system and, armed with this specification, you are in a better position to choose the most appropriate equipment and software than if you place yourself in the hands of a computer salesperson whose interest will be in selling his or her particular brand of equipment.

It is certainly wise, when selecting hardware, to go for equipment which has potential for expansion. The experience of most organizations is that once the system becomes fully integrated into the administration routine, existing memory capacity, for instance, is quickly filled. Partly this is because users tend to be dilatory about 'pruning' or removing from memory obsolete or redundant data and partly it is because such systems seem to create more information.

As far as software is concerned, off-the-shelf is cheaper than tailor-made. However, with a large and complex organization, the tailor-made program will almost certainly be required, whereas with a smaller and less complex organization, existing software packages for financial information, enrolment, timetabling and student data will be available. Such packages provide what is essentially a kind of template that can generally be adapted to individual school requirements, though the advice of a consultant will often be needed in order to do this successfully.

One of the primary factors to consider in the choice of software is whether or not, to use the familiar jargon, it is 'user friendly'. Because of the considerable commercial competition which exists in the software field, most packages for word and data processing, including such financial planning software as spread sheets, are now as easy to use as the state of the art can make them. Even so, there are differences in software packages, and it is wise to take consumer advice, either from a consultant, from other users or from the numerous publications now available. It is also wise to consider buying widely-used software rather than something exotic because advice on commonly used software is much easier to obtain.

It is also sensible to consider a service contract with both the hardware and software suppliers because computers are not infallible. As with all computer purchases, care should be taken in entering into a service agreement. Normally the charge is a percentage of the total cost of the installation and there are usually several levels of service, ranging from instant call-out to service within a specified time from call-out, which can be as long as a week. If your computer system is going to be at the heart of your office organization, even a day can be a long time to have the computer immobilized.

Although computer-based systems can provide information speedily, and while they enable the manipulation of data in ways which can be enormously helpful to all parts of the organization, paper-based records will still be required because of inherent limitations in electronically presented information and the restrictions of access to data stored in a computer. Experience, even with sophisticated mainframe computer-based systems, has shown that paper-based records of such things as registration information will be both essential and more convenient when quick and easy access is needed for such purposes as answering telephone inquiries. So, while student records can usefully be maintained on a data base, the old-fashioned card index with student information arranged alphabetically by student family name will still have an important role to play even in the electronic office.

Paperwork can be usefully saved, though, in other areas. For instance, if there are large numbers of weekly payments to be made to host families, computer-generated cheques will save hours of work in comparison with manually written cheques. Thus, for running a large accommodation scheme, a computer-based system, backed up with paper-based records, will be virtually essential.

A computer-based office system will be a major investment, and so requires careful financial planning (see Chapter 12). To the initial cost of the hardware should be added the cost of software, staff training and servicing of the system. Whatever you do, take the best local advice available and give a great deal of thought to what your office and administrative systems are before purchasing. Do not make the mistake of buying a computer system and then finding a use for it!

5.5.1 Training

The implementation of a computerized system will require running in and training time, both of which will need to be budgeted in costing new installations. Although hardware and software suppliers will usually offer training, there is almost always a cost involved, so some thought will have to be given to choosing staff who will be given the benefit of training. While initial training is useful, experience shows that it is only after a new system has been in use for a period that users realize what the problems are, so that in-service or refresher training may be more useful than a massive dose of pre-service training. In any case, it is essential that the supplier is able to provide a quick response to the teething troubles which inevitably arise with new systems, a point which it is important to clarify with suppliers when commissioning a new system.

Conclusion

Running a school's administration requires a systematic approach so that areas of responsibility are clearly delineated and procedures for running administrative systems are established, understood and used by all.

Running administrative systems is an exercise in information management, whether dealing with timetables or filing and retrieving correspondence. In some areas, such as the design and setting up of computerized systems, specialized advice is needed, while the application of new systems will require time and training.

Follow-up activities

The International Association of Teachers of English as a Foreign Language (IATEFL) has two Special Interest Groups (SIG) of interest to school managers: ELT Management SIG and Micro Users in English as a Second Language Institutes (MUESLI). Both publish newsletters and run events. Further details may be obtained from:

IATEFL
3 Kingsdown Chambers
Kingsdown Park
Tankerton
Whitstable
Kent
England CT5 2DJ

1 Do a time audit of your own, following the procedures outlined in section 5.1.
2 Apply some of the time management principles to your own time management. This will require some discipline and dedication if you are not used to being systematic about how you plan and use your time. If used on a day-to-day basis, planning priorities and making a daily list of things which must be done will become a matter of habit.
3 Make out your own action plan on the basis of your time audit.
4 Make a time review the subject of a staff meeting. Discuss how time is

being used and how each person could make better use of their time, not necessarily to increase productivity but in order to make their work easier and less tense.

5 Review your own timetabling procedures in the light of the scheme outlined in section 5.2. What improvements could you make (a) to your own procedures, and (b) to the scheme outlined here?

6 Make a plan of the administrative system of your school along the lines of the one given in section 5.3. Carefully review the distribution and allocation of responsibilities and consider how to improve the present system. You may find that there is ambiguity in some areas; or you may find that there are some tasks which fall to several hands.

7 Review the records that are maintained in your school. How are they organized and who is responsible for which areas? Are there problems with the present system? If so, what are they? And how could these problems be sorted out?

8 Review the system for typing and photocopying. How does it work? Are there any problems? You may not be aware of any, but it may be that other staff are – consult them. How could these problems be overcome?

9 What are the registration procedures at your school? Review the last registration period – if necessary, consult your colleagues – and consider how the system could be improved. Does it require changes in organization, provision of more resources or time, introduction of new hardware, or what? Sometimes a very simple change in a system will bring about huge improvements, so don't go for major changes first as the way of solving whatever problems have been revealed.

10 Review the systems which could benefit from computerization. What are the benefits of computerization for this aspect of your operation? What would happen if you didn't computerize?

11 This is an in-tray activity.

It is 0830 on Friday 13th. You are Felicity Peacock, the Principal of the Kennet School of English. The school is incorporated as a limited company and you are one of the directors. The original founder of the school, Gerald Maxwell, is the Chairman of the Board, of which there are four members.

The Chairman maintains regular contact with the school, and tends to drop in from time to time. There are monthly board meetings, at which the financial and professional state of the school is reviewed. The main shareholders are concerned with the state of their investment, and one of the board, Mrs Veronica Harwick, tends to take an unduly mercenary interest in the profit margins of the school.

In the school, there are the following staff:

Laura Henderson	*Administrative assistant/Bursar and accommodation manager*
Brenda Maddox	*Secretary/receptionist (full-time)*
Jo Crosby	*Secretary/typist (part-time)*

Bill Pearce	*Caretaker/handyman*
Betty O'Donald	*Cleaner*
Andrew Cook	*Director of Studies*

Full-time teachers

Charles Hardy
Helen Johnson
Julia Marks
Henry Kelly
Paula Wilson
Sandra Keyes

Part-time teachers

Jake Caldwell
Cynthia Jones
Trish Barber
Oliver Haymarket

The full-time staff teach 20 hours per week, the part-timers 15, which yields a total of 180 hours per week over all staff. At the moment, you have the following numbers of classes:

6 × 15 hours per week	*90*	
2 × 25 hours per week	*50*	
2 × 20 hours per week	*40*	
Total hours		*180*

There is a total of 155 students in the school, distributed among these classes. Of the students, there are the following groups:

Japanese college students (number in class: N = 11) doing a 20 hour general English course.
German engineers (N = 13) doing a 15 hour per week EOP course.
Lebanese undergraduates (N = 9) doing a 15 hour per week EAP course.
Mixed nationalities (mostly young continental students) doing 15 hours per week of general English.
Mixed nationalities (mostly Italian and Spanish) doing an FCE course.
Mixed nationalities (mostly Latin American) doing a CPE course.

You have been away on Thursday, attending a committee meeting in London, and you arrive in your office on Friday morning to find a full in-tray.
How would you plan your day and what would be your priorities?

Bahasan International College in U.K.

Downs Road, Reading, Berkshire RG1 5AQ England

Telephone: 0734 310897 Fax: 0734 310459

12th November, 1991

Miss F Peacock
Kennet School of English
Reading RG1 5DE

Dear Miss Peacock

As you know, the Bahasan College has been established on the Downs Road site of the University. In April next year, 150 students will be arriving to begin a first year English language course. Until now, this course has been provided by the Centre for Applied Language Studies at the University. Because of some problems with them, we have decided not to continue our connection with CALS, and we are looking for another organization to help run the first year language programme.

Professor Yamanabe, the head of the college, will be in Reading next week. Would you be able to have a meeting with us to discuss matters?

Yours sincerely

T. Kasanimbe

T Kasanimbe
Bursar

Memorandum from	To
LH	FP
KENNET SCHOOL OF ENGLISH	

SWISS BANKERS

You will remember that we negotiated the fees for this course on the basis of 12 students, but only 11 have turned up. Someone at the Cultural Attache's office phoned today. You'd already left so I couldn't tell you, as you might have been able to call in on the Embassy while you were in London.

Anyway, they are disputing our invoice (which is for the agreed number of 12 students). They say that as only 11 have come, they will only pay for that number. I pointed out that the costing was for a minimum of 12, and that this had been agreed, and I quoted the relevant correspondence.

I'm afraid that this is something only you can deal with, as they obviously won't take any notice of me! Just a reminder: the Swiss fee is £130 per week, so losing one student's fee will cost us £3,900.

Thursday.

Miss Felicity,

Betty was complaining to me about the lavatories. I cleaned up the gents this afternoon after one of the Italian students complained to me.

Bill

WILLOW COTTAGE

Moreton on Marsh,
Nr Rollright,
WARWICKSHIRE

12th November, 1991

Dear Felicity,

How are things going this term? Busy as ever I suppose. I've just been on a Spec. Tour to Latin America. Very exhausting, but great fun. Ophelia in Curitiba sends her greetings, and all of the Anglo staff in Uruguay asked me to give you their regards.

On my return, I've been checking through my records, and I can't find any payments for the two weeks I did for you during the summer - the Polish students course. I'm sure there's been some oversight. Could you check as I am rather short this month - the builders have been working on an extension to my kitchen and they need paying.

I hope you will be up this way before the end of the year. Come and admire my kitchen and have a meal.

Yours,

Donnie

Memorandum from	To
JC	FP
KENNET SCHOOL OF ENGLISH	

Inspector Henderson from the local CID left a message. He wants to see you on Friday about 'something urgent'. He wouldn't say any more than that. You can call him on 98076 Extension 469.

THAMES BOOKS LIMITED

Bridge House
Bridge Street
Reading
Berkshire

12th November 1991

The Principal
Kennet School of English
Kendrick Road
Reading

Dear Ms Peacock

As you know, we have been supplying your school with books ever since we started up in business, some five and a half years ago, and our association has been a very happy one. Unfortunately, a recent incident has marred this relationship, and I am now writing to you direct in the hope that we can resolve the matter.

In September, we received an order from your school for 28 copies of THEMES student's book and one copy of the teacher's book. The publisher was slow in supplying copies, and we informed your administrative assistant that stocks would not be available until early in October. We were told that this would be alright.

When the books came in, they were delivered to the school on 17th October, with an invoice for payment. A week later we received a message to collect the books, since they were not required. I contacted the administrative assistant, with whom we normally do all of our business, and the discussion became somewhat strained.

We have not so far collected the books; nor have they been returned. But then nor, on the other hand, has our bill been settled. Naturally, we do not wish to push for payment, but you will understand our position.

I should welcome some clarification on the matter and look forward to hearing from you shortly so that we shall be in a position to accept further orders from your school.

Yours sincerely

S. Urquart

Simon Urquart
Manager

COMFISEAT **LIMITED**

Hardy Bottom

Oldham

Lancs

12th November 1991

Ms Felicity Peacock
Principal
Kennet School of English
Kendrick Road
Reading RG1 5DV

Dear Ms Peacock

We have pleasure in enclosing our new brochure describing our latest range of institutional seating. You will note that we have introduced a new line, the ComfiClassroom Chair, which is stackable.

If you are able to place an order with us by 20th of the month, we can give you a special introductory discount of 10% on this range.

We look forward to hearing from you shortly, and assure you of our attention at all times.

Yours sincerely

Richard Robinson

Richard Robinson
Sales Manager

Encl.

In Confidence

Felicity,

As you know, my wife and I recently became parents for the first time. We have received some lovely gifts from staff and students, but we were quite nonplussed when Hakim, one of the Omani students, turned up at our house the other evening with a pram! It was a brand new Mothercare one which cost about a hundred quid.

Anyway, I didn't know what to say, so I accepted it; but of course, we don't want to keep it as we can't accept that sort of present. (He said things about it being 'our custom' and 'the Arab way' and so on— all very charmingly done.) How can we return it to him without offending him? I'd like your advice on this, as we'd like to sort things out before the weekend, if we could, because Jane's mother is coming to stay— and she's bringing a new pram as a present from her and my father-in-law.

Harry

HENRY WILKINS MANAGEMENT

Registered office:
12 Rivermead, Reading, RG1 1SB
Telephone Reading (0734) 52026/8

Your Reference
Our Reference MET/WH
Date 12th November 1991

PRIVATE AND CONFIDENTIAL

Felicity Peacock,
Principal,
Kennet School of English

Dear Miss Peacock,

Julio Rodriguez,
14 St. Johns Crescent,
London E5

The above proposes to rent accommodation through our agency for a period of twelve months at a rent of £700.00 per calender month.

Your name has been given as a referee and we should be grateful if, in confidence, you would supply the following information;

Period of his/her employment

Position held

Permanency of Position

Salary

Please would you also let us know whether or not, in your opinion, the above named would make a suitable tenant.

We would be grateful for an early reply.

Yours faithfully,

Henry Wilkins Management

Memorandum from
JM
KENNET SCHOOL OF ENGLISH

To
FP

CHINESE DELEGATION

17.00 hours

I've just taken a phone call from the Chinese Embassy. Two representatives are coming tomorrow, Friday, on a fact- finding visit. They said that they had contacted you about it some time ago. They're due to arrive at 11.30 so I suppose you'll have to take them to lunch. Shall I book a table at the Peking Palace?

12th November, 1991

Dear Felicity,

Veronica phoned me the other day to say that she was worried about the figures from last month. I tried to reassure her, saying that we were having the best Autumn term in our history, but she wouldn't be persuaded.

Could I suggest that we have lunch on Friday to chat about how to deal with this situation? Naturally, I'll back you all the way, as I'm very happy with our current financial situation, but I think I need a few more facts and figures so as to deal with Veronica's worries.

Give me a call at the office to confirm lunch.

Yours,

Gerald.

LABOLING
2 Queen's Chambers
Queen's Road
Reading

12th November 1991

The Principal
Kennet School of English
Kendrick Road
Reading

Dear Ms Peacock

You will recall that we met at an ARELS/FELCO weekend earlier this year and we agreed that it would be admirable if we could collaborate on a project, given that we run our operations in the same town.

Recently, we were approached by a foreign embassy with a view to running a large course for participants from their country. The project is larger than we can handle, particularly as it involves some prelimanary work in the country. However, we are reluctant to turn away business, so I am wondering if we can take our earlier idea of collaboration a step further?

The embassy wants a reply immediately - they always do, of course! Could we have a chat about it either on Friday or on Monday so that I can respond to their request early next week?

I'll look forward to hearing from you.

Yours sincerely

E. Portman

Ernest Portman
Principal

Felicity –

Laminex rep. called – wants to know when would be a suitable time for him to come + demo the laminating machine that Andy wanted to order.

JD

KENNET SCHOOL OF ENGLISH

Kendrick Road

Reading

Felicity Peacock — 12th November 1991
Principal
Kennet School of English

Dear Felicity

I am writing on behalf of the staff regarding conditions of service.

All full-time teachers are contracted to teach 20 contact hours per week. There is nothing in our contracts specifying other duties, except a statement to the effect that we shall be "required to undertake such marking and preparation as are necessary for effective teaching" and that we shall be expected to accompany students on "excursions and visits which shall from time to time take place."

Since the beginning of the current academic year, we have all noticed that our contact hours have been increased (we are now all working a 25 hour week) while the running of the new self - access centre has been added to our existing commitments - some of us are doing an hour a day there, over and above our teaching load. This means that we are doing considerably more than our contracted contact time.

Although we regard some additional work as a part of our professional role, there is a widespread feeling that this recent increase is, to quote one colleague, "the thin edge of the cost cutters' wedge." Strong words, perhaps, but symptomatic. Furthermore, a rumour to the effect that the school has just had its most successful summer operation for the past ten years has done nothing to allay a sense of financial exploitation.

Naturally, I have done all I can to reduce such feelings, but I feel that it is now imperatve to discuss these issues with you so that we can restore staff - management relations to the happy atmosphere which has always typified this institution.

Yours sincerely

Charles

Charles Hardy
Staff Representative

Copy to: Andrew Cook, DOS

Inland Revenue Accounts Office (Shipley)

BRADFORD

West Yorkshire BD98 8AA

Date 12th November 1991

Old Reference 558 DA 18890

New Reference 487 DA 94933

Ms Felicity Peacock
Principal
Kennet School of English
Kendrick Road Reading RG1 5DV

Dear Ms Peacock

It has come to my attention that three of the 'self - employed' teachers at your school are in fact only employed by yourself and no one else. They are:

Jake Caldwell
Cynthia Jones
Patricia Barber

Their respective periods of 'employment' with you are:

2 years 3 months
1 year 5 months
1 year 7 months

We cannot, on any account, classify these people as self - employed. This means that you are at fault for not deducting PAYE and accounting for National Insurance contributions for their past period of employment. It is essential that you commence deducting PAYE and accounting for their National Insurance immediately and that arrangements are made to pay the arrears of unpaid PAYE and National Insurance.

I should be grateful if you would get in touch with me as soon as possible to discuss this oversight. I will also inform you of the sums involved.

Yours sincerely

Jon Snowdon

Jon Snowdon
for Collector of Taxes

TELEX

KENSCHOOL
READING

TEACHERS GROUP ARRIVING FRIDAY 20TH AND NOT REPEAT NOT SUNDAY 22ND
PLEASE ARRANGE COLLECTION GATWICK 0920 ARRIVAL BRITCOUN PARIS

Felicity,

Don't forget there's a staff meeting at 4.30 Friday afternoon. Some people have given me some items for the agenda:

Installation of Muslim ablution facilities
Video equipment
Oxford examination
Algerian firemen course

Can you see me before lunch so that I can type up the agenda?

Laura

Dear Miss Peacock

I am sorry but I am resigning.

For the past few months, I have had a lot of trouble in keeping the lavatories clean because some of the students just don't know how to use them decently. Today was the limit. I put a notice on the door saying Keep Out. While I was cleaning the men's lavatory, one of them came in and started going while I was there. I came out very shocked. I cannot work like this any more.

Yours obediently

Betty Jordan

Felicity

I'm trying to fix up some mock interviews for my Lebanese students to prepare them for university interviews - Could you do some of them? They don't know you (except by sight) so it would be good for them to have a new person instead of those of us who teach them. Would Friday morning be OK?
Julia

12th

Felicity

Trouble at Mill! There's been a bit of a set-to in Paula's class with the bankers. One of them is a bit of a **** and he said something to Paula yesterday which upset her. She made some remarks to him about machismo and attitudes to women, which, although I don't think he or the group really understood it, didn't go down very well. So, one minute I had a deputation to complain, and Paula in tears the next.

I'm not surprised that this has happened, but I hoped we could keep things on an even keel till the end of term, when we could change classes round. I think that I'll have to alter classes as from Monday, but this may mean that I'll have to bump up the hours of one or two of the part-timers.

Can I see you tomorrow to sort it out?

Andy.

Memorandum from	To
BS	FP
KENNET SCHOOL OF ENGLISH	

GROUP OF YEMENI AGRONOMISTS

Julie Grant from ETCU phoned to ask if we could take a group of about 10 Yemeni agronomists in three months for between 6 and 9 months tuition. They would like to have full details of fees, course content, accommodation, excursion programme, etc., early next week so that the Foundation, which is funding the students, can compare our costings with others before deciding where to send these students.

Brenda.

59 Robin Drive
Earley
Reading
November 12th 1991

The Principal
Kennet School of English
Kendrick Road
Reading

Dear Madam

My family has been on your accommododation register for three years now and we have taken a lot of your students as boarders. At the moment we have Julio, a young man from Colombia, staying with us. He is very nice, but I am very worried about him. He isn't eating, he complains of headaches, and he is missing classes. We have tried to make him feel at home, and my son and daughter, who are a similar age, have tried to take him out of himself.

I have spoken to the lady who is in charge of your accommodation register, but she hasn't done anything about it. The trouble is, Julio's depression is having an effect on my own family and on me, too. I don't know what the best thing is to do.

Yours faithfully

K. Scriven (Mrs.)

Friday,

Miss Felicity,

I took a call early this morning from the hospital. One of the students... Chantel Genet... was taken in this morning. They would'nt say what it was. I said I'd ask you to call them when you came in

Bill

TELEX

PRINCIPAL
KENSCHOOL
READING

COSTINGS FOR 4 WEEK COURSE FOR JAPANESE TEACHERS REQUIRED BY 20TH AS PER OUR LETTER OF 1ST. JACKSON CIEE.

6 MANAGING CURRICULUM DEVELOPMENT AND INNOVATION

Aims

The aims of this chapter are:

1 to place curriculum development within the context of management.
2 to exemplify curriculum development through Skilbeck's situational curriculum development model.
3 to work systematically through this model.
4 to relate curriculum development to the management of innovation.
5 to review factors which facilitate and hinder innovation.
6 to outline a sequence of stages in managing the implementation of innovation.
7 to apply some of the principles and procedures given in the chapter to the analysis of past or the planning of future curriculum innovations.

Introduction

One of the problems we meet when discussing management within an educational context is that schools in general tend to differ from the commercial organizations in which most management theory and practice are grounded. In comparison with such institutions, the aims of a school are difficult to define, being vague, value-loaded and open to debate, whereas those of a commercial organization are relatively clear-cut. A further complicating factor in ELT is that there is an important distinction between the public or state-funded and the private sectors. Whereas the measurable outputs of the former will tend to be in terms of academic achievement, the outputs of the latter will necessarily have to include the financial as well as the academic, since a privately-funded language school will have to generate profits in order to remain financially viable. Another complicating factor as far as both sectors are concerned is that it can be argued that the most significant objectives of schools are those which cannot be quantified and that, furthermore, their importance lies in long-term rather than short-term effects.

Yet another problem concerns the teachers themselves. They share a common professional background and they claim a measure of autonomy in the teaching/learning process. Indeed, such autonomy is often built into the system and may even be guaranteed by legislation. As professionals, teachers expect and may even demand participation (and at very least consultation) within the decision-making process.

One difficulty with involving teachers in decision-making lies in the fragmented organizational and management structure within the school and between the school and other organizations in the wider community. The autonomy of the teacher and the fragmentation of school organization tend to go hand in hand, and in some contexts are such that there is virtually no contact between staff teaching the same subject. Unfortunately, a lack of collegiality of this kind greatly inhibits the effects of curriculum renewal, which is inevitably a team exercise, whether it is a team involving the teacher and students, or a team consisting of the professional peer group within a school or educational system as a whole.

An absence of collegiality means that it is virtually impossible for any initiatives to come from the staff themselves, while the implementation of even centrally controlled initiatives will face problems because of the absence of an organizational structure within which to diffuse such changes. For some educational systems, a social interaction model of change may not be an appropriate one, even though it is clear that social factors are crucial in the acceptance and implementation of successful curriculum change. Furthermore, in the commercial and industrial world, team work and the dispersal of management among networks of teams is now being seen as the most effective way of operating (see for example Naisbitt and Aburdene, 1985). It would be ironical if, during a period in which exciting and challenging new management concepts and practice are evolving, management in ELT was to isolate itself from such potentially enlightening influences.

A collegial school culture would seem to be essential to any school-based curriculum innovation, and it is such school-based curriculum renewal to which Malcolm Skilbeck (1984) gives priority in his situational model of curriculum development, to be discussed further below. This model is based on the assumption that, firstly, curriculum development will be something internal to the institution, not imposed from outside, but that at the same time 'the curriculum should not be parochially conceived' because any educational institution is part of a network of relationships which includes stakeholders other than the members of the school itself.

In advocating school-based curriculum development, Skilbeck shows an awareness of the effects of controls which are extrinsic to the school and he observes that

> neither the independent initiatives of the school nor those larger external forces in the curriculum are by themselves sufficient for achieving the system wide kinds of changes that are needed. Imposed change from without does not work, because it is not

> adequately thought out, or it is not understood, or resources are not available to carry it through, or because it is actively resisted. Within-institution change is, by its nature, situation specific, often piecemeal, incomplete, of mediocre quality and so on. Each process requires the other, in a well worked out philosophy and programme of developments. (Skilbeck 1984:5)

So, while initiatives may be school-based, support must be system-wide. In practice, this will mean that those responsible for the management of the education system will need to collaborate with those from whom the initiatives have come.

Finally, most teachers and managers in schools have very little time for management. For most, it is a free or part-time activity, squeezed into an already busy schedule whose priorities will tend to be pedagogical and pastoral ones. As Bush (1986:7) says,

> This time limitation has serious implications for the nature of management in educational institutions with decision-making often reverting simply to those who are available.

Clearly, then, management within a school faces a number of significant constraints and it may well be that simply overcoming these constraints will constitute a change as in, for instance, modifying organizational structure to provide such participative machinery as committees, departments or sections. Indeed, it may well be the case that establishing the mechanisms for implementing innovation – such as setting up a committee or a working party – could be as far as the change process goes, while the structures themselves may give rise to outcomes quite different from those originally envisaged. For instance, a working party, finding that the task for which it was originally set up fails to materialize, may then set about inventing new tasks to perform. Thus, a group which is brought into being to develop a new type of course which is then aborted may turn its attention to an alternative initiative which results in a new teaching programme quite different from that for which the group was set up to develop.

6.1 Curriculum development

The ELT teacher will be familiar with the process of planning, setting up and running courses. Likewise, the academic director of a school will know about designing syllabuses, making choices of content and materials, and assessing student performance. All of these are aspects of curriculum development (CD). What differentiates CD from syllabus and course design is the breadth of scope of CD and the demands it makes on management.

A curriculum should not be regarded simply as a kind of super syllabus; there are qualitative differences between the two. A syllabus tends to be a sequentially organized specification of what is to be taught, partly justified on theoretical grounds, and partly shaped by practical considerations. Traditionally, the focus in a syllabus has been on the selection and organization of content.

A curriculum, in comparison, covers not only the content, but also the goals of the teaching programme as well as the activities which will form part of the learning experiences for a given group of students. In short, curriculum is concerned with objectives and methods as well as content. Finally, the matching up of outcomes with objectives involves evaluation. The four main elements which traditionally form the basis of the curriculum are summed up in Figure 6.1.

Figure 6.1 Curriculum model

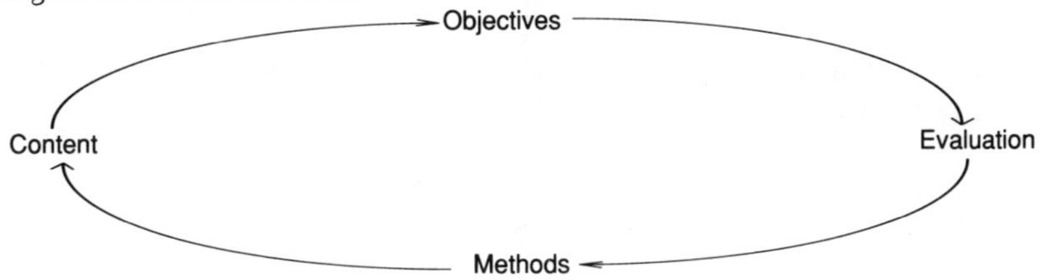

This cycle, which forms the basis of the so-called means-ends model of curriculum associated with Taba (1962) and Tyler (1949), can be represented as a flow chart (see Figure 6.2 overleaf), in which the parallels with a systematic approach to management, will be clear.

A systematic approach begins with the specification of objectives, followed by a plan on how to achieve the objectives using the personnel and resources available, the outcomes to be evaluated by comparing achievements with objectives. Both the curriculum model above and the systematic approach to management discussed in section 6 of Chapter 1 are rational planning models based on the assumption that it is rational to specify the goals of an activity before engaging in the activity itself. Indeed, the processes of curriculum development in a language school or a department within a more broadly based educational organization are not essentially different from the practices of good management which are applied to any kind of project. This similarity will become more obvious as we work through Skilbeck's model of curriculum development.

6.1.1 A curriculum development management model

Of all the numerous activities which we engage in as human beings, education is value-loaded; that is, there are values and beliefs which determine very profoundly the aims and methods realized in the school curriculum. So, any curriculum model is an expression of a particular ideology and language teaching is no more immune to the influence of such ideologies than any other subject (Clark 1987).

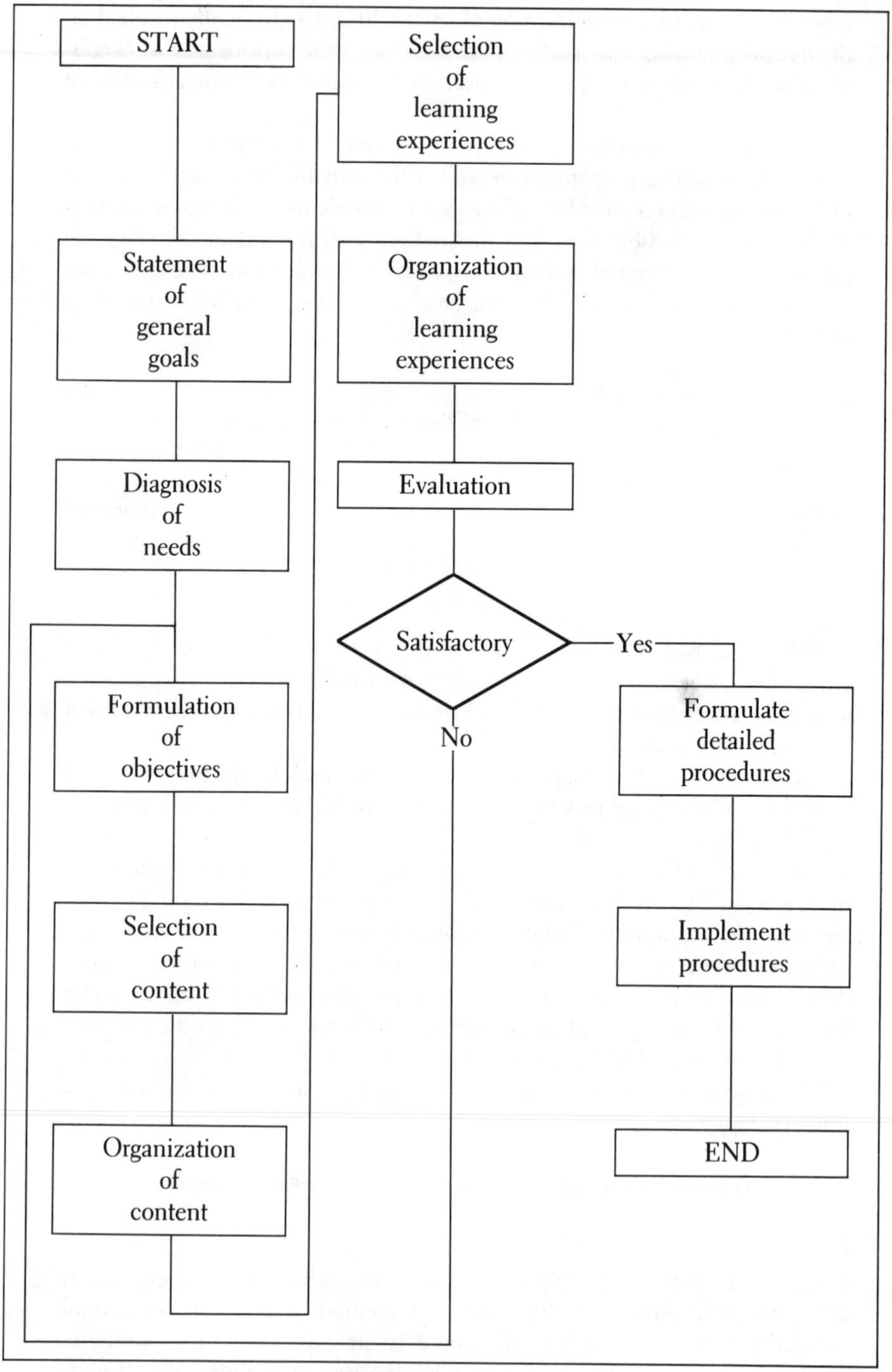

Figure 6.2 Flow chart of means-ends curriculum development model

One view of education is that it is concerned with the transmission, intact, of an esteemed cultural heritage, while another view is one which stresses the growth and self-realization of the individual. Yet another view sees education as an instrument of social change. The first viewpoint will give rise to a curriculum in which the emphasis will tend to be on conformity to set norms; in other words, the learner has to adhere to prescribed canons of correctness and acceptability, and the language curriculum would consequently stress the learning and application of grammatical rules and, quite possibly, the study of prescribed works of literature as products of the esteemed cultural heritage. The second viewpoint will tend to err towards an approach which encourages individual achievement, possibly at the expense of conformity. One manifestation of such an approach would be the attitude expressed in such statements as 'it doesn't matter how you say it, so long as you express yourself/get your message across'. The third viewpoint may have a strong political orientation because education – and specifically, language – will be seen as having an empowering function by helping individuals or groups to achieve status or power, or it may be seen as a means towards encouraging economic, political or cultural exchange and integration.

The ideological differences among these three approaches may not be obvious in practice, especially as in ELT in particular, there is a tendency towards eclecticism, particularly in methodology, which can obscure fundamental differences in the ideological basis of different language curricula. The surface similarities, notably in respect of methodology, can be deceptive, however, and it will be found that fundamental differences in value systems among the players in the ELT game can give rise to substantial problems when it comes to the management of curriculum development, and particularly the management of innovation. Indeed, curriculum development and the introduction of innovation tend to go hand in hand, since the planning and introduction of new curricula are generally concerned with introducing something new rather than simply recycling something old. These are questions which we shall address in a later section. Meanwhile, we shall exemplify the process of curriculum development by working through Skilbeck's situational model, summarized in Figure 6.3.

Figure 6.3 Skilbeck's situational curriculum model

Analyse the situation
Define objectives
Design the teaching-learning programme
Interpret and implement the programme
Assess and evaluate

As Skilbeck (1984:231) himself points out, 'such a diagrammatic representation of the process of curriculum making must simplify and risk distortion by its very brevity and orderliness' and he suggests that we should 'be ready to take concurrently or even in reverse what may suggest themselves to the orderly-minded as items for step-by-step progression'. The value of the sequence depicted in Figure 6.3, in Skilbeck's view, is that it provides for the following:

> First, we may use it to provide a resume, a kind of prospectus of tasks to be accomplished. Second, it can be the basis of agreed action and hence help in reducing arbitrary or authoritarian decisions, a matter of some importance when hierarchies may feel challenged by unstructured reviews and evaluations. Third, it will be useful if it encompasses, in simplified ways, crucial and productive kinds of action . . . Fourth, what is proposed is useful if it helps in the presentation and communication to interested parties of what is planned and is happening in the curriculum. (Skilbeck 1984:232)

Each of the stages in Skilbeck's model gives rise to a set of questions which provide a basis for information gathering or action. We shall take each stage by turn.

6.1.2 Analyse the situation

The questions to be dealt with here are concerned with clarifying the current situation *before* looking to the future. It is only by analysing the current situation that problems, if there are any, will be revealed. When the whole issue of innovation in methodology tends to operate as a bandwagon, it is very easy to apply a solution to a problem which may not exist, or to bring about problems which a fashionable solution will have called into existence.

WITHIN THE SCHOOL

1 What is the existing curriculum including the school rules, rituals and value sets? This includes not only the rules which relate to students, but to staff as well. And they include unspoken rules as well as those which are codified in, for instance, staff contracts or a school handbook. Other clues to the curriculum can be found in the classroom: how teacher and students interact with each other, and how students interact with students. Repeated patterns of behaviour are especially significant in revealing the basis of the curriculum.
2 What is the students' experience of, performance in and perception of the curriculum? This viewpoint is one which teachers probably give little attention to, partly because it is difficult to obtain a students' eye view of

what is happening to them. Direct questioning of students may not be very helpful, whereas attending to what students say to each other and how they react to lessons and materials will reveal more.

3 What is the curriculum context within the school (i.e. social climate, patterns of conduct etc.)? The school context will vary considerably according to the type of school. Thus, a state school which is part of a national education system will be in a very different position from a private language school in Britain; and both will be different from a private language school on the Continent.

4 What are the strengths and capacities of the staff? What are the staff qualifications? What are they good at? What special skills and abilities do they possess? (See the discussion of job descriptions and personal specifications in Chapter 2.)

5 What are the available resources for the curriculum? This includes material and human resources and will take account of both the obvious material resources, such as textbooks and hardware like video recorders, and the resources available in the community outside the school walls.

THE WIDER ENVIRONMENT

1 What kind of neighbourhood, community, society are we serving? Again, a distinction will be made between state and private institutions. A private language school in England will give rather different answers to this question from a state school in a non-English-speaking country.

2 What are the key educational policies to which we should be responding (Local Education Authority, national, international etc.)? These policies can be highly significant and market research will be responsive to changes in education policy. It is increasingly the case that language policy is a significant part of educational planning and all schools, whether private or state-funded, will be influenced by such policy.

3 What kinds of resource/support can we draw upon? This includes local or state educational authorities, teachers' centres, teachers' associations and publishers' workshops, as well as research and publications.

4 What are some of the changes, proposals and developments in curriculum practice and ideas that could be useful for us here? This includes ideas from outside ELT as well as developments within it.

Skilbeck's set of questions can be supplemented by a scheme devised by Roger Bowers (1983), see Figure 6.4 overleaf, in which the systems most directly related to curriculum development are displayed. The significance of such an interlocking set of elements will become even more obvious in later discussion of factors facilitating and hindering innovation.

Figure 6.4 Bowers' scheme of elements in curriculum development projects

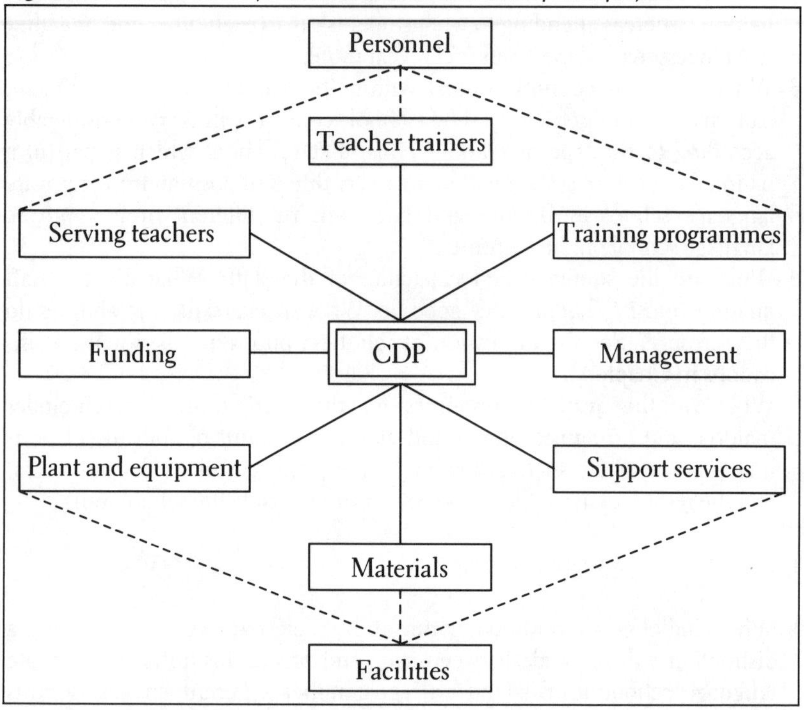

In the meantime, if we look back to Skilbeck's set of questions, it will be clear that some adaptation or extrapolation will be needed according to circumstance since his model was developed with state-funded educational systems in mind, whereas in ELT there is, as we have already noted, a substantial private sector which exists outside and independently of the public sector. Even so, no great powers of imagination are called upon to extrapolate to the private language sector, while some consideration of the questions can lead to valuable insight into the precise nature and function of a school. For instance, the question, 'What kind of neighbourhood, community, society are we serving?', though not having obvious reference to a language school serving clients from a multitude of countries of origin, draws attention to a very important factor, both for curriculum development within the school and for defining the present and future market for the school's services.

6.1.3 Define objectives

Defining objectives is a critical stage in any operation, and in curriculum development as elsewhere, the question of defining objectives will occur at more than one stage. Furthermore, defining objectives tends to need much more time and discussion, while also giving rise to more dispute than most other parts of the process. Skilbeck makes the following points about objectives:

1 Objectives in a curriculum should be stated as what it is desired that students will learn and as actions to be undertaken by teachers and those associated with them to affect, influence, or bring about these desired objectives; they need to be clear, concise and to be capable of being understood by the learners themselves.
2 Objectives are directional and dynamic in that they must be reviewed, modified and if necessary reformulated progressively as the teaching-learning process unfolds.
3 Objectives gain their legitimacy by being related systematically both to general aims and to the practicalities of teaching and learning, and by the manner of their construction and adoption in the school . . . it is desirable to try to show that the objectives have a rational and legitimate basis.
4 There are several types of objectives: broad and general versus specific; long- and short-term; higher order cognitive versus lower order information; subject-specific versus global; and so on. Working groups . . . need to select and plot types of objectives.
5 The construction of curriculum objectives has to be participatory, involving students as well as teachers, parents and community as well as professionals.

It is notable, in view of the importance given in current management practice to the participation in decision-making of those affected by the decisions, that Skilbeck pays particular attention to the participatory nature of defining objectives. It is also notable that he stresses the importance of demonstrating their rationality and legitimacy. Important though this undoubtedly is, rationality alone is not sufficient for achieving acceptance of objectives (Nicholls, 1983). Even so, the opportunity for people to work out their understanding of what is involved is undoubtedly an important factor in achieving acceptance.

6.1.4 Design the teaching-learning programme

Here Skilbeck refers to aspects which clearly fall within the domain of management, particularly with respect to the organization of people, resources and time. He lists the following:

1 The fundamental orientation of the curriculum, as for example areas of experience in a core curriculum, or academic specializations or leisure interests in the elective part of the curriculum.
2 The groupings and combinations of subject matter.
3 The groupings of students, for example mixed ability, or special interest groups.
4 The relationship of learning in the different subject areas to the overall objectives of the curriculum (a particularly important point in ESL contexts or in English for Specific Purposes programmes).

5 The scope, sequence and structure of teaching content.
6 Space, resources, materials, equipment.
7 The proposed methods of teaching and learning.
8 Staffing needs and allocations.
9 Timetabling and scheduling.

6.1.5 Interpret and implement the programme

Interpreting and implementing the programme is the most challenging step because it is here that misunderstandings can – and do – occur. People's ideas differ, and there may be resistance or indifference to the curriculum proposals which have been put forward. It is very important to take account of these variations in people's understandings and attitudes, which are quite normal, because they can destabilize even the most praiseworthy attempts at curriculum development. This is a recurrent theme in any discussions of change and development, and one to which we shall be returning.

6.1.6 Assess and evaluate

A distinction is to be made between assessing, which is concerned with making judgements on students' learning potential and performance, and evaluation, which is involved with collecting evidence on and making judgements about the curriculum as a whole, including planning, designing and implementing it. In fact, evaluation will characterize each stage of the curriculum design process, as is illustrated in Figure 6.5.

Figure 6.5 The place of evaluation (from White 1988, adapted from Bramley 1986)

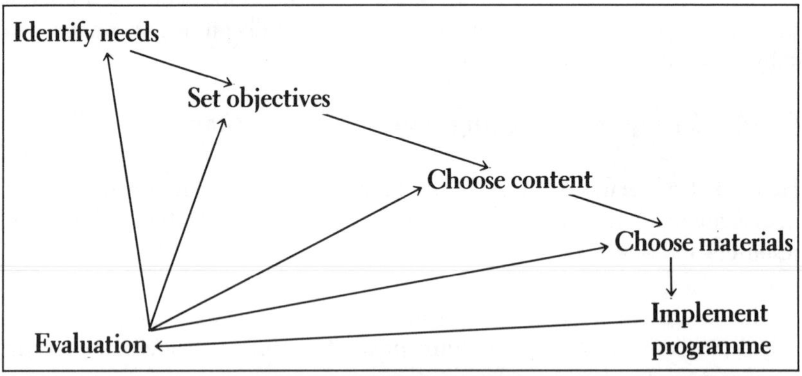

In this scheme, evaluation has a formative as well as a summative role. In other words, evaluation can modify the shape of things during the process of development. Indeed, evaluation as feedback is crucial and is part of good management practice since it is foolhardy to assume that because something has been set in motion, it will automatically reach a desired conclusion. Keeping an eye on things is a vital function of evaluation.

It is also important to build in evaluation from the beginning rather than add it later on because the definition of objectives (*What should we be able to do at the end of a given stage?*), the specification of success criteria (*What are acceptable levels of performance or achievement?*) and the evaluation of outcomes (*How can we measure or demonstrate effects?*) form an inseparable trio.

As in defining objectives, what has characterized recent trends in evaluation is a concern to involve everyone. As McCabe (1987:1) says,

> Everyone's view is important. Evaluation is a continuum embracing everyone in the learning business, teachers, pupils – and even evaluation consultants. Evaluation, according to this ideal view, involves everyone in learning more deeply than before. Its harnessing makes everyone's view valuable, and it makes alienation less likely, in the sense that students or teachers who feel that they can influence what is being done, who know that their views are being heard are more likely to feel responsible for and committed to their education. Where learning is truly negotiated between student and teacher, or educational innovation involves an effective partnership between administrator and teachers, evaluation plays an integral part.

Because evaluation may be perceived as a threat, most notably by those responsible for developing and implementing a new curriculum, it is vital that evaluation should focus on *issues* and not individuals. It is also important that the aims of the evaluation are clear to all involved and that the evaluation should be as impartial as possible. Parties to the evaluation should be assured of confidentiality and control over the information they provide, and all parties should be consulted and involved in the planning and running of whatever evaluation procedures are used. Finally, *all* levels of the organizational hierarchy should be accountable; that is, evaluation should not simply be a calling to account of teachers, who will tend to be at the 'sharp end' of implementing curriculum changes, but also of academic administrators and management. After all, if teachers have been starved of funds needed for new materials, those responsible for budgetary planning are as accountable for the unsuccessful outcomes as the teachers whose work was restricted by inadequate resourcing.

Impartiality may be assured by bringing in an outside evaluator whose role and terms of reference have to be agreed in advance by all who are party to the evaluation. There may well be practical and financial constraints on employing an outside evaluator, particularly if the development to be evaluated is small scale. In most cases, the evaluator (in the sense of someone with that role) will be a member of the home team. Again, their terms of reference should be quite clear and reached by consensus. Furthermore, the evaluator should not be placed in a position of having to carry out an evaluation of an unrelated controversial issue under the guise of evaluating current curriculum development.

6.2 Implementing innovation

Curriculum development is necessarily concerned with making changes in some or all aspects of teaching. Consequently, curriculum development can be regarded as an instance of developing and implementing innovation. We can view innovation from two different perspectives. First, there is what we can call a *macro* view, which sees innovation as concerning fundamental aspects of the organization, be it a department, a school or a complete state system. Second, there is a *micro* view, which looks at innovation as being concerned with one element within a broader context.

On a macro level, we have the kind of innovation involved in a major policy review within a school or education system in which the mission of the school or the aims, content, methods and forms of evaluation of a national system are redefined, as has been the case in Britain in the late 1980s. A policy review in a school, a change of ownership or management, the need for a response to changing market forces (see Part Two), or an increased concern with accountability through evaluation and teacher appraisal (Chapter 3), will also involve such macro level innovation. On a micro level there are the kinds of innovation which often occur on a small scale basis when individuals within a school introduce new hardware or new techniques, either in the office or in the classroom. What all such innovations involve is an act of learning on the part of those concerned with using them, and unless we take this important fact into account, the implementation of an innovation can be at best disappointing, at worst a catastrophe.

Indeed, the first difficulty lies in the nature of innovation itself. Unlike change, which is any involuntary alteration between one time and another, innovation is planned and deliberate – sometimes inadequately planned and muddled, but nevertheless with an intention to bring about an improved state of affairs (Miles 1964:13). Audrey Nicholls (1983:4), in her book on educational innovation, has defined innovation as

> an idea, object or practice perceived as new by an individual or individuals, which is intended to bring about improvement in relation to desired objectives, which is fundamental in nature and which is planned and deliberate.

Nicholls notes that there are a number of problems associated with innovation. Her first point is that because innovation, as she has defined it, is fundamental in nature, it will involve changes in teachers' attitudes and practices. Secondly, innovation will almost always lead to an increase in teachers' workloads. Thirdly, there will also be an economic cost in terms of time and funds.

What is most significant, however, is the way in which innovations are perceived by all of those involved with them. It has to be realized that the view of an innovation differs according to where you stand in the system. There are two quite different viewpoints: that of the *change* agent – the person advocating the innovation – and that of the *receiver* or *changer* – the person who is being asked to put the innovation into effect. It would be scarcely surprising if their perceptions of the innovation did not differ. To take a parallel instance, no two readers will bring the same interpretation to a text, and today it is widely accepted that the meaning of a text only partly inheres in the text itself because meaning is also provided by what the reader brings to the reading of it. As a result, the meaning which is finally arrived at derives from the negotiation which has gone on between the perceptions and understandings of the reader and the meanings and intentions of the writer as revealed in the text.

Similarly, an innovation in language teaching, be it a syllabus, a textbook or a method, will have different meanings to the inventor and to the change agent on the one hand than they will to the client or receiver, in this case a teacher, on the other. Likewise, changes within an organization or changes in working relationships – as will occur on the introduction of a teacher appraisal scheme (Chapter 3) – will also mean different things to different people. Thus, the introduction of an appraisal scheme which is seen as an application of sound management principles by senior management as change agent may be perceived to be a threat by teachers as receivers, especially if the innovation is linked to a merit-related pay or promotion scheme.

Whatever his or her status in the organization, a change agent (Havelock 1973) is the person who introduces the innovation to the system or organization in which it will be implemented. Typically, a change agent is someone who has been introduced to the innovation on a course or at a conference. In hierarchical organizations, the change agent will usually be someone in a higher position, such as the Principal, Academic Director or Director of Studies. The change agent can also be someone lower down in the hierarchy. It is not unusual, for instance, for new teachers to be change agents by importing ideas into the school which they are joining. Whatever the status of the change agents, it is vital that they can understand the receivers' viewpoint of the innovation, a point which Everard and Morris (1985:171) make in their discussion of change.

> Effecting change calls for open-mindedness and a readiness to understand the feelings and position of others. Truth and reality are multifaceted, and the reality of other people's worlds is different from yours. Most people act rationally and sensibly within the reality of the world *as they see it.* They make assumptions about the world, and about the causes of things, which differ from yours, because their experiences are different, and they even experience the same event in different ways. Hence innovators have to address

themselves not just to the world they see, but also to the world other people see, however misguided, perverse and distorted they may think the outlook of others to be.

Failure to take the receivers' viewpoint into consideration will almost invariably lead to difficulties because in the process of dissemination and implementation, an innovation will tend to be 'reinvented' by the adopters. An obvious example which comes to mind is the way in which communicative language teaching has been adapted in widely different ways by those who claim to have adopted it. In fact, as has already been noted, such reinvention is a necessary part of coming to terms with the innovation, even if it is disappointing or infuriating to the inventor or to the change agent. So that the people adopting the innovation can come to terms with it, they will almost always need retraining and this will require them not only to work with the innovation, but also to reflect upon the experience of attempting to apply it. In other words, experience and theorizing will need to be combined in a mutually enriching fashion.

It will be clear from this account that two key words in this process are *understanding* and *negotiation*, both of which take place through *communication*. It is this process of communication which seems to be essential at all stages, no more so than at the beginning of an innovation process (Bowers 1983), although this is often the point at which pressure to get on with things rather than with sorting things out is very great. This is understandable because it is the task goals – or getting results – which often assume priority in people's minds, and it has been observed (Beckhard and Harris 1977, cited by Everard and Morris 1985:167) that too often people fall into the trap of moving to the action stage too quickly. Such pressure should be resisted because failure to sort things out can, later in the process, lead to problems, the worst of which can be a complete disintegration of the team when hitherto submerged differences in understandings surface.

What will characterize successful management under these circumstances is maintaining in balance three sets of needs and functions discussed in section 2 of Chapter 1: task, group and individual. What is striking is how some of these needs would not be not out of place in approaches to education which have a basis in humanistic psychology. Developing a team spirit, giving a sense of purpose, attending to individuals' problems, and making them feel valued are as much attributes of good management as they are of good educational practice. Similarly, providing individuals with the skills needed to perform a given task is a management as well as an educational requirement. And all are very important when seeking to implement an innovation.

6.2.1 Factors in innovation

Although, especially in ELT, our knowledge of how innovation is effectively disseminated is still incomplete (though see Flenley 1988, Henrichsen 1987, 1988, Kennedy 1987, 1988, Tomlinson 1990), we do know from a considerable body of research and theorizing carried out in other fields that there are factors which either facilitate or hinder the implementation of innovation. Applying insights from the field of innovation studies, Flenley and Henrichsen independently studied innovations in Japan. Lynn Henrichsen (1988), investigated the unsuccessful attempts at implementing curriculum change in ELT in post-war Japan under the aegis of Charles Fries, one of the leading figures in the development of Audio-lingualism in the USA during the 1940s and 50s. Tony Flenley (1987), surveyed innovations in Japanese senior high schools. Thus, we have one study on a system-wide level, with the other at the level of the individual school and teacher. Their research enabled them to devise models of innovation, of which Henrichsen's (Figure 6.6 overleaf) is the more complex and comprehensive.

In both models, the factors which are defined as facilitating or hindering the implementation of an innovation are present within the innovation itself, some within the resource system, some within the intended user-system, while others are inter-elemental. As is so often the case, the constraining and facilitating factors which they list seem obvious, yet the very large number and range of them indicate the enormous complexity of any implementation process. Given such complexity, it is hardly surprising that bringing about change can so easily go wrong.

ANTECEDENT CONDITIONS

Among the factors given in Figure 6.6, Henrichsen points out that there are antecedent conditions which have to be taken into account, and which are part of the situational analysis that makes up the first stage of Skilbeck's curriculum model reviewed earlier. These are:

Pedagogic traditions
Pre-existing conditions and forces: social, economic, political, educational.
Perceived need for innovation.

The first two of these relate to the wider environment of the school, while the last one concerns members of the user-system, that is, the members of the organization which will adopt the innovation, which in most cases will be an individual school, although it can, of course, be a nationwide education system.

CHARACTERISTICS OF THE INNOVATION

A number of characteristics of an innovation influence its acceptability and

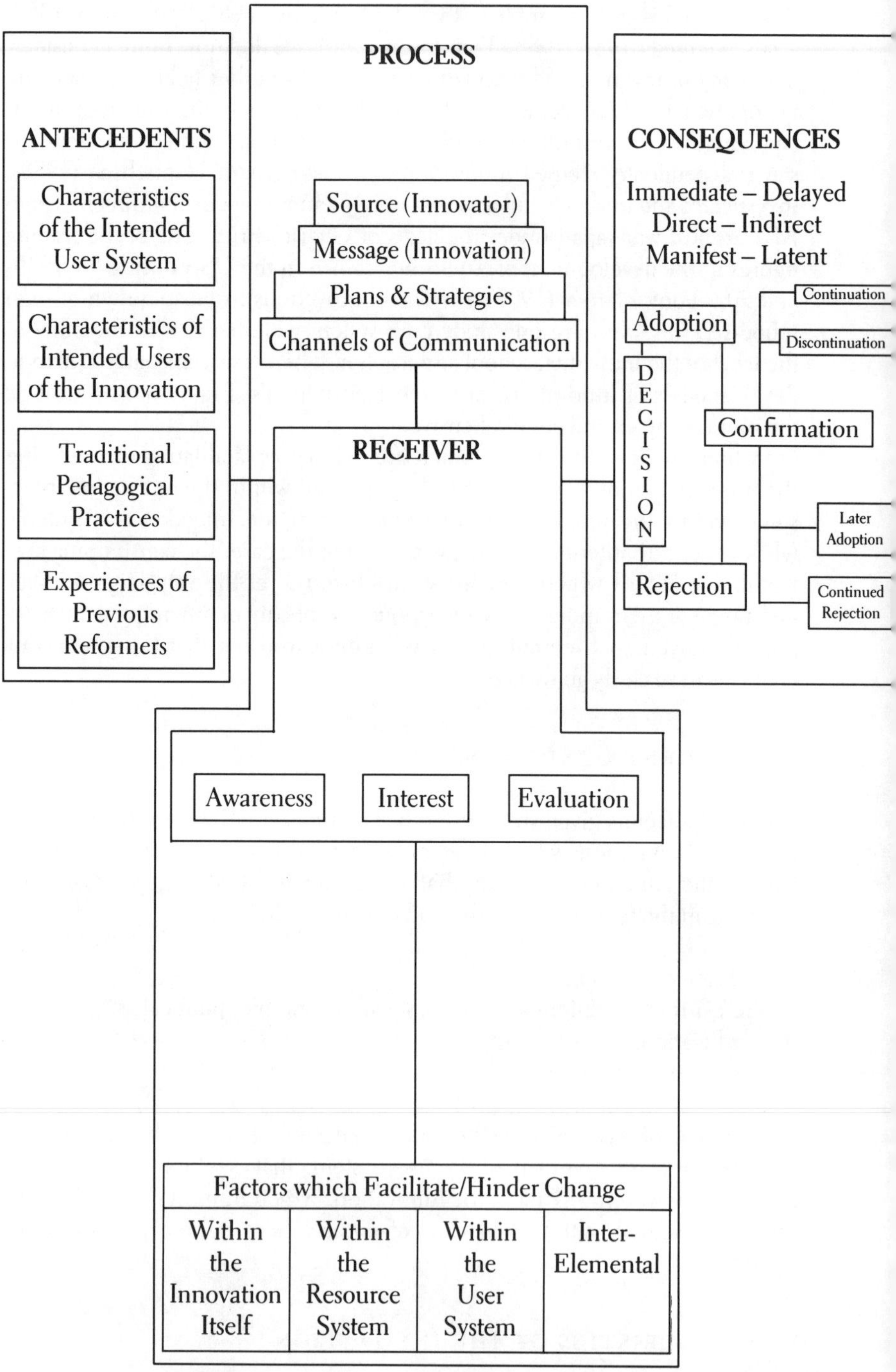

Figure 6.6 The hybrid model of innovation (from Henrichsen 1988)

implementation. They include originality, complexity, explicitness, relative advantage, trialability, status, practicality, flexibility and form.

If an innovation is highly original (which means that it is very unlike current practices), there are likely to be compatibility problems. Computer and word processor users will be familiar with this problem as data stored on one system may not be readily usable on another. Examples of pedagogical incompatibility include the mismatch between a new syllabus and materials on the one hand and an existing examination on the other; or between the practices advocated to teachers by course providers contrasted with the rather different beliefs and directives handed down to the same teachers by members of the inspectorate.

The more complex an innovation is perceived to be, the less likely it is to be adopted. It should be noted that it is the perception of the innovation which is crucial here. An innovation is not necessarily any more complex than existing practice, but because it is *different*, it will tend to be perceived as more complex. Undoubtedly one of the reasons computers are resisted by some teachers and administrators is that they are perceived as being complex, although such perceptions will no doubt change as more and more people have experience of using computers in daily applications.

Another important point to keep in mind is that all innovations involve deskilling and relearning to some extent, so that when complex changes are required in teacher behaviour, it is more difficult to bring about the successful adoption of an innovation in teaching methods. There are also time and financial cost factors to consider. A complex innovation will require more retraining time, which in turn will lead to higher costs. The adoption of communicative language teaching methods which call for an alteration in teachers' behaviour is a typical instance.

Explicitness is an important characteristic of an innovation. If an innovation can be clearly described, people are more prepared to take notice of it. Also, if the innovation is well developed and in tangible form, it will be more acceptable. For this reason, teaching innovations which have been worked through into actual published materials are more likely to be adopted than those which remain at a conceptual rather than a tangible level. This is a point which is not lost upon publishers who are able to provide innovations in methodology in an acceptably packaged form. Radical innovations, such as the process syllabus, are not able to be packaged in textbook form and so tend to languish in the minds of those who have conceived of them or in the papers that they publish.

Finally, the specificity of goals and objectives as far as the implementation programme is concerned will help encourage adoption. When explicitness is low or lacking, the result is confusion or scepticism in the minds of the potential adopters and a lower rate of adoption. Utopian proposals tend to suffer from such lack of specificity and as a result, few are taken up.

The relative advantage of an innovation over existing practices in terms of economics, social prestige, convenience etc. can be a significant factor, although as the history of innovations shows, the demonstrable superiority of an innovation does not necessarily ensure its adoption (Nicholls, 1983). The superiority of structured small group and pair work in promoting active use of the language is both obvious and well demonstrated, but this has not ensured its acceptance beyond a comparatively limited range of schools. Furthermore, appeals to research evidence in support of an innovation may not necessarily secure adoption. Indeed, invoking research evidence may only harden people's rejection of the innovation. In fact, what is important is the *perceived* advantage relative to that which is to be superseded. When an advantage is perceived – or when people are persuaded of an advantage – an innovation is more rapidly taken up. So, when teachers perceive advantages in group work – and the advantages may not necessarily be in the students' favour – group work will be adopted.

Whether or not an innovation can be tried out on a limited basis is important. Small-scale trialling or experimentation limits the risks involved in wholesale, wide-scale adoption without trial. For this reason, a new method neatly packaged in a textbook can be trialled with one or two classes before making a decision to adopt and it is common for schools to trial a newly published course before either adopting or rejecting it. Related to such trialling is observability. If the favourable results of an innovation are visible to others, then its adoption and spread are more likely. Staff room gossip can be a potent influence here.

The status of an innovation is important. If an innovation is associated with a higher social level or a group or individuals to whom potential adopters refer as models, then the innovation is imbued with legitimacy and it gains attention. *Homophily* – 'the degree to which pairs of individuals who interact are similar in certain attributes' (Rogers 1983) – is an important factor in ensuring acceptance. If a change agent or an early adopter is seen to be 'like us' by other potential adopters, then implementation rates are higher.

Even with such factors as the above taken into account, there still remains the practicality of the innovation. Can the user system – that is, the system in which adopters work – meet the demands of the innovation? For most people, the user system will be their school. An innovation which places heavy demands on the school in terms of time, personnel and money will be less likely to be taken up than one which has realistic demands. A related point here is that the system changes needed to accommodate an innovation may require supplementary inputs and unless such provision is made, system overload can simply inhibit implementation. The experience of the British school system in the late 1980s is a case in point. Changes on a macro level placed demands on existing systems and individuals which required increased resourcing to enable teachers and administrators to meet the demands and deadlines placed upon them.

If an innovation is flexible and can change to fit new situations, it will have a greater chance of success than one which is inflexible. Such flexibility is related to the question of 're-invention', whereby the adopters alter the innovation in ways which match their own understanding and capacities. Undoubtedly one reason why some ELT methods have not spread widely is because in their orthodox form they require an inflexible adoption of a codified set of procedures. It is only when adopters alter the method to their own circumstances that innovation occurs, and then often in a form which will be repudiated by the original inventor or the change agent.

Another reason why smart new methods or hardware do not always appeal is because we tend to retain our first resource systems longest, especially in circumstances where tradition and loyalty are valued. So, primacy will be an important factor in inhibiting change. The familiar, tried and true will often seem preferable to the novel.

Whenever an innovation is proposed, it is important to ask the following questions, adapted from White (1988) and Everard and Morris (1983):

What is the innovation?
Is it an innovation in hardware, software, materials, methods, forms of assessment, appraisal or evaluation etc.?

What do we mean by the terms we use when discussing the innovation?
For instance, what do we mean by *task-based learning?*

Why are we carrying out this innovation?
Are we carrying it out because other stakeholders have told us to; or is it in response to problems that have arisen through a drop in student motivation or achievement; or is it to relieve teachers' boredom; is it to conform to the latest fashion; or what?

What is it for?
Is it to improve learning in particular skills; is it to raise examination performance; is it to improve the school's public image etc.?

Who is it for?
Is it for the benefit of students or teachers? Is it for clients and sponsors? Who are the intended beneficiaries of the change?

Do we actually need it?
Can we really justify the innovation in terms of improvements and cost? Is it relevant to this particular school? Has the relevance been established? Can it be presented as practical in the short-run, not too costly and potentially helpful to the teachers? Is it needed more than other changes, the implementation of which will use the same (usually scarce) resources?

What justifications are there for it?
Can we give a principled justification for the innovation? Is it sound? Is it actually feasible? If a new syllabus is introduced, are there opportunities and funds for any necessary in-service training?

Basically, we need to go on asking and attempting to answer the question *Why?*

THE RESOURCE SYSTEM

Second in Henrichsen's scheme, we have the resource system from which the innovation proceeds. If the resource system lacks the power, prestige, capacity and structure to promote and support the innovation, implementation will be limited. Likewise, the degree to which the resource system is open to feedback and the extent to which there are harmonious relationships among the members of the organization and between them and the intended user system will influence the success of implementational efforts. In other words, if the resource system, such as a section in a ministry, operates a one-way communication system in which teachers have no voice, there is a tendency for teachers to *accept* the innovation without necessarily *implementing* it. In such a context, teachers will give verbal agreement to the innovation, but their classroom practice will not change. A simple instance may suffice. The inspectorate tells teachers that from henceforth, they must use only English in their classrooms. This is accepted by teachers (who are they to challenge the inspector?), but, unless the inspector or some other authority figure is present, the teachers continue to use the vernacular in the same way as they did before the directive was issued.

If, however, the resource system responds to user needs and aspirations instead of merely transmitting ideas without adaptation, success is more likely; that is, teachers will be more likely to *implement* the innovation in actual teaching behaviour rather than verbally *adopting* it. Such openness is important when innovations are being taken from one culture to another, as is often the case with methodological innovations, as Harold Palmer discovered in the 1930s in his unsuccessful attempts to transfer his oral method, developed by a native speaking teacher in European classrooms, to Japanese classrooms, where non-native speakers of English were working within a very different culture.

THE INTENDED USER SYSTEM

The third element in Henrichsen's scheme is the intended user system, which in most cases means the school within which an innovation is to be implemented. Everard and Morris (op cit.:188) point out that 'it is quite possible to overload any system or organization with change, so the issue of priorities and sequencing changes is a vital strategic decision for any manager'. Systems are like people. No one can accommodate too many changes at the same time, and over-zealous attempts to implement too many changes at once can lead to stress on the system's capacity to cope. This will be revealed in people's behaviour: dissatisfaction, complaints, anxiety, stress, even illness and absenteeism.

In addition to the capacity of the system to cope with the innovation, there is the openness of the system to change and the harmony of relationships among members of the organization. If, for instance, there is already discord among members of staff, introducing an innovation is not likely to create harmony, while the innovation itself may become a weapon used by one faction against another. At best, a disunited staff may combine to reject the innovation – in which case, of course, the implementation will have failed.

It is also important to look at the history and culture of the organization. Everard and Morris list a number of questions relating to the organization itself:

> Does the school have a track record of successfully implementing innovation?
> Or is there a succession of unsuccessful experiences, which has created an atmosphere of cynicism, disillusionment and apathy?
> Are there people in authority who can facilitate change, such as well-respected advisers with time available?
> Are there problems that could be simultaneously helped by implementing the change?
> What is the Principal's attitude to change?
> Are the teachers relatively confident in their own ability, yet open to suggestions from colleagues on further improvement?

INTER-ELEMENTAL

Finally, we have the relationship among the various elements listed by Henrichsen. Basically, if there is a good degree of fit among the elements, change will be facilitated. Furthermore, if there are rewards for implementing the change, success is more likely to be achieved. Such rewards need not be financial ones – although money is always a powerful incentive. Even so, as Maslow's hierarchy (Chapter 1) indicates, when a need is satisfied, it no longer serves as a motivator, so if pay scales are accepted as being reasonable, simply giving people another increment may not in itself achieve the results that were anticipated. One of the things a manager needs to establish is the kinds of rewards which are meaningful and motivating to the people being asked to make implementational efforts. Job satisfaction may, in some circumstances, be a more powerful reward than a pay increase.

Implementing change is both a social as well as an individual process, and the social organization of a school as well as the individual beliefs and practices of teachers will be disturbed by a proposed change. It will be necessary to enlist group and individual commitment to change and it is important to provide for both organizational as well as individual development as part of the change process. Indeed, as has already been discussed in Chapter 3, staff development is part of the good management practice which enables an organization to respond to a changed environment. Furthermore, as Fullan (1982) points out, effective educational change cannot occur without improvements to the working life of teachers. Change must not simply add to their problems.

Researching North American schools, Fullan and his colleagues found that those which were good at change were characterized by openness of communication, a high level of communication skills, a widespread desire for collaborative work, a supportive administration, good agreement on educational goals and previous experience of successful change. In short, the schools were characterized by the kind of collegiate culture which was noted at the beginning of this chapter as being a key factor in successful curriculum development and innovation. Although no comparable body of research exists for schools specifically dedicated to ELT, it would be surprising if they were to be substantially different from those studied by Fullan and his colleagues. Impressionistic though the picture is, the one emerging from the British Council's Recognition Scheme for UK language schools is in line with Fullan et al.'s findings.

6.2.2 Transition management

All of the above points may be subsumed under an information-gathering or reconnaissance phase in an implementational sequence. The second phase is describing the future in answer to the question, 'What do we want to happen?'. In the case of macro-level change, this involves helicoptering over the organization and looking at where it will be in, say, five years time. While this future scenario should ignore present difficulties, it should take account of operational factors – it shouldn't just be a dream scenario, and it should be specific. What this means is taking into account such factors as finance and stakeholders (staff, students, parents, governors, employers).

As a counterpoint to the ideal future scenario, it is a good idea to produce a 'doom' scenario, which is the picture that will emerge if things are simply left to drift. A comparison of the two scenarios will help reveal what needs to be done.

The next step is to describe the present in the context of the future. Everard and Morris suggest three questions:

1 Where is the system now?
2 What work is needed to move it?
3 Where are we, the initiators, in all this?

The answers will give a list of what has to be done. As part of this process in the context of a policy review, it is advisable to define what the organization exists for – what is its 'core mission' – and what is the environment in which the organization exists. Bowers' diagram (Figure 6.4) provides a list of some of these environmental factors. In addition, there are stakeholders such as the following to be taken into consideration: the unions, parents, clients, employers and education authorities. Each stakeholder has a particular interest in the school, and these interests may be in conflict. For instance, while unions are interested in preserving teachers' jobs and improving their conditions of service through regulating hours of teaching and rates of pay, management may be more concerned with reducing costs and increasing profit margins, while an education authority (local or national) may wish to achieve better results with fewer resources.

An analysis of these various elements most relevant to the change being planned will form the basis of an environmental map. Then the typical demands of each element should be listed. After this, the typical response of the organization to these demands will be considered. For instance, if the unions typically seek a reduction in teachers' hours while retaining existing pay scales (in effect, a pay increase), what is the school management's typical response to such a demand? If a client requests more content but without increasing time, how does the course planner usually respond?

Having identified the demand-response relationships between the school and stakeholders and the environment, it is important to identify the key individuals, groups, force or systems that could influence the change, either positively or negatively. We should then consider (Everard and Morris, op cit 194):

1 How *ready* is he/she/it to change in the desired direction (high, medium, low)? Readiness is to do with willingness, motives and aims.
2 Irrespective of readiness, how *capable* is he/she/it of making or helping the change? Capability is about power, influence, authority and resources such as equipment and skills.

Management of the day-to-day running of a school is one thing; managing the transitions involved in implementing innovation is another. We have seen that innovations don't just happen; they are – or should be – planned. We have also seen that implementing change is a social process and that it will impinge on both the social needs of the organization and the individual needs of personnel. We have also noted that an innovation must have credibility, and what will help to give it credibility is the source from which the innovation comes and the status of the individual or individuals promoting the innovation. If the stimulus for change comes from an individual who is 'one of us' (i.e. is homophilous with the potential adopter) and, in addition, has high status and credibility, an innovation is more likely to be accepted than if the reverse is true. Likewise, if an innovation is implemented by such a person who is also a member of the organization, adoption by others is encouraged.

What will be needed in transition management for the implementation of innovation is a management structure which has the authority to mobilize and direct people and resources, the communication skills needed to persuade changers to adopt the innovation, and time to plan and act. There is no recipe for creating such a structure, any more than there is an infallible recipe for implementing innovation. The choices range from the Principal acting as a project manager to establishing a task group composed of representatives of different parties in the organization to choosing natural leaders from within the organization. It is very important that the Principal's support is actively displayed, particularly in an organization in which the Principal occupies the peak of a hierarchy from which authority normally flows. Flenley, in his account of innovations in Japanese senior high schools, reports one successful attempt in which the changes obtained the Principal's support at an early stage in their attempts to introduce change in English teaching in their schools. Without his support, their efforts would probably have come to nothing.

It may also be helpful to engage an outside consultant. Bringing in such a consultant should not be regarded as a sign of failure: such use of consultants is increasingly common in commerce and industry because the outsider will bring both expertise and a viewpoint which will be lacking within the client organization. The role of consultants is to counsel and facilitate rather than to provide ready-made solutions, and they may be involved from the very earliest stages in helping to identify the need for change, through the transition process to the final evaluation of outcomes.

Transition management will require a carefully thought out management plan which will state:

1 Goals and priorities.
2 Specific activities to be carried out and who will be responsible for them. This is the WDWW stage: What has to be Done by Whom and When.
3 The costs involved: time, money, people.

The definition of goals and priorities will, as we have already noted, require considerable discussion and clarification, with as much consultation and participation as possible. Drawing up a chart of WDWW is best done by only a few people and the resulting plan should be circulated to all concerned. Such a chart provides everyone with an agenda and a guide to action. Finally, budgeting time, money and people provides guidelines for monitoring implementation. No organization has endless resources and monitoring expenditure under all three headings will indicate where there is danger of depleting resources before implementation is complete or where additional resources need to be supplied.

6.3 Evaluation

It is important to be sure that an innovation has in fact been implemented and to ascertain what the effects are in relation to the success criteria stated in the 'future scenario'. An evaluation will also be a way of building upon successes achieved and avoiding problems in the future. A published case study of the implementation may also be valuable for others.

Bell (1982) has devised a useful series of questions as the basis for planning evaluation:

1 What are the purposes of the evaluation?
2 What programme, instructional material or issues are being evaluated?
3 Who are the potential audiences of the evaluation?
4 What particular characteristics of the context may be relevant?
5 What are the particular questions to be answered in order to achieve the purpose?
6 What types of information will be collected and from whom?
7 What techniques and instruments will be used for gathering the information?
8 Who is to be involved in conducting the evaluation and in what capacity?
9 How are time and funds to be allocated?
10 What is to be the form of reporting?
11 What difficulties, compromises and side effects do you anticipate?

As to the methods of evaluation, these will depend on the type of data being collected. Figure 6.7 summarizes some of the main methods of data collection.

Figure 6.7 Methods of evaluation

Type of data	Method
Methods, classroom procedures	Observation, diaries, interviews, peer appraisal, questionnaires, ranking and rating scales
Content	Questionnaires, interviews, document analysis, textbooks, syllabuses, tests, ranking and rating scales
Learning achievement	Tests, assignments

Finally, it is a good idea to thank all the people involved in the implementation process. Thanks and praise fulfil significant individual needs and help to maintain the crucial balance among the task, social and individual needs which is so important to the successful functioning of an organization.

Of course, the fact that an innovation has been implemented does not mean that efforts stop at this point. Innovation is not something which is necessarily ever complete or finished, a point stressed by Miller (1967:17):

> Too often an innovation is introduced as 'the answer' rather than as something good but not perfect that can be improved with experience and careful study.

Curriculum innovation may be best thought of as being on-going and developmental rather than as the installation of ready-made and complete solutions in a system ready and waiting to receive them. Indeed the implementation of an innovation may be only the beginning of a process of adaptation, adjustment and refinement and the innovation may require continuing support before it becomes institutionalized as part of the routines of the organization. At which point, no doubt, further innovations will take its place in the queue of things requiring management decisions and action.

Conclusion

Management is not simply concerned with maintaining the status quo. Indeed, as will be clear in the chapters dealing with other aspects of management, an organization which fails to adapt and move with the times is one which will fall behind and eventually expire. The importance of pre-empting the effects of environmental change means that a school has to be innovative, though not to the point at which the whole organization is in a constant state of flux and confusion. Nowhere is innovation more important than in the area of curriculum because it is the provision of effective teaching and learning that is the raison d'être of a school. But, developing and implementing new curricula are not only matters requiring academic and professional knowledge and skills; managerial expertise is also called for. And as we have seen in this chapter, the management skills required in developing new curricula or introducing innovation are of essentially the same nature as the skills called for in other aspects of management. The skills of choosing, motivating, organizing and communicating with people, of controlling resources, of monitoring on-going performance, of responding to changes suggested by such monitoring, of evaluating outcomes – all of these are fundamental to good management in general and to implementing innovation in particular.

The innovation sequence described in this chapter can be summarized in the five-step sequence of educational innovation proposed by Trump (1967):

1 Analyse cooperatively reasons for present practice.
2 Discover what people want that is different from what they are doing.
3 Make tentative decisions about the priority of proposed changes.
4 Plan the innovation carefully in terms of teacher preparation, student preparation, procedures to be followed and the anticipated effects of the innovation.
5 Determine the times and techniques for evaluation.

Follow-up activities

1 Analyse the curriculum in your own school and describe in terms of the four elements given in Figure 6.1.
2 Apply the procedures presented in the flow diagram in Figure 6.2 to the

development of a curriculum for an existing or, better still, a new language programme in your own school.

3 Analyse your own situation, within the school and within the wider environment, by applying Skilbeck's questions. To do so will require careful thought and discussion with colleagues. Some of the information will, in fact, be hidden and may only be revealed by considering critical incidents when, for instance, the unexpected has occurred or unspoken rules have been broken.

4 Use Bowers' 'spider web' (Figure 6.4) to analyse further the factors involved in any curriculum development project within your own school system. Make a list of the information you would need to gather in order to gain an in-depth picture of the elements in the spider web, and consider the knock-on effects on other parts of the system of a change in any one part. You may find it helpful to refer to actual instances within your experience.

5 Review the objectives of your present curriculum. How are they expressed? How were they arrived at? What principles, if any, were used or could be referred to in justifying the objectives? How fixed are the objectives? Have they been subject to change and if so, what brought about the change?

6 Ask as many of your colleagues as possible what they believe to be the objectives of one of the courses they teach. Compare what they say. What differences and commonality of statements do you find? What do these differences and similarities tell you about people's perception of what they are doing as teachers?

7 Refer back to the team tasks outlined in the activities section of Chapter 1. If you have already done one or two of these tasks with colleagues, analyse how the group went about defining its task objectives. If you haven't already done one of these tasks, try to do one with a group of colleagues, and then analyse the objectives setting stage. In fact, you may find that the groups proceeded very quickly to the action stage without agreeing on objectives. If so, what happened? What lessons do you learn from this for curriculum development?

8 How collegial is the culture of your school? Consider the organizational structure and the forms of communication within the school. (See Chapter 1 on organizational structure and Chapter 4 on communication within the school.) How can you foster and build on existing collegiality or how can you foster such collegiality if it doesn't exist? What practical measures can you take, e.g. frequency and style of staff meetings, setting up discussion or task groups for specific functions, newsletters and bulletins, provision of meeting areas etc.

9 Teachers have little time for management; yet time is needed for management. Consider how to make time for management, both for yourself and for teachers. Refer back to Chapter 5 and organizing time.

10 Apply Skilbeck's scheme to the analysis of an existing learning-teaching

programme within your school, or to a future programme. Consider each heading in terms of the information-gathering, decision-making and action which you, as an academic manager, have had to make or would have to make in the detailed planning of such a programme. Refer back to Chapter 5 on timetabling.

11 Review how you evaluate courses at the moment. What kinds of information do you seek? How do you collect it? What do you do with it? How useful is it? How could evaluation be improved? Refer to the performance/importance survey technique outlined in Chapter 7.

12 Take a set of objectives for a given programme within your school and plan ways of evaluating these objectives, that is, of judging whether or not they have been achieved and to what level of achievement. Consider the ways of putting the evaluation into practice.

13 Take an example of innovation within your own organization. The innovation can be a pedagogical or an administrative one. Make as detailed a case history as you can of how the innovation arose, who was associated with it, what happened as it was introduced, how people reacted and what the outcomes were. Refer to Henrichsen's model as a way of organizing your case history. If the implementation of the innovation is generally considered to have been successful and the innovation is now a routine part of the organization, consider carefully what it was that enabled the implementation to be successful. If the implementation was a failure, consider why it was rejected and what might have made the implementational efforts successful.

14 Relate Adair's diagram of task, group and individual needs to your own situation. Consider instances in which the balance among these three sets of needs has been disturbed. What was the effect? How was the balance restored? What lessons for yourself as a manager can be derived from looking at instances where the balance was disrupted? How could you try to keep the three in balance in future?

15 What are the rewards which teachers in your school obtain through having made implementational efforts? Are these rewards what they want? If not, what rewards would they be happy with? If rewards are inappropriate, what changes – or innovations – would have to be made within the management of the school to provide relevant rewards to teachers who make the effort to implement new curricula?

16 Identify teachers within your school or community to whom colleagues refer as models. What characterizes these teachers? What has been their role in introducing new ideas into the school? How could they be co-opted to future innovation efforts?

17 Looking at your school in the light of broader developments, particularly in the market, prepare future and doom scenarios. If you can, discuss these with your colleagues and work towards preparing an agreed action plan for reaching the desired future state outlined in your plan.

18 Apply Everard and Morris' three questions to your present organization:

Where is the system now?
What work is needed to move it?
Where are we, the initiators, in all this?

Use the answers to make a list of what has to be done.

19 Make an environmental map of your organization. Relate this map to an actual or imaginary innovation and consider how the elements in the environment would facilitate or hinder the implementation of the innovation.

20 Develop a plan for the management of an innovation during the transition stage. Keep Henrichsen's model in mind, and take account of information produced in earlier activities. In particular, take account of the teachers identified in activity 16, and the environmental map developed in activity 19.

21 Plan how you will evaluate the innovation being dealt with in activities 19 and 20. In particular, consider how you will make use of the information you obtain.

PART TWO: MARKETING

7 WHAT IS MARKETING?

Aims

The aims of this chapter are:

1 to introduce the topic of marketing.
2 to demonstrate the fundamental importance of having a clear definition of business and a clear set of business objectives.
3 to outline a framework for the consideration of marketing issues.
4 to outline the bases of market research.

Introduction

The marketing of professional services tends to be more difficult than that of tangible goods since most professional people like to think their services don't need marketing and they themselves don't want to be marketed.

The following arguments are those normally advanced:

Our teaching is better than anyone else's. Students will recognize this and the school is full.

This assertion, frequently heard in ELT schools, carries with it the fatal implication that, even if the school is forced to close through low enrolments, it will be those students who will lose out. It is a defensive argument which overlooks the fact that, important as the teaching in the school is, there are many other factors operating in the minds of students if and when they decide to enrol: price, location, environment, timing and duration of lessons – to name but a few.

Our school is full, so we don't need marketing.

The marketing response to this is to ask whether the school is also profitable (since some ELT schools are full but only just break even), whether it is sure that it will be full and profitable next term and in the future and why the school is not aiming to expand.

If it is full, profitable and aiming to expand, it is very probable that the school is already marketing-oriented and unlikely, therefore, to make a statement like the one above.

Even if we needed marketing, it would be better for us to do it ourselves.

This wrongly assumes that anyone teaching or administering can automatically turn his or her hand to marketing and that there are no real skills, knowledge and techniques to be learnt. Both of these propositions are patently untrue.

However, whilst it is unwise to put anyone untrained in charge of a school's marketing function, there are specific tasks which academic staff may undertake which may help to market the school.

The underlying philosophy of the whole of this section of the book is that professionalism in marketing must match the professionalism to be marketed.

The marketing approach concerns the investigation of customers' requirements and desires, followed by a decision as to which of these wants the institution wishes to satisfy and consideration of how it can be done profitably. The antithesis is to determine what products or services the school wishes to offer and then to try to sell them. In that marketing concerns the generation of profitable business by meeting customer needs, its role is as crucial to the ELT business as it is to any other commercial operation, whether making widgets or offering consultancy services.

The barriers to entry into ELT are low. It is not obligatory to be qualified to teach nor to possess a large amount of capital. Some entrants are wealthy, experienced and qualified and can pitch their school at the top end of the market, well-equipped and staffed on luxurious premises, others begin with two or three rooms on one floor of a building in a cheap area of town doing most of the teaching themselves. This openness means that it is rare to find an area of the world where ELT institutions do not have to compete fiercely for students – to persuade them, firstly, of the value of learning English and, secondly, of learning it at a particular institution. Simply to sit and wait for applications and students to turn up is to invite them to stay at home or leave them to the inducements of the competition.

The key question for all those with a market- and marketing-orientation will always be: why should customers buy our services rather than those of the competition?

7.1 Defining the business

It may sound trite to begin by stressing the fundamental importance of a clear definition of the business the institution sees itself as being in. However, without such a definition setting out but constraining its area of business, it is impossible to determine objectives and to meet those objectives.

An example may provide the best illustration. A small ELT-based school has been established in Barcelona. Its definition of business might be:

1 We are in the business of teaching English.
2 We are in the business of teaching English as a foreign language.
3 We are in the business of teaching EFL in Barcelona.
4 We are in the business of teaching business English to executives in our premises in Barcelona.
5 We are in the business of providing a wide range of ELT services in our premises in Barcelona.
6 We are in the business of providing a top-quality range of ELT services in our premises in Barcelona.
7 We are in the business of providing a wide and top-quality range of ELT and other language learning services in our premises in Barcelona.
8 We are in the business of providing only profitable ELT services of top quality to our clients in our premises or elsewhere in Barcelona.
9 We are in the business of providing services in ELT and other, not necessarily linguistic areas, at an overall profit in our premises.
10 We are in the business of providing mainly profitable services in ELT and other related areas to clients either in our premises, elsewhere in the country or abroad.

Various themes recur and it should be clear that the business will differ greatly according to the chosen definition. Recurrent themes are:

a) the services to be offered:

- ELT
- ELT plus related linguistic services
- business English
- English with other non-linguistic services

b) the range of services:

- wide
- top-quality

c) location

- in our premises
- on-site, off-site or overseas
- in our premises or elsewhere (off-site)

d) profit

- only profitable
- at an annual overall profit
- mainly profitable

The definition of the business must not be too wide or too narrow. It should encapsulate a specific area of work for which there is believed to be a (profitable) market and which the overall assets and skills of the institution wish and are able to operate in.

7.1.1 Setting business objectives

Any institution that is not progressing is either standing still or regressing. In order to advance, an institution must have direction and to achieve this, it must have objectives that relate to the institution's definition of business. These objectives must take closely into account market needs and be agreed and accepted by owners, management and staff alike. Only then can all involved in the company know and understand how to channel their own efforts and the resources at their disposal as well as appreciating how their work and the work of others contributes to the attainment of the company's aims.

The objectives under consideration here are *business* objectives only. There may be many other worthwhile aims for an institution to espouse but they fall outside the range of this work. An aim such as 'the improvement of international understanding' is worthy in itself but cannot be accepted as a *business* objective any more than 'the promotion of British culture'. Such aims are too broad and intangible.

Business objectives should meet all of the following criteria. They should:

1 relate closely to the definition of the business.
2 be achievable.
3 be specific.
4 be measurable.

There is no 'ideal' number of objectives, but it is likely to be the case that the more objectives a company is trying to achieve at any one time, the more likely it is that some will militate against others with employees attaching highest priority to the objectives they espouse most warmly. For this reason, the set of objectives, once drawn up, should have priorities attached so that no one is in any doubt as to what are the most important goals.

In a typical ELT institution the most common inner tension in setting and prioritizing *business* objectives lies in the balance between commercial and academic perspectives. The following example highlights this:

1 Our aim is to make 15% profit in each school and on each of our activities quarter by quarter.
2 Our aim is to increase the number of students we teach by 5% per year to the point where we have 50% of the private ELT market.
3 Our aim is to be model employers.
4 Our aim is to achieve a higher examination pass-rate than our competitors.
5 Our aim is to build and maintain a solid, high-price but top-quality image.

In this case it will be clear that there is conflict inherent in having 15% profit as the prime aim, allied to 5% growth, alongside the desire to be model employers and this demonstrates the need for clearly thought-out objectives, to be understood and accepted by all.

Many established ELT institutions carry with them 'the burden of tradition', customs that have grown up over the years and are now established even though they bear no relation to customer or market needs and may well depress growth and profits, as well as helping to present a dowdy, unenterprising image. In trying to draw up the best set of objectives for your institution, arrangements made more for the convenience of the staff than the students will have to give way to new conditions so that the institution, its staff and students, can reach their full potential. In fact, one possible aim for a given year may be to identify and find ways of resolving such potentially thorny issues.

7.1.2 A framework for marketing

Many who are new to marketing have the impression that it is the same as selling but with frills. This is *NOT* the case. Marketing differs from selling in that a sales-oriented company looks at things from the point of view of the producer: 'This is what we produce: can we persuade you to buy?' On the other hand, the marketing-oriented company will first find out what the needs of the market are and then decide if it can and wants to satisfy them profitably.

Thus everything that has some impact on the client can be considered part of marketing and marketing the institution profitably is essential to its survival. It is vital, therefore, not only that senior management understand the importance of marketing and are seen to be leading, or at the very least, supporting the activity, but that *all* employees both understand and practise an approach that is oriented towards the client. It is misguided to think that an institution can appoint a Marketing Manager and then assume that all responsibility for marketing efforts and activity can rest on someone else's shoulders. The Marketing Manager can be the focal point of the institution's marketing activities but cannot be expected to re-orientate the company single-handed.

Good marketing is primarily a matter of attitudes, organization and orientation rather than intelligence or ability. Its essence lies in a real belief running throughout the *whole* organization in giving the customer superior value for money, offering dedicated *service* as well as good-quality *services*. It is not just a combination of activities like advertising and public relations, but a total approach to the business and in that way should permeate everything.

The figure on the facing page gives a broad framework into which most marketing considerations will fall. It can also provide the outline base for drawing up the marketing plan.

Figure 7.1 Outline of the marketing process

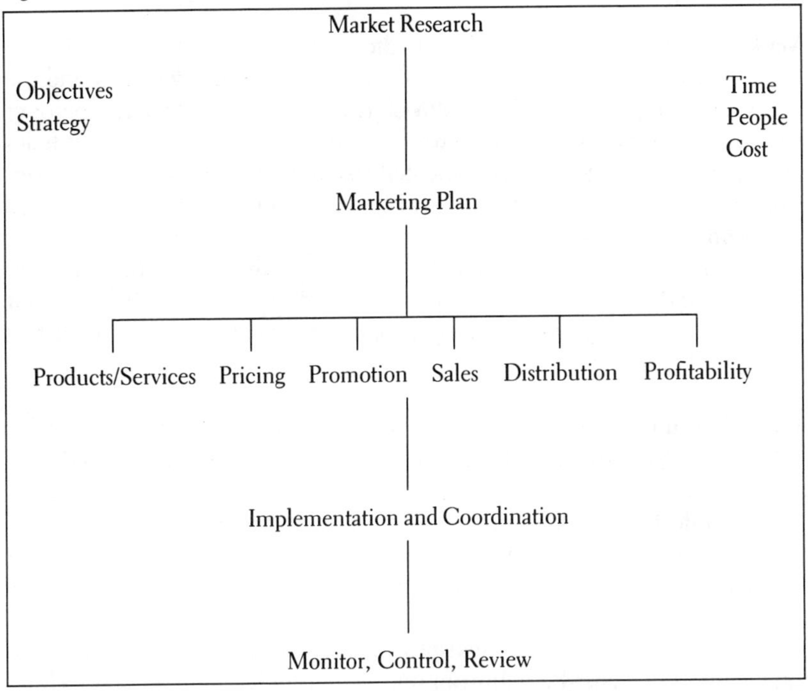

The distribution function has been included for completeness, but it has a much less important role in the provision of ELT services than, for example, in a manufacturing company.

It is the functions of developing products and services, pricing, promoting and selling at a profit, outlined above that make up what is called the 'marketing mix'.

Marketing plans are normally drawn up annually. Each section – market research, pricing, promotion etc. – will have its own objectives to be met and its own chosen strategy. Ideally, decisions on all such items should stem from and be informed by market research, although in practice in ELT institutes it is more likely that decisions will be made on the basis of some market research, current practice and managerial hunch. Nonetheless, it must not be forgotten that:

1 each item carries a cost.
2 someone must be made responsible for making things happen.
3 it will take time to assemble meaningful data.
4 there should be a detailed programme of action for each function.
5 the coordinating function is crucial. Each component for the framework must hang coherently together with the others. There is no more point in having excellent salespeople with low quality services than having excellent services that the market is unaware of.

7.1.3 Market research

Market research is the means used by those who offer goods and services of keeping themselves in touch with the requirements of those who buy and use those goods and services. The health of a school from the business point of view depends very much on its capacity to interpret the behaviour, attitudes and needs of the customers and potential customers who make up its market. Without market research, decisions will be based on a mixture of informed guesswork, hunches and prejudices.

Formally, market research may be described as the *systematic* gathering, recording and analysis of data on marketing and marketing-related issues for the purposes of improved decision-making and control in the marketing function. Its aims are:

1 to reduce uncertainty and minimize risk when plans are being made.
2 to monitor performance when and after plans have been implemented.

Data collected may be 'primary' when it emanates from new research or 'secondary' when it is drawn from published market research sources; it is 'internal' when it refers to matters within the organization and 'external' as regards the competition. A further categorization involves 'quantitative' research which aims to give statistical analysis of factual information and 'qualitative' research which aims to uncover customer attitudes and feelings via questionnaires, interviews and discussions.

Most ELT schools conduct little market research even of the internal variety, which ought to be available at very low cost. Whilst it would be unwise to try to do too much from scratch, it is advisable to undertake some systematic qualitative *and* quantitative research: to have statistics facilitating good decision-making but also to be able to see the people behind the numbers and to understand their feelings, needs and attitudes.

It is important always to bear in mind that market research produces data, not decisions. It will always be necessary to add the ingredient of judgement, but this can only come when there is actionable data available. Some in the ELT world become disillusioned with market research as a whole because their efforts have produced only information from which little can be concluded and no new initiatives taken. This is not the fault of the function but of the functionary who drew the survey or study up. In the design area of market research there are two main sins when drawing up a framework:

1 The sin of omission: not treating a topic in sufficient detail.
2 The sin of commission: collecting data which proves to be immaterial or unactionable.

Bearing this in mind, it is valuable at the outset to have a framework of research in which an external and internal audit can be conducted. The data provided by these will be the bases for the marketing plan. In order to avoid the dangerous sin of commission it can be useful to write down alongside each research item the justification for its requirement, the reason why you wish to have it and the kind of action it might require once it is in your possession.

It is unlikely that all requested items can be researched simultaneously and it will be necessary, therefore, to attach priorities, as well as giving an estimate of the cost, the time it will take and the person responsible for carrying it out.

The kind of research which schools could usefully undertake in an internal and external audit is given in the preliminary checklist below:

INTERNAL AND EXTERNAL AUDIT CHECKLIST

1 Size of market
- is it increasing or decreasing overall?
- size of identifiable segments
- purchasing criteria
- demography
- geographic
- market share

2 Institute profile

2 classes	CPE 2	16 students
5 classes	CPE 1	45 students
10 classes	FCE	81 students
24 classes	POST-INTERMEDIATE	256 students
34 classes	INTERMEDIATE	442 students
39 classes	PRE-INTERMEDIATE	573 students
45 classes	JUNIORS	698 students
Total: 159 classes		2111 students

3 Services
- breakdown by customer type
- breakdown by product range
- breakdown by source of students
- breakdown by course duration
  - returners
  - drop-outs
- new service development

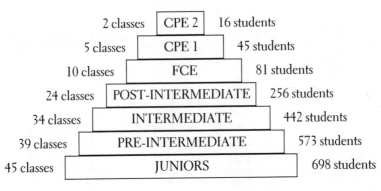

4 Promotion
– cost-effectiveness of each promotion activity
– image of organization as perceived by (a) staff (b) students (c) outsiders
– coherence of publicity material
– is it in line with desired image?
– collation of data on all listed media and advertising rates

5 Plant utilization
– the following grid gives a view of plant utilization

Figure 7.2 Plant utilization at the Lucanda Cultura, N.E. Brazil

	Room 1	Room 2	Room 3	Room 4	Room 5	Room 6	Room 7	Room 8	Room 9	Room 10	Room 11	Room 12
0900 – 1000	J1 15	J2 15	J3 15	B1 15	B2 15	B3 13	I1 14	I2 14	UI1 15	UI2 14	FCE1 15	CPE1 15
1000 – 1100												
1100 – 1200												
1200 – 1300	B1 10	B2 10										
1300 – 1400	CPE2 8	FCE2 8	I1 14	UI1 12								
1400 – 1500	J1 15	J2 13	J3 11	B1 14	B2 15	B3 14	I2 12	UI2 13	PI1 13	PI2 14		
1500 – 1600	J1 13	J1 12	J2 14	J3 13	B1 14	B1 13	B2 12	B2 12	B3 10	I1 12	UI1 13	
1600 – 1700	I2 14	UI2 14	I1 13	UI1 10	FCE1 11	PI1 14	PI2 15					
1700 – 1800	FCE2 9	CPE2 9	CPE3 8	B1 12	B2 12	PI1 13	PI2 13	I1 10	FCE1 10			
1800 – 1900	B1 11	B2 12	B3 11	PI1 13	PI2 12	I2 12	UI2 13	FCE1 10	CPE1 9			
1900 – 2000	CPE1 8	CPE3 8	FCE2 10	UI1 10	I1 9	B1 10	B2 10					

First Term 1988 *Mondays and Wednesdays*
Total Students 864 *Classes 71* *Class Average 12.16*

6 Prices
– will your services sustain a premium price? If not, are they really the best?
– breakdown of prices/services by segment
– relationship between price increases/discounts and sales
– relationship between sales and currency fluctuations

7 Selling
– cost-effectiveness of all sales activities and sales promotions
– value of sales per salesperson
per call
per overseas visit
as broken down by type of course

8 Profitability
– overall profitability
– profit contribution by school/by course
– profit margin

This checklist may be applied first within the organization, then as far as possible with reference to the competition. Finally, the two sets of data should be integrated and analysed so as to give an appreciation and appraisal of the organization's position, standing and image in relation to the overall market.

PERFORMANCE/IMPORTANCE SURVEYS

Performance/Importance (PI) surveys are a flexible, simply administered tool for quickly gauging opinions. They are simpler to put together than questionnaires and allow for much greater variety. Moreover, the results can be charted very easily, although care must be taken to ensure that false conclusions are not drawn from unrepresentative samples and that students complete the survey in an honest and sincere manner. It may be instructive to progress in a survey from general to highly specific topics in order to uncover real and detailed opinions.

The following example should illustrate the procedure clearly. A class of 14 students were asked to give scores from 0–10 on how they viewed (a) the performance in school and (b) the importance of various functions.

A score of zero signified very bad performance and extremely low importance, whereas scores of ten meant excellent performance and that the students viewed the topic as very important. The mean scores were as follows:

	Performance	Importance
Teaching	7.2	8.5
Newsletter	2.4	3.1
Language laboratory	6.1	6.0
Social programme	8.0	6.9
Pre-course administration	4.4	7.2
Examination preparation	7.1	8.3
School café	7.9	2.6

Axes can then be drawn up for management action:

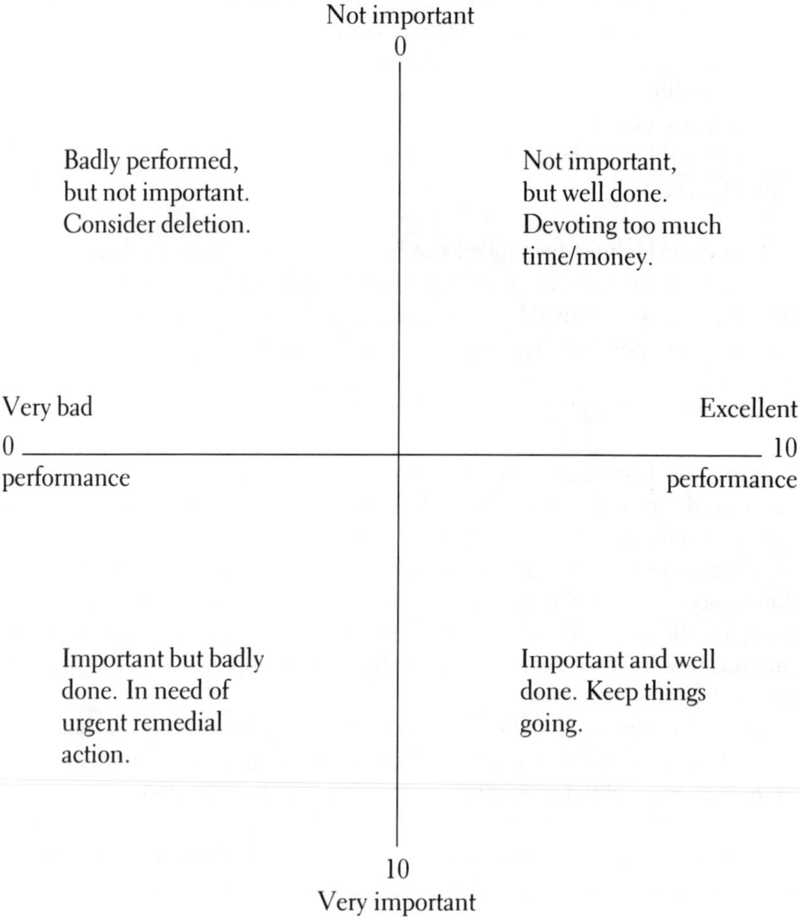

In conducting Performance/Importance surveys, it is worth bearing three other items in mind:

1 Whilst it is easy to compose and distribute questionnaires, it is less easy to produce really effective ones. It is also very time-consuming adding up the points for each of twenty items when a large number of students are being

surveyed. To ask the teacher distributing and collecting in the questionnaires to 'tot up' the figures for each item on the papers collected is a valuable time-saving device.

2 Some legitimate items do not lend themselves to this type of survey. For example, it is not possible to find out whether a school prospectus serves its purpose by putting the word 'prospectus' in the left-hand column and effectively asking students to answer the question 'Is it well done?'

3 As in much of market research, the survey should identify the areas needing attention, but may not show exactly what is being done wrong. More detailed research may be necessary for this to emerge.

This may be most easily achieved by conducting in-depth interviews with a number of 'focus groups'. Each interview should be structured along the same guidelines and delve deeply into the item under scrutiny, both from the point of view of where current arrangements are failing and as to how improvements may be brought about. Groups of 6–10 students interviewed for 30–45 minutes should provide valuable information.

In the case of the example given above, the results would show:

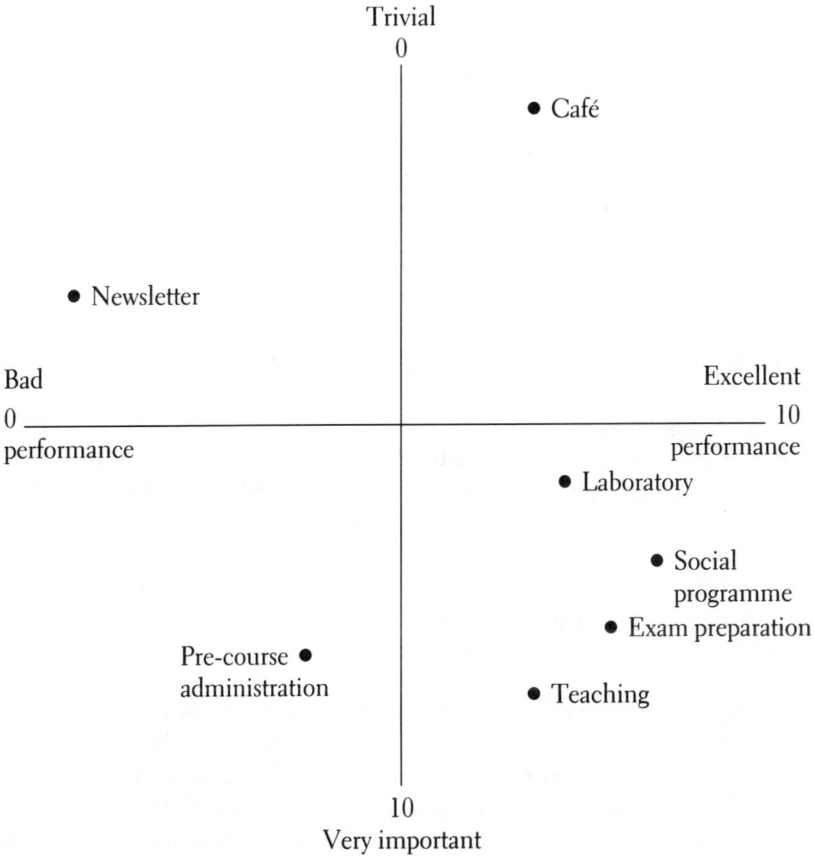

Conclusion

Marketing is central to a business in that it aims to satisfy customers' requirements profitably. In order to do this, an institution must define precisely the business it sees itself in and must set itself achievable, specific and measurable objectives. The marketing mix is made up of the co-ordination of service, pricing, promotion and sales into a profitable business operation. But it is more than an amalgam of such functions. In essence it is a belief permeating all of the company in giving the customer superior value for money: *services* and *service* together. Leading the market is preferable to following in the footsteps of others: market leadership is attained by the integrated development of academic prestige, premises, personnel, profits, pricing and product development.

Follow-up activities

1 Consider the school you are working in. Define its business. State briefly your reasons for using this definition instead of other possibilities. What are its implications?
2 Draw up a list of business objectives for the school and put them in order of priority. What are the key factors for success? Are the objectives specific, achievable and measurable?
3 Put your definition of the business alongside your list of objectives. Do the two match neatly? Are some objectives incompatible with your definition?
4 Make a list of items, preferably allied to improved profitability, which would make the school more customer-oriented.
5 What working practices, pedagogical or administrative, which are contrary to market needs or customer requirements, exist in the school? Why do they continue?
6 Ask some of your customers why they buy your services rather than those of your competitors. Do your services sustain a premium? If not, are they really better than those of your competitors?
7 Draw up a framework of all the data necessary for improved decision-making. Attach to this an estimate of the cost involved, the time it is likely to take and the person(s) responsible.
8 Who is buying what, when, where and how from the school? Is the market growing or decreasing? What are the main market segments and what are their purchasing criteria? How can these needs and wants be met? Are you going to try to serve all segments? Is that the best strategy? Are there some segments the company would like to serve but are not serving at present? What is necessary in order to satisfy them?
9 Conduct an internal and external audit. What decisions do the results

lead you to take? If the data are not actionable, what are you going to do to improve data collection?

10 Conduct a Performance/Importance survey. What do the results tell you? What are you going to do about the findings?

11 What is the image of the school as seen by (a) staff (b) students (c) outsiders? What can be done to bring these 3 images into line with the image that management wants to project?

12 What is the ratio of enquiries to sales? How does this compare from school to school? What is the breakdown of enquiries by type?

13 What is the comparison from school to school of drop-outs and returners? Why do people drop out? Why do they return?

14 How do clients evaluate your service and services against those of the competition?

Teaching	Class size
Location	Prices
Course duration	Staff
Image	Administration
Premises	Course materials

15 Which schools do profits come from?

16 From the data collected is there evidence that new products may be profitably developed?

17 What are the main sources of students? Are they stable? Are you giving them an efficient service which represents good value? Are there sources one would expect but which are not represented? Could your existing customers buy other products from you?

8 THE MARKETING MIX

Aim

The aim of this chapter is:
to investigate and analyse the importance, role and contribution of each of the main components of the marketing mix: services, promotion, pricing, selling and profitability.

Introduction

Each of the items that make up the marketing mix plays a crucial role in its own right. The decision-making should be underpinned by market research findings and directed towards improved long-term profitability. Each item also holds separate approaches, strategies and techniques for marketing a school creatively and effectively.

8.1 Services

A school whose business is primarily ELT may define its services as everything that has a direct impact or makes an impression on the customer or potential customer. This will vary from school to school, but the following checklist may be helpful in illustrating the number and range of items and areas this comprises.

8.1.1 Inventory of services

1 *Exterior*

- overall appearance
- car parking
  - space
  - size
- notices/signs
  - banners
- use of logo
- gardens
  - appearance
  - use of
  - furniture
- entrance area

NB: *Convenience of location*

2 *Interior*

- reception area
  - layout/design/colours
  - decoration/design
  - furniture
  - use of logo/name
  - availability/display of promotional literature
  - carpets
  - newspapers/magazines
- telephones
- ashtrays
- 'bell' – begin/end of classes
- student facilities
  - common room/chatting area
  - furniture/carpets
  - size
  - papers/magazines
  - music
  - telephones
  - video
- notices/noticeboards
  - size
  - design/layout/display
  - contents/orientation
- cloakroom
- toilets
- labelling/signs
- cleanliness/lighting/heating
- photos/titles of staff
- coffee/lunch area
- flower arrangements
- wall coverings

3 *Classrooms*

- size
- heating/lighting/cleanliness
- furniture
- decoration
- equipment
- use of logo/name

- library
  - book stock
- self-access centre
  - tape stock
  - materials
- computer centre
  - hardware
  - software

4 *Administration*

- staffing
  - appearance
  - warmth
  - language
  - efficiency
- map for reaching school
- joining instructions
- registration forms
  - procedures
  - dates
  - times

- giving course information
- answering the telephone
  - – speed
  - – language
  - – warmth
  - – knowledge
- dealing with complaints
- responding to enquiries
- end-of-course questionnaires
- student reports
- certificates of attendance
- performance/importance surveys

5 *Accounting*

- methods of payment
  - – convenience
  - – clarity
- invoicing
- discounts
- refunds
- pocket money

6 *Transport*

7 *Accommodation*

– quality/level
– proximity to school
– warmth
– heat/light/clean
– smoking/pets/children
– details given well in advance
– food
– student's bedroom
– number of students
– language
– extra voluntary involvement
– welcome (procedure)

8 *Teaching*

- equipment
  - – books
  - – tapes
  - – videotapes
  - – cassette recorders
  - – computers
- examinations
  - – range prepared for
  - – staff orientation towards
  - – administration
  - – efficiency in posting results
- courses
  - – objectives
  - – content
- social/cultural
  - – range
  - – attendance (staff)
  - – frequency
  - – orientation
- staff
  - – appearance
  - – committment
  - – punctuality
  - – lesson preparation
  - – homework
  - – materials preparation

- group size
- skills focus
- range
- duration
- progression
- age range
- timing
- frequency/intensity

9 *Marketing*

- promotion
  - advertising
  - PR
  - advertorial (editorials which advertise)
  - stationery
  - logo
  - typeface
  - design
  - layout
  - prospectuses/leaflets
  - posters
  - video
  - newsletters
  - direct mail
  - exhibitions
  - image
  - coordination
  - cohesion
  - clarity
  - attractiveness
  - brevity
  - photos
- selling and sales promotion
  - sales visits
  - presentation and speed of quotes
  - sales promotions
- gimmicks
  - pens
  - bags
  - T-shirts
  - diaries
  - bookmarks
  - year-planners (with free advertising)
  - hats
  - calendars
- pricing
  - clarity
  - presentation
  - well in advance

10 *Communication systems*

- internal
- external
- hardware

8.1.2 Standardization

One of the main differentiating features of services, as opposed to products, is their intangibility. Overall marketing considerations remain the same, but the very nature of services means that certain modifications have to be made.

Intangibility makes it much more difficult to develop unique selling propositions. This in turn makes it of paramount importance to build a reputation for excellence in all the services offered.

Uniformity and standardization are almost impossible to achieve. In buying a product such as a car it is assumed that one built to the same specifications will be the same whether bought in Bath or Birmingham: a bar of chocolate will be exactly the same in Glasgow or Greenwich in a way that an ELT class or enrolment service will never be entirely uniform.

Some schools try to make their services as standardized as possible by imposing:

- a uniform teaching style
- prescribed syllabuses and teaching materials
- standard decoration of the reception area and classrooms
- provision of uniforms for secretarial and administrative staff

8.1.3 Differentiation

Another typical strategy is to take the view that since uniformity of intangible services is impossible, it is unwise to strive for it. If a school has several branches in the same city or a company several schools in one country, the physical construction of the buildings is bound to vary. It is therefore wisest to abandon the goal of complete uniformity and instead pursue active differentiation within a corporate framework. It can be made clear that advertisements, neon signs, logo, banners, stationery, colours, typeface etc. adhere to the corporate identity, whilst schools can still differentiate themselves according to the segments and services offered. For example, those schools offering junior courses can develop a specific image and service by way of room decoration, furniture, teaching approach and materials, course length, intensity and progression, group size and price.

In some countries strong centralization can be a major selling point. If a company with branches country-wide wishes to give its executives English training, it may well be attracted by the prospect of placing them with a chain of schools which will give the same amount and type of training to each executive regardless of whether he or she works in Kyoto, Nagoya, Tokyo, Hakata or Hiroshima.

On the question of uniformity it is bound to be important to control the quality of *services* and *service*. In considering this, what is meant by the quality of services and service? In terms of service, this is as intangible as its partner but would normally include:

- ★ reliability
- ★ competence
- ★ ready availability
- ★ uniformity
- ★ warmth/sympathy
- ★ speed and clarity of response
- ★ efficiency
- ★ interest/willingness
- ★ appearance

In all schools service may be as important as services and a programme should be drawn up for the monitoring, control and improvement of service alongside that of services.

It is continuously necessary to review the range, development and improvement of the services offered. Questions worthy of consideration will include:

1 Are there some courses which both lose money and do not even add to the school's academic prestige and reputation?
2 Is the range of courses too large? Would it be more profitable to cut the range down and concentrate on fewer courses and segments?
3 What are we doing to improve services? Are these improvements going to be appreciated by *customers*?
4 What efforts are being made to develop new courses/services? Are we sure there is a profitable market?
5 Which services are you going to:
– maintain – improve – harvest – exit – enter?

8.1.4 Service development

It is now axiomatic that small improvements matter. A press-button digital telephone may appear only slightly different from a dial phone but standard dial telephones form only a small percentage of the market nowadays. Taken together several small improvements can amount to a major advantage as seen from the customers' point of view.

Moreover, since those with the true marketing approach believe in giving the customer superior value for money in services and service, it will normally follow that superior services can be developed. Digital telephones with a meter showing the cost of each call and the accumulated amount for the current quarter are sure to be popular with consumers, if they are offered at an acceptable price. In the ELT business the superior features developed will vary from school to school, but the true marketing ethos should transmit itself quickly to customers. If customers show little appreciation of allegedly superior benefits – and the 'bottom line' in this concerns whether improved profits can be made from the new features – then management must question whether it has been allocating its resources in the most cost-effective way.

Presentation is important. A school may have excellent teaching staff and administrative services, but if its prospectus is bleak or badly produced, or its reception area scruffy or unattractive, this will not attract potential students.

In developing new services, it should always be remembered that:

1 services are pathways to *consumer* benefits.
2 superior services can usually be developed.
3 presentation is important.
4 profit improvements should be looked for.
5 small differences matter.

The standard framework around which most service and market developments focus is the Ansoff matrix (1984:84). This is given below and may serve to categorize the different broad strategies and opportunities available.

Figure 8.1 The Ansoff matrix

	Existing Products	New Products
Existing Markets	Present activity	Product improvement and/or extension of product lines
New Markets	Development of present markets and/or entry into new markets with existing products	Diversification, entry into new markets with new products

8.2 Promotion

8.2.1 What is promotion?

Promotion may be thought of as all the activities involved in:

1 raising customer awareness of what the school offers.
2 attracting customer interest.
3 stimulating desire.
4 keeping the school and its services in the minds of all those involved in the decision-making process.
5 reassuring those attracted but uncertain.
6 giving information about the school and its services.
7 reinforcing feelings of satisfaction with services already bought.

Its aims will be to:

- ⋆ give information
- ⋆ reassure
- ⋆ familiarize
- ⋆ remind
- ⋆ make aware
- ⋆ overcome inertia

Its targets will be:

* ★ customers
* ★ potential customers
* ★ influencers
* ★ sponsors
* ★ decision-makers

8.2.2 What can promotion do?

Inevitably most advertising is of a general nature and cannot therefore answer all a consumer's information needs; it cannot elaborate on specific points considered significant by an individual nor resolve doubts as to appropriateness in a particular situation.

However, amongst the items and issues it can contribute to are:

1 developing the image of a company.
2 developing the image of a specific service.
3 selling the company's services.
4 selling supporting factors or basic services.
5 selling the reputation and expertise of the company.
6 improving the level of consumer knowledge.

It must nonetheless be recognized that the credibility of advertising is not enough in itself. In the short term an expensive advertising campaign full of superlatives may attract students, but if the teaching is ineffective and the other services lackadaisical, word will quickly spread and it is highly improbable that the school will do well regardless of the advertising budget. By the same token a poor advertising campaign can do a great deal of harm to a good school.

In the ELT world promotion in general, and advertising in particular, has a chequered reputation. Some schools spend between 5%–10% of turnover advertising on buses, railway stations, trams, on radio and TV and in many magazines. It is a cornerstone of their marketing and recruitment policy. Others spend almost nothing, preferring to use resources in sending academic staff to give seminars and producing modest prospectuses to give dates and fees. There is no automatically right answer; each school must decide what it wants to achieve, how it intends to do it and what part promotion and advertising are to play in the overall strategy.

It is a common mistake to believe that if advertising is effective, sales increase and, as a corollary, if sales go down, it must be because advertising is ineffective. In reality the process is much more complex with many variables working towards or against an increase in student recruitment. The quality of services and service, the price, the location, timing and course duration will all play their part.

Each component of the marketing mix must have its own objectives and this applies to the sub-component of advertising as well as to overall promotion. In setting objectives for advertising, the question must be asked:

can advertising achieve this objective *alone*? If the answer is negative, then the advertising objective is inappropriate. It must always be remembered that sales reflect the impact and effectiveness of the marketing mix as a whole – NOT just one part of it.

Bearing these things in mind, advertising can:

1 convey information
2 make customers aware of services offered
3 change attitudes and perceptions
4 stimulate desires
5 attract enquiries
6 overcome prejudice
7 reach people inaccessible to salespeople
8 remind and reassure
9 give reasons for buying
10 reinforce positive sentiments
11 encourage switching from the competition
12 achieve sales
13 encourage returners/bringing friends
14 keep the school in customers' minds during the 'off' season

8.2.3 Methods

All schools will agree that the best way of filling is through word-of-mouth recruitment. Unfortunately, few schools can rely on this to make or keep them profitable and it is a risky strategy even for those with a first-class reputation and a large band of satisfied customers.

Nonetheless, direct enrolments may be actively encouraged by mailing former students, newsletters, PR and social activities and events. A good school will attract a high percentage enrolment with only a modest amount of advertising and promotion, but a market-oriented school is unlikely to be satisfied with that. It will wish to build on this solid foundation and grow by attracting new customers with new, improved or extended services and it will recognize that in order to do this it will need to promote itself and its services.

Its *internal* efforts must ensure that all its printed and public matter is well-presented and coheres:

- ⋆ stationery
- ⋆ visiting cards
- ⋆ compliments slips
- ⋆ typeface
- ⋆ logo
- ⋆ slogan
- ⋆ neon lights
- ⋆ banners
- ⋆ design and layout

To have one of these items out of harmony with the remainder will inevitably detract from the overall image. Of all of these items, a school's brochure, prospectus, its leaflet(s) and poster(s) are perhaps the most visible and prominent and must convey the desired image. All too often no framework has been laid down to cover:

- ★ design
- ★ colours
- ★ size and match of photos
- ★ text
- ★ size
- ★ length
- ★ quality of papers
- ★ typeface
- ★ print run
- ★ translation
- ★ main selling points and categories of essential information

A lack of policy and direction automatically lead to an incoherent proliferation of documents of different shapes, sizes and designs. In order to achieve coherence in promotion and printed matter one person with a high level of authority within the organization must be given overall responsibility.

With regard to *external* advertising, it must be borne clearly in mind:

1. why you are advertising: what you wish to achieve.
2. who you are trying to reach.
3. what message you want to convey:
   - it should try to stress a major customer benefit, preferably one no competitor can match.
   - it should NOT try to cover too many points in a short time.
4. when it is best to advertise.
5. how the message can be conveyed so as to stick in the target's mind.
6. what the most suitable external promotion media are:

   - national press
   - films/video/cinema
   - local press
   - outdoor billboards
   - professional magazines
   - direct mail
   - radio
   - sponsorship
   - TV

8.2.4 Budget

There is no definitive answer to how much should be spent on advertising, but it is important to remember that it is only a part of total promotional costs. These may include the expenses of the marketing staff, other publicity material and sales promotions.

The traditional ways of setting the budget are:

1. *Arbitrary* What we think we can afford.
2. *What the competition spends* This should not be ignored but it can be misleading since (a) it assumes other companies know what they are doing and (b) many companies have quite a different promotion mix.

3 *Percentage of sales* This is easy to calculate, but it is harder to decide whether it should be this year's, last year's or next year's. In any event the underlying assumption, which has been dismissed above as invalid, is that either the level of sales is directly determined by the level of the advertising budget or that advertising is a luxury you buy according to how much profit you make.
4 *Task basis* Perhaps the most satisfactory method is to decide what tasks need to be performed, assess advertising needs and work out a programme and budget to achieve the task. In principle, this is a good approach but there are many ways of achieving a desired objective, often with wildly varying costs. It is not a simple matter to decide what amount of advertising is required in order to achieve a particular result – and most marketing people are likely to err on the side of the expensive and conservative!

8.3 Selling

It is symptomatic of the problems attached to the marketing of professional services that 'selling' should often be diluted to 'recruitment' as if there was something inappropriate about wanting to attract customers actively. Whilst it can be readily agreed that direct enrolments are to be encouraged as actively as possible and a high level of students enrolling through word-of-mouth recommendation suggests a school has a high reputation, it is risky and unwise to rely on filling a school simply by word-of-mouth. Moreover, even if the school is thus filled over a long period, this is still not a reason for complacency but rather it should trigger consideration of whether the school should not be expanding from such a solid base. The market-oriented school will always be engaged in some active selling since it complements other marketing activities.

Personal selling has a number of advantages over other forms of promotion in that:

1 it gives the customer the opportunity to ask all the questions most relevant to his/her situation.
2 the sales message can be adapted much more flexibly.
3 the salesperson can counter objections and negotiate on prices.
4 the salesperson can suggest purchase of other services.

At the outset each school must decide to what extent active personal selling will play a part in its overall marketing mix and even within its sales strategy. Apart from personal selling, other sales-oriented activities may include:

- Mail shots
- Open days/exhibitions
- Sales promotions
- Telephone sales

It was established earlier that the marketing of professional services is made more difficult than that of products by their intangibility and non-uniformity. In selling terms this gives the salesperson three main tasks to perform:

1 Minimize any uncertainty the prospective customer may harbour.
2 Show that the customer's needs and requirements are understood and appreciated.
3 Demonstrate the professional competence necessary for proposing solutions to the customer's problems and satisfying his/her needs.

It may be helpful to elaborate further on these points. In aiming to minimize uncertainty in the mind of the prospective customer, the salesperson can adduce 'physical' evidence to support his/her statements of the benefits of the purchase:

1 the building and its facilities and equipment.
2 the reputation of the organization as a solid, established, reliable, efficient, effective institution – all soothing adjectives to the minds of sceptics.
3 the prospectus and publicity material, presenting services attractively and backing up verbal promises in writing.
4 materials produced for a learning need similar to the customer's.
5 the qualifications and experience of the staff.
6 the convenience of the location and its accessibility.
7 the convenience of the method of payment.

For a large part of the ELT market these factors are more important than the price of the course. Only a minority segment will be quite insensitive to the price, but many will pay a somewhat higher price for something they feel confident about and as provided by an organization with which they feel a personal link in the salesperson. If anything goes wrong or is unsatisfactory he/she can be called upon to put it right. There are also those customers who are suspicious of the lowest prices as likely to offer the lowest quality and offer what is perceived as the highest risk.

In order to show understanding of customers' language problems and needs it is helpful for the salesperson to have experience of language teaching. This will establish an accepted competence in the eyes of many customers where lack of it will engender only suspicion. Sellers of professional services may thus be seen as different in certain ways from those of tangible products. They should:

1 know their own services – benefits and applications – thoroughly and be able to present them attractively.
2 know competitors' services and how they compare.
3 grasp quickly the essence of customers' businesses as well as understanding business in general.

The combination of knowledge, skills and attributes required of a good ELT salesperson may be seen as:

Figure 8.2 The ELT salesperson

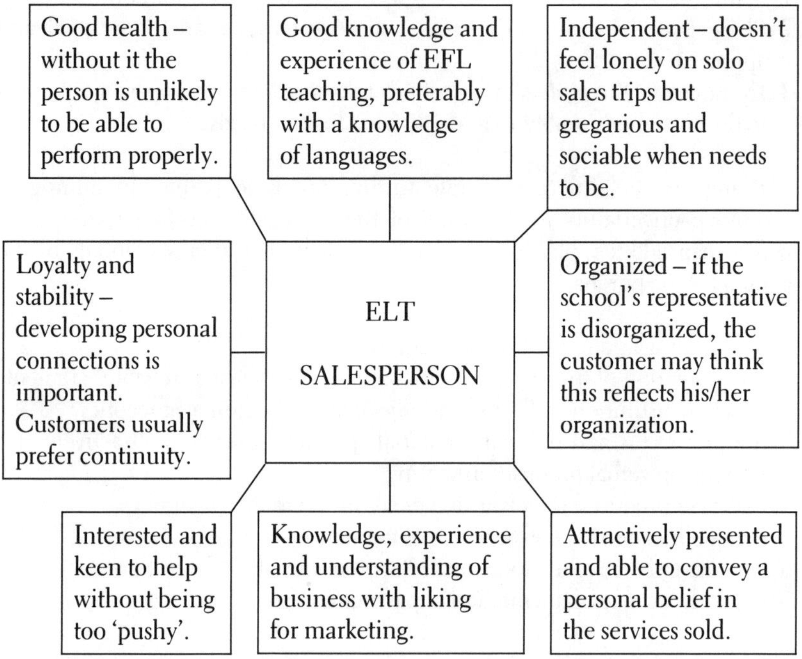

Good health – without it the person is unlikely to be able to perform properly.
Good knowledge and experience of EFL teaching, preferably with a knowledge of languages.
Independent – doesn't feel lonely on solo sales trips but gregarious and sociable when needs to be.
Loyalty and stability – developing personal connections is important. Customers usually prefer continuity.
ELT SALESPERSON
Organized – if the school's representative is disorganized, the customer may think this reflects his/her organization.
Interested and keen to help without being too 'pushy'.
Knowledge, experience and understanding of business with liking for marketing.
Attractively presented and able to convey a personal belief in the services sold.

The professional salesperson will also ask for a 'referral', try to elicit a new lead or two, at the end of each visit.

In the business of ELT direct mailshots are more prevalent than campaigns to sell courses by telephone. This is *not* to suggest that many schools find cold mailshots very fruitful, but rather that keeping students and former students up to date with the school's activities is a good base for keeping direct enrolments as high as possible.

Telephone sales may perform a different function in that they provide a closer link with an individual. One way in which this may be used to advantage is to call up 'drop-outs' from the previous term or course and try to encourage them to enrol again. Even if an enrolment is not immediately forthcoming – and the reason for the call may ostensibly be to enquire why the student withdrew – the activity can provide valuable market research data on why customers do drop out, whether they simply stop taking English lessons or re-enrol with the competition and the reasons for this.

Other ways in which the telephone can help with selling are:

* finding new leads
* renewing subscriptions
* making appointments for salespeople
* maximizing mailshot responses
* pursuing enquiries
* giving invitations to launches and seminars

This leaves salespeople more time to concentrate on selling.

8.3.1 Sales promotion

Sales promotion activities are defined variously by different people, but all aim to do what the name implies – promote sales. McDonald (1984:110) calls it 'the making of a featured offer to defined customers within a specific time limit' i.e. the company wishes to increase sales at a given time or of a certain product and to this end makes a special offer of something or some service that would not normally be available. The incentive may be immediate, for example, a straight price cut or delayed as when the buyer must collect coupons or vouchers, solve a puzzle or enter a competition.

Since sales promotions are generally of short-term duration they are often thought to be merely tactical. However, there is no fundamental reason why they should not be properly integrated into the overall marketing strategy, if the promotion is enduring and flexible.

It would be wrong to think that sales promotion is concerned only with increases in sales volumes. This may be the case, but it is also possible that its aim is to turn favourable attitudes into actual purchase, to encourage switching from one school to another, to reward loyalty, to move preferred buying time, to buy more or to use more quickly.

Apart from price reductions to encourage enrolments at certain off-peak times, sales promotion is not very much in evidence in ELT and may be considered 'unprofessional' by some. In other businesses typical promotions would be:

* price cut – 10p off your next purchase
* coupons – collect 10, send them off and win a prize
* premium offers – buy 12 and get one free
* free goods – buy window cleaning liquid and get a free cloth
* competitions – answer these questions and win a holiday in Moscow
* bonus commission – payable to top-performing agents.

Although not currently prevalent, sales promotion may be an area where, used flexibly and inventively, ELT schools could benefit greatly.

8.4 Pricing

Pricing is important since:

1 it affects the profit margin through its impact on revenue.
2 it affects the quantity sold through its influence on demand.

Figure 8.3 Factors affecting the pricing of services

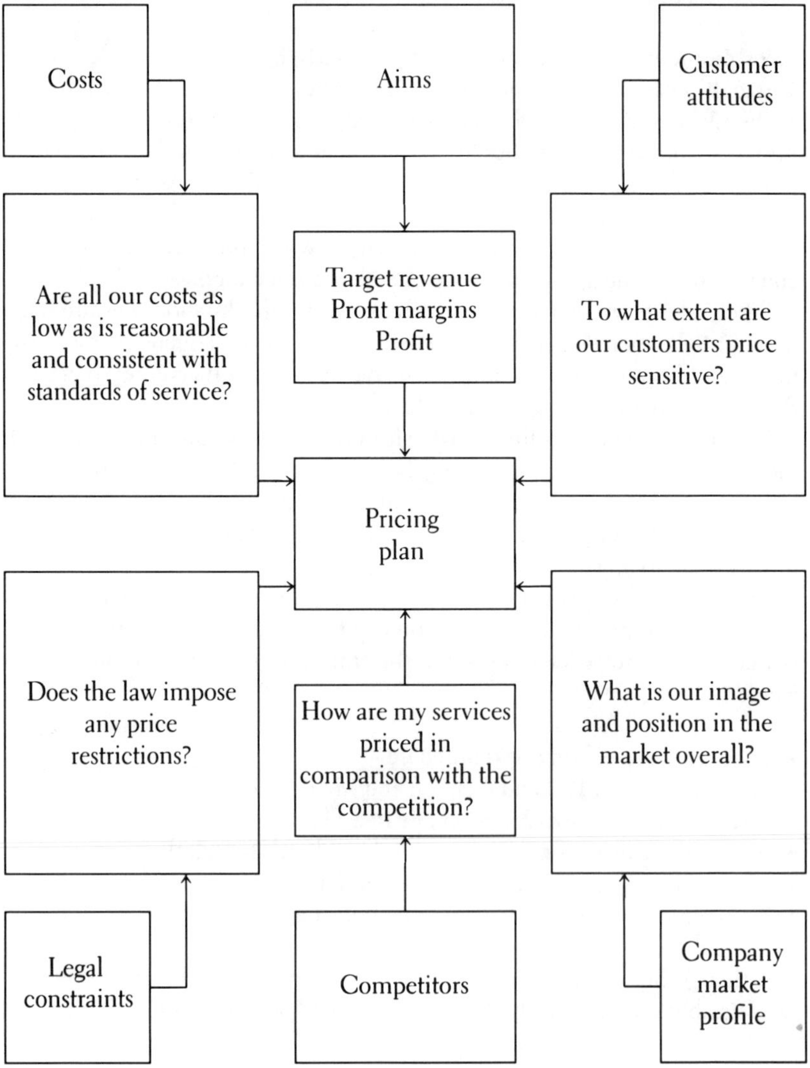

It must always be remembered that demand only exists at a certain price.

At the outset the school must decide on its *pricing aims*. These may be divided into long-term and short-term aims and should bear in mind that most services industries e.g. hotels, airlines or telephone services have patterns of uneven demand and devise programmes and pricing structures to take account of this with a view to maximizing use of capacity and thus profitability.

In the short-term prices may be set so as to:

- recover cash outlay rapidly
- meet the competition
- attract new customers
- secure key contracts
- use spare capacity

Longer-term aims in setting prices may be to:

- maximize return on sales/return on assets
- realize target market share
- operate strategic pricing in different markets
- stabilize the price/margin relationship

All marketing textbooks advise that prices should be market-related NOT cost-related. This is easy to say but hard to do. It assumes that schools have a clear idea of what the market will bear whereas in most cases schools know what their costs are, add on a profit margin and in that way arrive at a price.

Small companies have no adequate way of measuring what the market will bear, but those prepared to make an effort to find out will be helped by:

- sales force reports
- customer reports on the competition
- competitors' price lists

Larger organizations might try out one or more prices in different areas and then compare sales and profit results. They might also conduct some market research asking questions concerning past actions rather than future intent.

In advocating market-related pricing the point is correctly made that costs give you the bottom line only. They should NOT therefore be used alone in determining prices. The market is a far more powerful instrument in deciding selling prices than the costs of production.

Similarly, it is argued that schools should offer something unique which the competition cannot match.

Naturally, schools ought to try to develop unique selling propositions (USPs) which the competition cannot offer, and then price them according to what the market will bear. This often implies selling at a higher price and if such USPs can be maintained and are viewed as valuable *by the customer*, then premium pricing should apply.

However, in practice it is difficult for schools to offer something quite unique. Moreover, their costs are likely to be heavily dependent on staffing quality and levels. Further, once an edge is achieved the competition will be swift to move on price.

In reality, therefore, the best that schools are likely to be able to achieve is:

1 to aim to be the first in innovations perceived as valuable by customers. In this way the image of an entrepreneurial market leader may be developed.
2 to work on many service fronts at the same time rather than concentrate on one proposition. Many new services will be more difficult to match.
3 to pitch prices so as to emphasize value rather than go as high as possible in a 'creaming' strategy and then go lower and lower as the service is copied. Real value will be hard to match.
4 to recognize that winning strategies must be developed, but wear out quickly.

8.4.1 Different pricing methods

STANDARD COST PRICING

Most schools set their prices on the basis of the so-called standard cost pricing. This basically means calculating the total costs per unit and adding on the target percentage profit per unit to arrive at the final price. It has the virtue of simplicity but has many disadvantages.

1 It supports the myth that costs are the thing which cause people to buy. However, the market has no interest in cost. The market wants to satisfy its needs at a competitive price. Perceived value is far more important than cost.
2 This pricing system can disguise inefficiencies in costs.
3 It pays no attention to the competition.
4 The system is very dependent on the sales forecast, which is necessary to calculate total cost per unit.
5 Since the market doesn't know or care about costs, if these are too high in comparison with the competition, the price will have to be reduced in any event because the course will not sell.

The system may be used for producing a base line figure.

MARGINAL PRICING

Marginal pricing is normally used on the basis that it is better to have the business at variable cost than not have it at all. This may be true, but should not blur the fact that it should be done as an extraordinary measure acceptable at off-peak times but should under no circumstances be seen as the norm or used to attract marginal business at the expense of full-profit recruitment.

Marginal pricing theory is that the price is set at a point where marginal cost equals marginal revenue. (See Chapter 11 for more detailed analysis of marginal pricing.) In the ELT world this will normally mean the actual cost of providing a teacher in a classroom and pitching the price at a level whereby these basic costs will be met by the students attending the class. Normally it would be done on the basis that the classroom cannot be filled at normal prices and it is thus better to have a class making a financial contribution to overheads than to have an empty classroom.

Apart from the dangers mentioned above, there are certain other caveats to marginal policy. These are that it should be avoided if:

1 it will set a long-term precedent with big customers.
2 it will spread and all others want similar treatment.
3 it entails extra capital costs.
4 full-profit business has to be turned away to fit it in.
5 it costs in cash flow as well.
6 too many people are involved.

It is NOT being suggested here that costing procedures should be abandoned. Careful scrutiny of costs is important in evaluating the profitability. The recommendation is that costs alone should not determine prices.

Finally, it should not be forgotten that the rich are always with us. They constitute a non-price-sensitive and potentially very profitable market. If the school is strong with the rich, it will make the task of the competition, fighting on the basis of price alone, more difficult.

Follow-up activities

1 Draw up an inventory of services for your school. Conduct a survey and make a list of how major and minor improvements can be made.
2 Assume you have responsibility for a number of schools. Thinking strategically:
   a) what items/services do you wish to be the same within each school?
   b) what items/services should be different from the core but the same from school to school?
3 What exactly is meant by quality of services? How would you monitor quality of service?
4 What new products/services may be profitably developed? Could your school sell extended services to existing clients?
5 Are your promotion activities:
   a) meeting their objectives?
   b) cost-effective?
6 What is the organization's promotion policy?

7 Investigate the image the organization has in the minds of (a) clients (b) non-clients. Is the publicity material produced in line with the desired image?
8 Collect together all the publicity material the school produces. Does it project a coherent picture and conform to an obviously coherent framework?
9 What are the school's advertising objectives? Can they be achieved by advertising alone?
10 Collect data on all the listed media and advertising rates. Which media reach which audience? What is the size of the audience reached and is it the one your school is targeting?
11 Draft a statement of the school's sales strategy and state how it fits in with the school's overall marketing mix. What is the actual sales programme:
 – who is to be visited? Are there any other good sales targets?
 – when will the visit(s) take place?
 – what is the salesperson trying to sell?
 – can the school provide it if he/she is successful?
 – who will do the selling?
 – is he/she the best person?
 – what is the cost of the programme and how does this compare with the results?
12 Assume you are trying to sell your school's services to a bank training manager. He wishes to put ten of his staff, who need English to work in the foreign exchange department, on a 4-week course five days per week eight hours per day. They are all beginners, except one who has intermediate English, already more than adequate for the job. The training manager has a rather jaundiced view of the ELT institutes having had his fingers burned early in his career.
13 Think of two sales promotions that could be offered attractively at your school and explain how they should make a useful contribution to profitability.
14 Review the school's pricing structure so as to ensure that prices are pitched at the right level for each course.
15 Take your school's accounts for the last quarter and sift through them item by item, ensuring that all costs are justified and as low as is reasonable. List potential changes. Then do a sales, cost and profit projection for the next courses based on the prices you would charge.

9 DEVELOPING AND IMPLEMENTING THE MARKETING PLAN

Aims

The aims of this chapter are:

1 to introduce the concept of segmentation.
2 to demonstrate the importance of market leadership.
3 to outline the prime stages of strategic marketing planning.
4 to show how a marketing plan is put together.
5 to illustrate the most important financial aspects in marketing.
6 to detail some of the prime considerations in creating a marketing department.
7 to investigate the costs and benefits of indirect marketing.

Introduction

The two previous chapters showed how the components of the marketing mix intermeshed and highlighted the kind of information necessary to draw up a strategic marketing plan.

This chapter demonstrates how such a plan is drawn up and looks also into areas of marketing which are aimed ultimately at increasing enrolments in a school, but the effect of which is impossible to quantify in the short-term.

It is not technically difficult to draw up a marketing plan, yet few schools have one either because:

- there is no one officially responsible for marketing or no marketing department.
- the marketing staff do not know how to put a marketing plan together.
- the marketing staff do know but are too busy with other tasks e.g. trying to book next term's enrolments. Sitting and writing a formal plan has lower priority.

All schools have it within their scope to produce a formal marketing plan if such a step is given sufficiently high priority. However, this presupposes a market- and marketing-led school of the type which rarely exists. It implies a detached and unsentimental appraisal of a school's resources and activities as well as the will to make the necessary skills, time and money available for implementation. As with market research, there are two particular evils to be avoided:

1 the plan without action – which in some ways is worse than action without a plan.
2 the plan which merely reiterates the status quo either because the writer has no idea of the future direction or because vested interest is so entrenched as to make any significant change impossible.

Amongst the benefits a sound plan can confer McDonald (1984:36) lists:

1 co-ordination of the activities of many individuals whose actions are inter-related.
2 identification of expected developments.
3 preparedness to meet changes when they occur.
4 better communication throughout the organization.
5 minimization of conflict among individuals.

9.1 Segmentation

Up till now 'markets' have been spoken of as if there was one distinct entity, the components of which all had the same needs. In practice, 'markets' are invariably made up of several segments, all with very different requirements and which must be catered for in very different ways.

The normally accepted criteria for what constitutes a viable market segment are:

1 it should be of an adequate size to provide a school with a satisfactory return for its effort.
2 segments must be reachable.
3 the members of each segment should have a high degree of similarity but be distinct from each other.
4 the criteria for describing segments must be relevant to the purchasing situation.

In ELT some of the most easily distinguished segments are:

- Business English/executive English: small groups/premium price
- One-to-one: highly specific/premium price
- Junior courses: primarily in the summer/care and welfare aspects of supreme importance
- Courses leading to public examinations: duration to coincide with the timing of the examination: published pass-rates can be influential
- English for academic purposes: price-sensitive/often recruited from different countries from other segments
- Native-speaker teachers' courses: recruited in UK/price-sensitive

Each of these segments has clearly differentiated academic and other needs and preferences: the executive will not wish to practise past examination papers any more than a 10-year-old junior will want to take notes from an academic lecture. For executives, parking space at the school may be important whilst for the parents of juniors the provision of transport between home and school may be a valuable service.

Failure to understand the differing needs of segments will result in failure to provide desired services at an acceptable price.

9.2 Market leadership

In marketing it is normally better to lead than to follow. Many institutions aim to lead their particular markets but few have a clear idea what constitutes a market leader and distinguishes it from its competitors. Figure 9.1 overleaf aims to illustrate an answer.

If a school cannot be market leader, it should try to move gradually upmarket so as to attain market leadership and/or try to be the best in selected segments.

9.3 Strategic marketing planning

In strategic marketing planning the prime questions to be answered are:

1 where are we now?
2 where do we want to be? (Objective)
3 how are we going to get there? (Strategy)

An objective may be seen as a destination; a strategy is the route chosen for reaching that destination and tactics are the vehicles selected for taking the traveller down the chosen route.

A crucial process in developing strategies is a sound and sharp SWOT/PEST analysis. Based on the internal and external audits conducted as market research, this analysis will appraise a school's:

Strengths		Political	
Weaknesses	and take into	Economic	factors
Opportunities	account	Social	
Threats		Technical	

A good SWOT will help to pinpoint the really important issues to be addressed and make concise statements which should in themselves lead to further action. It is likely to imply ways in which a school could try to

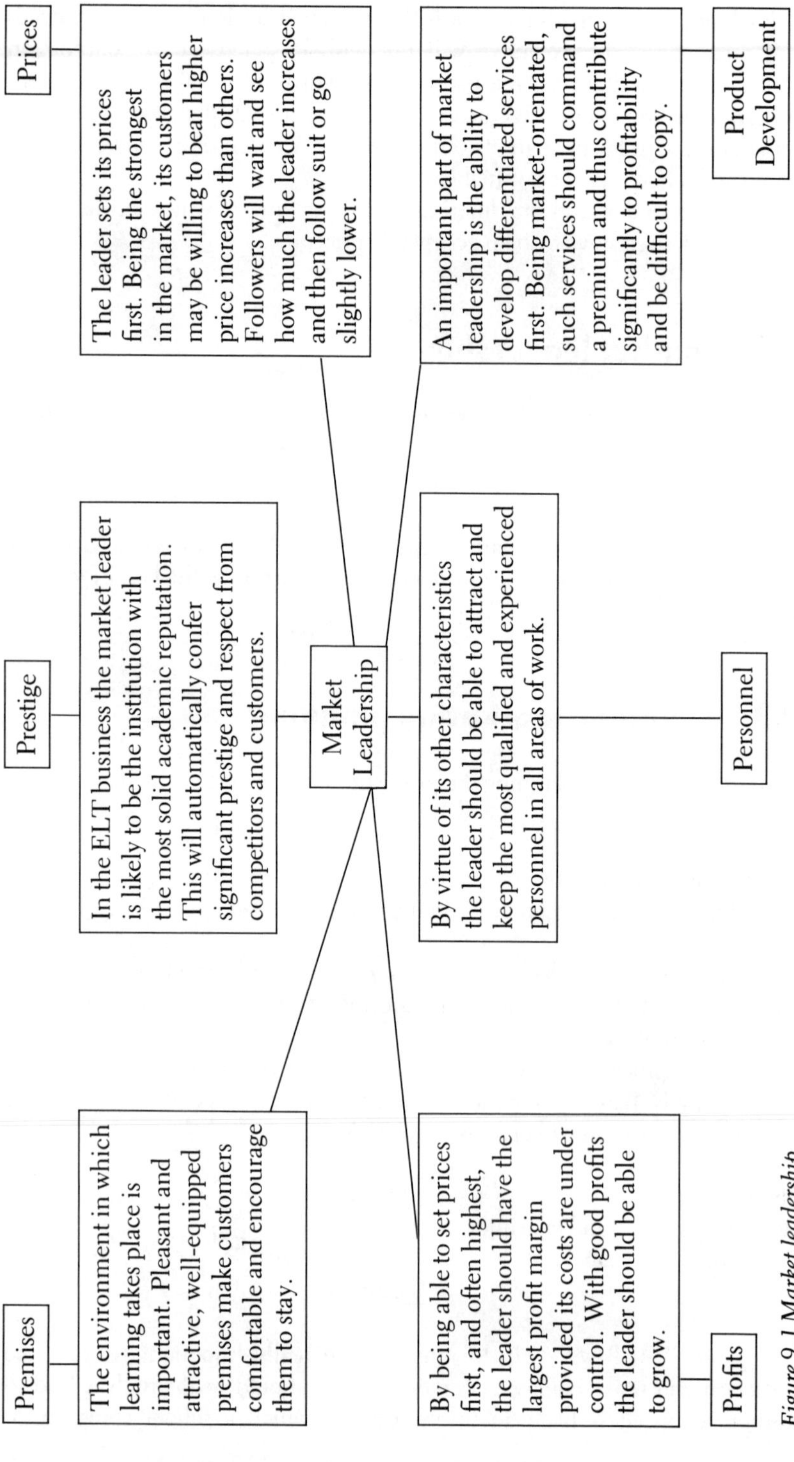

Premises
The environment in which learning takes place is important. Pleasant and attractive, well-equipped premises make customers comfortable and encourage them to stay.
Prestige
In the ELT business the market leader is likely to be the institution with the most solid academic reputation. This will automatically confer significant prestige and respect from competitors and customers.
Prices
The leader sets its prices first. Being the strongest in the market, its customers may be willing to bear higher price increases than others. Followers will wait and see how much the leader increases and then follow suit or go slightly lower.
Market Leadership
Profits
By being able to set prices first, and often highest, the leader should have the largest profit margin provided its costs are under control. With good profits the leader should be able to grow.
Personnel
By virtue of its other characteristics the leader should be able to attract and keep the most qualified and experienced personnel in all areas of work.
Product Development
An important part of market leadership is the ability to develop differentiated services first. Being market-orientated, such services should command a premium and thus contribute significantly to profitability and be difficult to copy.

Figure 9.1 Market leadership

differentiate itself from the competition by identifying gaps between demand and supply.

Valuable insights into how well a school is doing can be concluded from the internal audit and fed into the SWOT analysis. A legitimate objective of many schools is to fill as close to capacity as possible for as many weeks of the year as possible. Such a target ought to carry with it the maximum use of plant which should in turn work towards maximizing profitability. In considering the success or otherwise of a school's performance in this regard, four interconnecting touchstones may be investigated and conclusions about a school's strengths and weaknesses drawn from them:

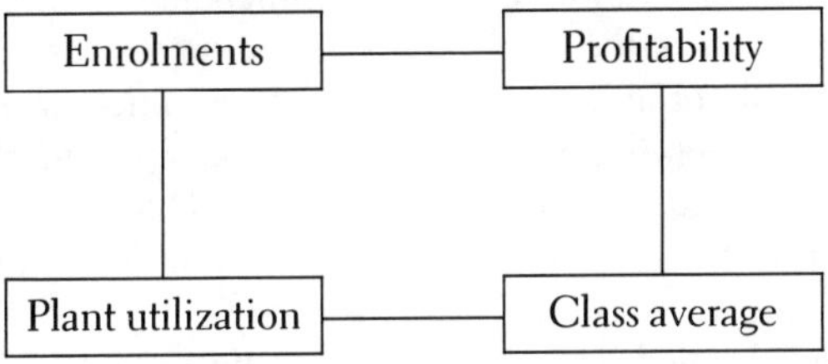

If all four of these items results in a 'high' figure or calculation, it is likely that a school is doing very well in commercial terms. But it is crucially important *NOT* simply to focus on one of these items and neglect the others. A high level of plant utilization does not in itself ensure profitability any more than a high class average implies good plant utilization. All four factors must work together to maximize a school's potential.

In a large institution valuable comparisons may be made term by term and branch by branch. In drawing up such analyses it is vital at the outset to set up fair parameters and to compare like with like. Three decisions here have great import:

1 Property costs: Some branches may be owned and thus show virtually no property costs in the accounts, whilst others will have their profitability substantially reduced.
2 Allocation of central overheads: Different companies allocate these in different ways. The fairest method may be to allocate on the basis of a school's student capacity.
3 Practical working day: Different branches are likely to have different enrolment patterns according to their location. The decision as to how many hours a day and how many days a week they are open and may reasonably be expected to fill will have a great bearing on the plant utilization calculations.

9.4 Marketing plans

Marketing strategies are primarily about products and markets. For each a spectrum of options is available:

Exit	Defend	Maintain	Attack	Expand

In a changing world it is inevitable that each institution will have a list of assets and products which represent where that institution used to be rather than where it is going. This must be viewed quite unsentimentally and the future potential assessed. Regardless of the level of investment made, earlier successes and glories, markets will not smile profitably on services which have long gone out of fashion or for which there is no demand. One of the most difficult decisions will be what to do about a school's weaknesses. Often it will be better to cut and bear the pain for a limited period than to allow a rash of unprofitable products to infect the whole company.

However, once it has been decided what is to be cut, the areas to be maintained and the sources of future profits, it should be possible to fit these strategic decisions into the Ansoff matrix. An example for a typical EFL school in Britain might be:

Figure 9.2 A product/market matrix for a UK EFL school

MARKETS		PRODUCTS: EXISTING	PRODUCTS: NEW
MARKETS	EXISTING	General English Summer courses ESP	Junior summer courses EAP 1:1 Executive courses
MARKETS	NEW	Brazil Argentina Taiwan Indonesia Malaysia	Native-speaker teachers' courses Foreign language courses for British executives Establish a school in France

9.5 Asset-led marketing

The marketing activities discussed so far may be seen as *market-led*. However, an *asset-led* approach can give an added dimension to marketing thinking and the following figure illustrates how the two approaches intermesh:

Figure 9.3 Market-led and asset-led marketing

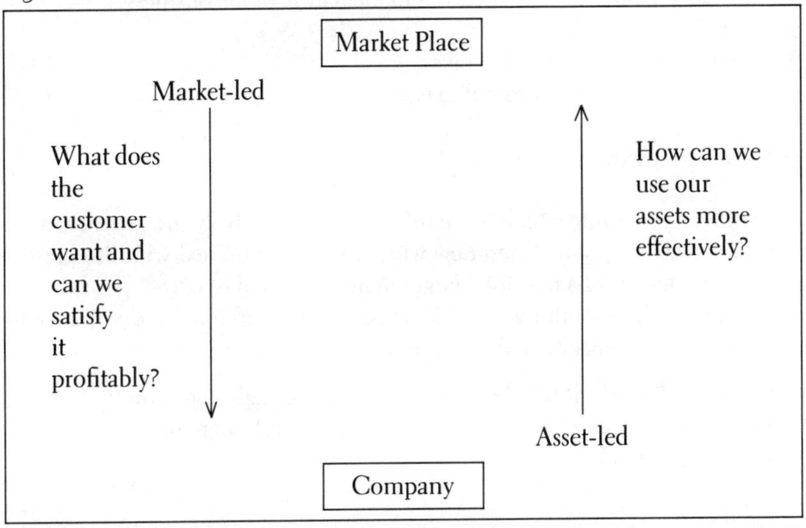

Both market-led and asset-led approaches may be pursued concurrently. It is equally possible to search the market-place for opportunities and then decide whether the school can handle them as it is to scrutinize carefully the school's assets and then look at the market-place to find ways of exploiting them. In order to do this it will be necessary to look in some detail into what the school's assets actually are. They can usually be broken down as follows:

Figure 9.4 Assets

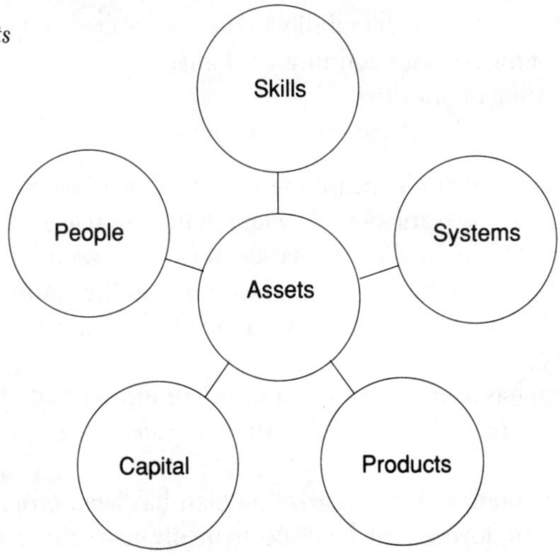

At this point it may also be worth considering in more detail *opportunities* and *risks*. Drucker (1964:230) has helpfully broken these down into the following categories:

RISKS

1 The risk one must accept as built into the nature of the business.
2 The risk one can afford to take.
3 The risk one cannot afford to take.
4 The risk one cannot afford *not* to take.

OPPORTUNITIES

1 Additive: something which more fully exploits already existing resources.
2 Complementary: something new which, when combined with the present business, results in a new total larger than the sum of its parts.
3 Breakthrough: something which changes the fundamental economic characteristics and capacity of the business.

In the ELT world it will be rare for a 'breakthrough opportunity' to arise, but in assessing opportunities it is a good idea also to appraise the level and type of risk attached.

9.5.1 The plan itself

Companies with effective marketing plans should enjoy the following benefits:

* widely understood objectives
* greater control and less vulnerability to the unexpected and unpredictable
* recognition of the need for continuous change
* an understanding of priorities
* minimum waste and duplication of resources

Marketing plans are rarely meant to be the final word on what the company will do during the relevant period. Plans tend to change as experience is gained and circumstances alter. However, they must be used and constantly referred to, if they are to have any significant role in the company's successful development. A flow chart for the development of a marketing plan is shown on the next page.

Once the plan has been written, it must be communicated. The communications necessary are likely to fall into two main categories:

1 Marketing orientation: If the marketing plan has been properly drawn up, the school's employees will have been involved in the process and will

already have a broad idea of what is proposed. However, there is still likely to be the need to explain the implications of a client-oriented approach and to ensure that the plan, its aims, strategies and priorities are understood and accepted by all.

2 Role in marketing: There will also be the need to agree with staff their role and contribution on a practical, day-to-day level. Here it should quickly become clear whether the client orientation has been fully accepted insofar as staff should be able to make an active contribution as to how their particular area of work could be improved. Passive acceptance is likely to suggest either lack of or only partial understanding.

Figure 9.5 The development of a marketing plan

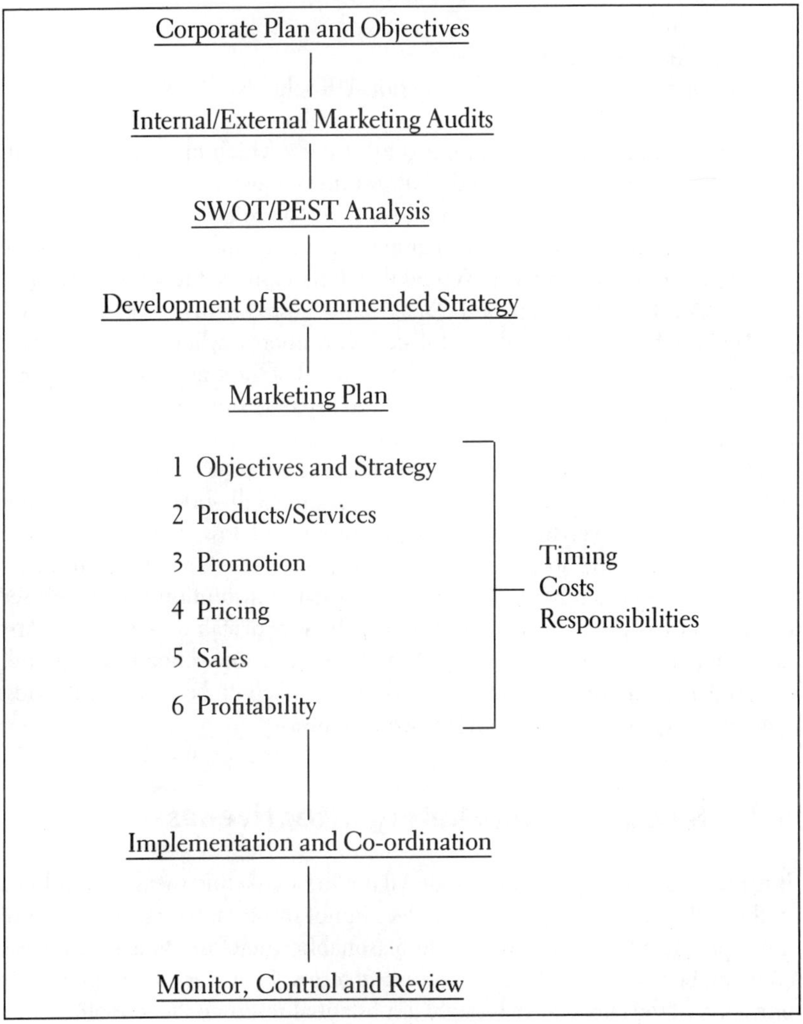

9.6 Indirect marketing

In ELT there are various activities which are undertaken for their inherent value but which, because they cost the school money, are sometimes presented as *indirect* marketing activities, ventures which may have a sales spin-off even if this is not their prime objective. Since an enrolment is frequently the result of a series of interlocking factors it is difficult to prove any results of indirect marketing in sales terms.

Amongst the activities falling into the category of indirect marketing are:

- ⋆ attendance at academic conferences
- ⋆ publication of books
- ⋆ seminars and British Council specialist tours
- ⋆ scholarships
- ⋆ marginally-costed courses
- ⋆ social and cultural programmes (in non-UK schools)

Attendance at conferences can lead to contacts which may put business in the way of the school. Would that business have come about without attendance at the conference? Similarly, a free place given to the son of the Personnel Manager of a multi-national company may bring a group of executives from that company. Would they have come to the school anyway?

It is often hoped that an initial marginally-costed course, e.g. for native-speaker teachers, will lead to full-fee enrolments when those teachers recommended the school to their students. In all of these areas there are many factors to be considered. It is impossible to separate out the 'deciding' items from items costing the school money unnecessarily.

The role of these activities will depend primarily on the school's philosophy. At one end of the spectrum, a commercially-oriented institution, which measures everything in terms of profit and loss, will not allow or undertake any of the above unless they show a direct return. This will rarely be the case. At the other end a liberal, charitable institution might well see the activities as valuable in themselves and by way of staff development. Any sales emanating would be a bonus. Assuming the school is financially sound, a considerable amount of indirect marketing is likely to be sanctioned. Most schools fall somewhere between the two extremes.

9.7 Measuring marketing effectiveness

It is inevitable that institutions undertaking the marketing measures outlined in these chapters will involve themselves in not insubstantial costs in terms of time, people and money. It is quite reasonable, therefore, to ask how these costs can be justified in strictly commercial terms. How is it shown, preferably proved, that the efforts have brought a substantial return to the school?

To attempt to answer this, calculations must first be done to determine what marketing costs have been incurred. They will normally include:

1 salaries and indirect costs of manager(s) and support staff.
2 overhead allocation for office space, equipment and other resources.
3 travel and entertainment expenses.
4 promotion literature.
5 advertising and attendance at exhibitions.
6 a percentage of mailing costs.
7 agents' commission.

Together these are bound to add up to a tidy sum and it is understandable that the immediate reaction of some in ELT is that the school would save itself a lot of time, effort and cash if it forgot marketing entirely, or did away with all such costs apart from the commission of the agents whose clients would fill the school.

The problem with the first solution is that if the marketing function is being performed properly and it is then dropped, enrolments will plummet and the school will enter hard times.

The difficulty with the second solution is that it contains an inherent dependence on agents and the suggestion that provided such agents are paid their commission, nothing else is required. In practice, agents themselves need support by way of promotion literature, information about the school and many other items. Unless the school is to rely on agents finding and selecting the school, a risky process, it is incumbent on the school to find and foster its representatives overseas. In an ideal world a school would eternally fill itself with direct enrolments and it is a prime aim of the marketing function to try to achieve this. Unfortunately, the competition is such that few UK schools attain this target and overseas the situation does not apply.

In scrutinizing marketing costs, the question is often asked as to what is the 'right' amount to be spent on marketing. Regrettably, there is no 'right' amount. Some schools spend next to nothing and survive. Others spend 15% of turnover and turn in variable performances. The questions ought rather to be:

- What do we want to achieve?
- How do we do it most cost-effectively?
- How are we going to monitor the effectiveness of each item?

The difficulty of measuring marketing effectiveness lies in the fact that it is involved in all aspects of the business and this makes it hard to separate marketing efforts from other functions in black and white terms. However, if money is not to be spent blindly, an attempt must be made.

As has been shown above, marketing costs can be broken down into identifiable segments and methods established for measuring effectiveness.

Whilst it would be unwise to spend an inordinate length of time on the item, the research can be of value in itself and offer important insights into the business.

Item	Method of measuring effectiveness
1 Salaries Travel Entertainment Overheads	1 Sales actually made. 2 Sales ensuing from marketing efforts but may have been made anyway.
2 Exhibitions	1 Make a special offer only for the exhibition. 2 Take a list of names of visitors to stand and try to match with sales.
3 Promotion literature	1 Sales made on accompanying application form. 2 In internal research test number of students who read brochure before enrolling.
4 Mailing	1 Relate overall mailing effort to sales realized. 2 Break this down further by country, agent and office.

It will be apparent that some of the above items overlap. Moreover, the results will not be final and absolute: a trip to a country from which the school hitherto received no students and from which sales are then made attracts greater credit than a visit to a well-established source. Nonetheless, these procedures will give the school as clear a picture as possible as to how its students arrive, and they will go a considerable way to evaluating the effectiveness of the marketing effort.

School accountants are likely to baulk at the yardsticks proposed here, suggest they fall short of the financial precision required and suggest a simpler, more concrete formula. This runs as follows:

Marketing costs are £25,000
School tuition fees per week are £120
Target profit is 15%

Thus, in order to justify this investment marketing must recruit:

$$\frac{25{,}000}{\pounds 18} = \underline{\underline{1{,}389 \text{ student weeks}}}$$

This is one, rather simplistic version of the truth. Its weakness lies in the fact that it fails to take into account the number of vacant places a school may have and thus revenue lost *entirely* if this investment in marketing had not been made.

It has been stressed throughout that marketing aims to increase profitability. It is, therefore, impossible to perform the marketing function properly without supporting aims, strategies and programmes with projected profit calculations. In this book such calculations and methods of calculating have been given over to the finance section. This is not to abrogate the responsibility from marketing but merely to avoid duplication. Marketers will normally support plans with a variety of calculations. Three crucially important items will be:

1. the direct and indirect costs of teacher provision – which will normally form the basis for the minimum class size figure.
2. the method of allocating overheads – which can radically alter the picture of whether a branch or a course is profitable.
3. the break-even point – which indicates the level to which a school must fill in order to cover its costs.

Conclusion

Markets are not one entity but rather are composed of many different segments with different needs and thus requiring different approaches and provision. Schools which are market leaders ought to be the most profitable. If a school cannot be overall market leader, its best strategy may be to lead in a selected segment.

A SWOT analysis is a crucial process in developing strategies. Alongside this, the four yardsticks of Enrolments/Plant utilization/Class average/ Profitability, will give valuable insights into a school's current position and thus where it might realistically aim to go. The marketing plan will make explicit the programmes and responsibilities for achieving objectives.

An asset-led approach to marketing can throw up new opportunities for business and increased profitability.

It is difficult to measure marketing effectiveness in black and white terms. However, there are methods of evaluation which ought to be undertaken and which in themselves ought to give valuable insights into the business.

Follow-up activities

1. Make a list of the market segments the school serves and the ways in which you treat them differently.
2. Research each segment's needs and wants in depth and draw up proposals for how they may be more closely met.

3 List the segments the school does not serve and state why you do not wish to attract that area of business.
4 Make a list of practical ways in which the school would either come closer to or maintain market leadership.
5 Do a SWOT/PEST analysis for the school.
6 Calculate figures for Enrolments / Class Average / Plant Utilization / Profitability. State the bases on which the calculations were made and give reasons as to how these bases were decided upon especially as regards treatment of:
 * Property costs * Overhead allocation * Length of working day
7 Draw up an Ansoff Matrix for your school and outline the bases on which the decisions for (a) new products and (b) new markets were made.
8 Give an account of the main assets of your business. What opportunities exist for developing it further and what are the risks attached?
9 What indirect marketing activities might be undertaken by your school? What *marketing* effect do you expect them to have?
10 Write a complete marketing plan for your school.
11 Construct a practical framework for evaluating the effectiveness of your school's marketing effort.

PART THREE: FINANCE

10 FINANCIAL RECORDS AND STATEMENTS

Aims

The main aim of this chapter is to enable readers to understand financial statements. The subsidiary aims are:

1 to introduce the topics of recording, adjusting and presenting financial information.
2 to explain the concepts of double entry book-keeping.
3 to demonstrate the method of double entry book-keeping.
4 to show how book-keeping information is summarized and adjusted to form the basis of conventional financial statements.
5 to explain the form and content of the profit and loss account and the balance sheet.
6 to outline the purpose and content of certain other non-traditional financial statements.

Introduction

This chapter deals with the conventional techniques of recording, adjusting and presenting financial information. Financial information is important. As an employee you may find that your salary or even your job itself depends on someone else's interpretation of financial information. As a manager your performance may be judged on the basis of financial information, and you will need to take account of financial information in making plans and decisions.

The chapter is intended to develop an understanding of financial information as it is conventionally presented – in a stylized format, using terms and ideas which may be strange and even counter to intuition.

Most of these terms and ideas derive from double entry book-keeping. We begin with a description of the principles of double entry, and show how the principles are applied to record transactions in the accounts of an enterprise.

Once recorded, the transactions of an enterprise must be summarized and adjusted to reveal the state of affairs of the enterprise, and the result of its transactions over a period. We show why, and how this is done in a way consistent with the principles of double entry.

Finally we show how the result and state of affairs of an enterprise are presented in conventional financial statements and consider the purpose and form of certain other non-traditional financial statements – the statements of source and application of funds and of value added.

The conventional financial statements of an enterprise are the profit and loss account and the balance sheet. This raises a question of terminology: a commercial business makes a profit or a loss, while an educational trust or a public sector body may generate a surplus or a deficit. There are other differences of terminology but the principles of recording and presenting financial information remain constant, whatever the nature of the enterprise.

For consistency we have chosen the example of a business which makes a profit. The differences in terminology are very few. A commercial business presents a profit and loss account, while a trust or public sector body may present a statement of income and expenditure. The owner's interest in a commercial business will be represented as capital and reserves, or equity. For a trust, the equivalent of equity will be a trust fund or funds. Public sector bodies may have no precise equivalent of equity, or may in its place have an account with the sponsoring authority to which their surpluses are returned.

10.1 Recording financial information

Accounting is at least the second oldest profession in the world. But while earlier professionals rapidly got to grips with basic techniques and even introduced refinements, it is remarkable that generations of tax collectors and merchants staggered on for thousands of years before finding a satisfactory general method of keeping a record of their affairs.

This should serve as a warning, The problem is common sense but the answer is not. It is highly contrived and in some respects still imperfect. It begins with a particular way of looking at a business which we present in the next section.

10.1.1 The accounting equation

A business may be pictured as a box. The box has contents and by virtue of owning the box, the owner has a claim to the value of the contents. Others also may have a claim on the contents, by virtue of having lent money to the business or of having supplied goods or services to the business for which they have not yet been paid. These are the creditors of the business.

As the business buys and sells goods and services, so the value of the contents of the box will increase or decrease, depending on whether the business makes a profit or a loss. These changes in value of contents must be equalled by changes in value of claims on contents. Specifically the claims of the owners will vary so that the total value of claims is always equal to the value of the contents.

Now we may list the value of the contents of the business box at any time, say down the left side of a piece of paper. On the right side we may list the value of claims on those contents. The claims of third party creditors will be known. The claims of the owners will amount to whatever is necessary to make the total value of claims equal to the total value of contents.

Such a list of contents (on the left) balanced by a list of claims (on the right), constitutes a simple balance sheet. A balance sheet is a presentation of the state of affairs of a business in a succinct, systematic and recognizable format.

Restating the original theory, with the picture of the business as a box, we can write

£ contents = £ claims on contents.

In accounting terms, this becomes

1) ASSETS = EQUITY + LIABILITIES

where assets are simply what is held in the business, equity is the claim of the owners, and liabilities are the claims of third parties.

By transferring liabilities to the other side of the equation we may write

ASSETS – LIABILITIES = EQUITY

or, using a technical term

2) NET ASSETS = EQUITY

Finally we may split equity into the capital originally put into the business and reserves. Reserves represent profits which have been reserved or kept in the business. The equation now becomes

3) NET ASSETS = CAPITAL + RESERVES

1,2 and 3 above are forms of the fundamental accounting equation. Readers should take the time to learn all three forms of the accounting equation. Remember that the equation does not represent an arithmetical accident. It is always true because it is a definition of equity. The working of the equation is shown in Figure 10.1 overleaf.

Figure 10.1 The accounting equation

A A business begins when its owners lay aside £10 for the future purchase of supplies and equipment. Apply the accounting equation to determine the value of both sides of the balance sheet.

There are no liabilities, and so

NET ASSETS = £10 cash
NET ASSETS = EQUITY
therefore EQUITY = £10

B After one year's trading the business has £20 cash. Sundry debtors owe £5 to the business and the business owes £8 to various creditors. What is the value of the equity?

NET ASSETS = ASSETS − LIABILITIES
= £20 cash + £5 debtors − £8 creditors
= £17
NET ASSETS = EQUITY
therefore EQUITY = £17

C After a further year the business has debtors of £15, an overdraft of £5 and creditors of £2. What is the value of the equity?

NET ASSETS = ASSETS − LIABILITIES
= £15 debtors − £5 overdraft − £2 creditors
= £8
NET ASSETS = EQUITY
therefore EQUITY = £8

10.1.2 Inflows and outflows

The accounting equation is a static representation of a business. It resembles a fast shutter photograph which freezes the action at one particular instant. Our intention is to create a dynamic view of a business, capable of recording events as they happen.

To do this we may view the business box mentioned above, not as a treasure chest with contents and claims, but as a reservoir at the centre of a series of inflows and outflows. Figure 10.2 demonstrates that the accounting equation approach can be comprehended within the more flexible inflow and outflow approach.

Figure 10.2 Inflows and outflows: the business as a reservoir

A business has cash of £30, debtors of £20, and creditors of £5.

---

1 Determine the value of equity using the accounting equation.

NET ASSETS = ASSETS − LIABILITIES
= £30 cash + £20 debtors − £5 creditors
= £45
NET ASSETS = EQUITY
therefore EQUITY = £45

---

2 Interpret the accounting equation in terms of inflows and outflows. We use this form of the accounting equation:

ASSETS = EQUITY + LIABILITIES

and thus

£30 cash + £20 debtors = £45 equity + £5 creditors

The LEFT side can be interpreted in terms of INFLOWS as:

£30 cash: any business experiences inflows and outflows of cash. At this instant the business holds £30 cash and therefore over the life of the business it has experienced a NET INFLOW of £30.

£20 debtors: these debtors will eventually pay the business in cash. The debtors amount can therefore be seen as a FUTURE INFLOW of £20.

The RIGHT side can be interpreted in terms of OUTFLOWS as:

£45 equity: this is the owners' claim and represents the amount the owners could take away if the business were closed at this instant. It is therefore a POTENTIAL OUTFLOW of £45.

£5 creditors: the business will eventually pay these creditors in cash. The creditors amount can therefore be seen as a FUTURE OUTFLOW of £5.

10.1.3 Transactions

Double entry book-keeping depends on the assertion (or convention) that every recordable event or transaction involves an inflow and an outflow of equal value. Both the inflow and the outflow must be recorded in the books of account – hence the name, double entry book-keeping.

In most instances the inflow and the outflow are observable and the equality in value is easily assumed. However the idea of a transaction as composed of an inflow and an outflow of equal value remains a convention and not a picture drawn from life. The examples below will show that some considerable stretching and squeezing is involved if every recordable event is to be forced into this mould.

TRANSACTION 1:

A business buys goods for £10 cash.
Inflow: goods value £10
Outflow: cash value £10

TRANSACTION 2:

A business sells the *same* goods for £15 cash.
Inflow: cash value £15
Outflow: goods value £15

Note that value is not intrinsic. It is determined by the transaction. The business bought these goods for £10 and so £10 was their value in transaction 1. In transaction 2, the goods are sold for £15 and so £15 is their value for transaction 2.

TRANSACTION 3:

A business buys goods on credit for £20.
Inflow: goods £20
Future outflow: to creditor £20

Note that the matching flows need not occur simultaneously. It is only important that matching flows should be recorded simultaneously.

TRANSACTION 4:

A business sells goods for £25 on credit.
Future inflow: from debtor £25
Outflow: goods £25

TRANSACTION 5:

A business receives fee for professional advice, £30 cash.
Inflow: cash £30
Outflow: advice £30

Note that the flows need not be of tangible items. The convention dictates that if there is an inflow then there must be an outflow of equal value, even if we cannot see it.

TRANSACTION 6:

A business pays salary, £35 cash.
Inflow: efforts of staff, £35
Outflow: cash £35

Note: you may think that your input to your employer's business is worth more than your salary, or that the input of some of your colleagues is of no value. The double entry takes a dogmatic stand on this issue. If there is an outflow of value then there must be an inflow of equal value.

TRANSACTION 7:

A business robs passer-by of £40 cash.
Inflow: cash £40
Potential outflow: to owners £40

Note that here the double entry system starts to become arbitrary. Under any common sense view of things the robbery represents an inflow of £40 cash in return for no outflow. However, the system must record an outflow to match the inflow.

The recording of a potential outflow to the owners can be justified in terms of the accounting equation. We know that equity is the total potential outflow to the owners, and that equity is given by the value of net assets. The inflow of £40 cash in exchange for nothing must increase net assets, and therefore increase equity. It therefore represents an increase in the potential outflow to owners, which is how it has been recorded.

TRANSACTION 8:

A business gives £45 to charity.
Potential inflow: from owners £45
Outflow: cash, £45

Note that once again common sense tells us that this transaction involves a one way flow. Once again the system requires us to invent a flow, this time an inflow to match the outflow.

Again the invented inflow from the owners is justified in terms of the accounting equation. The gift to charity reduces net assets and therefore reduces equity. Equity is a potential outflow to the owners. The potential inflow from the owners, as recorded here, thus serves to reduce equity.

TRANSACTION 9:

A business receives £25 cash from the debtor recorded in transaction 4.
Inflow: cash £25
Outflow: loss of claim on debtor £25

The outflow we have had to record here represents a negation of the inflow recorded in transaction 4.

TRANSACTION 10:

A business pays £15 to the creditor in transaction 3.
Inflow: part negation of outflow recorded in transaction 3, £15
Outflow: cash £15

Here the idea of an inflow as the negation or cancellation of a previously recorded outflow (or vice versa) becomes more clear.

Note that in respect of the creditor we have now recorded

transaction 3:	future outflow	£20
transaction 10:	negative outflow	£15
leaving now:	future outflow	£5

10.1.4 Recording transactions – debits and credits

We now have a system which the book-keeper can use to record any financial event as a transaction. Two entries in the records are always required – one to record the inflow and one to record the outflow. The entries are always equal.

The entry to record an inflow is called a *debit*. The entry to record an outflow is called a *credit*. In writing, debit can be abbreviated to the form DR (the R is an inexplicable impostor). Credit is abbreviated to CR.

Each transaction is a matched pair, inflow and outflow of equal value. For any transaction and in any set of financial records therefore:

1 a transaction is an inflow and a matching outflow.
2 the inflow is recorded by a debit.

3 the outflow is recorded by a credit.
4 for every debit there must be a credit.
5 for every credit there must be a debit.
6 total debits = total credits.

These six rules should be learned by heart as well as the accounting equation.

10.1.5 Double entry: an example

Having described the double entry system, we can now use and demonstrate it with a series of transactions. The transactions are as below:

A business begins with introduction of £1,000 cash by owners.
B business pays rent £200 for premises.
C business buys materials £100 on credit.
D business sells lessons for £300 cash.
E business pays £50 cash for advertising.
F business sells lessons for £400 on credit.
G business pays creditor £100 cash for materials (see C).
H business receives £350 from debtors for lessons (see F).
I business pays teacher's salary of £100, cash.

The first step is to sort out the debits and the credits – the inflows and the outflows.

Conventionally these are always listed with *debits on the left* and *credits on the right*. Again this convention should be learned by heart. There are mnemonics: credit has an 'r' in it and so is on the right; flows are across the paper in the direction of reading, with debits, inflows, on the left, and credits, outflows, on the right.

Figure 10.3 Transactions as debits and credits

transaction DEBITS (inflows)	DR £	CREDITS (outflows)	CR £
A *cash* introduced	1,000	*capital*	1,000
B premises (*rent*)	200	*cash* paid	200
C *materials*	100	*creditor* payable	100
D *cash* received	300	lesson *sales*	300
E *advertising*	50	*cash* paid	50
F *debtors* (amount receivable)	400	lesson *sales*	400
G *creditor* eliminated (see C)	100	*cash* paid	100
H *cash* received	350	*debtors* part eliminated (see F)	350
I teaching (*salary*)	100	*cash* paid	100
	£2,600		£2,600

The transactions are organized as debits and credits in Figure 10.3 on the previous page. Readers should study Figure 10.3 with reference to the description of the transactions and ensure that they understand the analysis of each transaction into debit side and credit side. Transactions G and H are noteworthy as examples of the use of a debit as a negative credit and vice versa.

10.1.6 Separate accounts

Figure 10.3 is of little use in itself. It would be more useful to identify the items we are interested in (cash, sales, debtors, creditors, etc.) and group all of the debits and credits relating to each item in one place. Thus we could compare the inflows and outflows of cash and determine how much cash was left in the business. Or we could add all the credits in respect of sales, and determine the total value of sales. Or we could compare the debits and credits in respect of debtors, and determine how much was still owed to the business, and so on.

This procedure is perfectly feasible. The place where we group all of the debits and credits relating to any particular item is called an account. The cash account groups all of the debits and credits relating to cash. The debtors account groups all of the debits and credits relating to debtors, and so on.

In Figure 10.4 opposite we have grouped all of the debits and credits in our example into nine separate accounts. Each account is ruled down the middle, and the left side by convention is reserved for debits, while the right side is reserved for credits. Readers should compare Figure 10.3 and Figure 10.4 and check that the debits and credits have been properly placed in the appropriate accounts.

The entire collection of separate accounts is known as a ledger. In olden days a ledger would resemble Figure 10.4 exactly, with separate pages for each account. Nowadays computers have introduced some changes. In particular computerized accounts list all entries in the same vertical column, identifying credits by a following minus sign.

Note that each entry in the accounts is identified with a reference to the original transaction.

10.1.7 Names of accounts

A business may open as many or as few accounts as it needs, and call them whatever it likes, although it is advisable to call an account by a name related to its contents. Some account names, however, are given by voluntary or thoughtless following of convention. Among these are some which cause grave distress to beginners in double entry and can subvert any understanding of the principles involved. Some examples will illustrate the point.

TRANSACTION 1:

A business pays wages of £100 cash.

CAPITAL

		A	1000

CASH

A	1000	B	200
D	300	E	50
H	350	G	100
		I	100

RENT

B	200		

MATERIALS

C	100		

ADVERTISING

E	50		

DEBTORS

F	400	H	350

CREDITORS

G	100	C	100

SALES

		D	300
		F	400

SALARIES

I	100		

Figure 10.4 Ledger accounts

J

Analysis: inflow: labour £100
outflow: cash £100

The inflow is in part an artificial creation designed to meet the demands of the double entry system. Disegarding that squeamish point we should open, say, a labour account and a cash account and make the entries:

DR labour account	£100	
CR cash account		£100

Unfortunately, the common name for our labour account is 'wages account' and thus the entries would usually be

DR wages account	£100	
CR cash account		£100

This is distressing to the beginner. Wages is a name for the cash the business hands over and so it seems that 'DR wages account £100' is somehow trying to record an outflow, when we know that the outflow is cash and that in any case a debit records an inflow.

TRANSACTION 2:

A business receives commission of £200 cash for placing students.
Analysis: inflow: cash £200
outflow: placement services £200

In this instance the outflow is artificial but we know for sure that the inflow is cash. We would record the transaction with these entries:

DR cash account	£200	
CR placement services		£200

However, the standard way of recording this transaction would be

DR cash account	£200	
CR commissions account		£200

Once again this is terribly confusing. We know that the inflow is cash and we call this cash our commission. The entry 'CR commissions account £200' therefore seems to indicate an inflow when we have already recorded the real inflow of cash, and we know in any case that a credit indicates an outflow.

These problems are caused solely by inappropriate naming of accounts. The strategy for dealing with them is to return to first principles, remembering that:

1 a debit always records an inflow.
2 a credit always records an outflow.
3 there is only one cash account and it is always called the cash account.
4 any account which bears a name which appears to describe the cash involved in a transaction, is actually concerned with the movement of the underlying service. This movement is in the opposite direction to the movement of the cash involved.
5 any account which bears a misleading name should be mentally renamed in a more rational fashion.

Some of the accounts which are persistently misnamed are listed below against the item which accounts under such names generally deal with:

account name	*item dealt with*
wages account	labour services
salaries account	staff services
sundry expenses account	sundry inputs to business
rent account	use of property
tax account	government services
fees account	the underlying service
commissions account	the underlying service
interest account	use of money

Note that the item dealt with is frequently one of the imaginary or intangible flows which the double entry system forces us to recognize – for example the outflow of cash to pay tax is deemed to be matched by an inflow of government services. To this extent the misnaming is understandable, but it should not be permitted to mislead.

Readers should review the list and for each account imagine a transaction that would involve its use. First identify the movement of cash as a debit (inflow) or credit (outflow). Then identify the opposite flow, however arbitrary or intangible, and complete the accounting entries, explaining the misnomer of the account.

Example: sundry expenses: you buy a drink for a business acquaintance, price £2, and reimburse yourself with cash.

1 cash movement: outflow, therefore credit cash £2.
2 opposite flow: inflow, say, benefit to business name.
3 accounting entries:

DR	sundry expenses account	£2
CR	cash	£2

4 misnomer: the sundry expenses account covers inflows of sundry small items of benefit to the business.

Readers who accept the logic of this discussion but remain puzzled as to why such misnomers persist, should review this section after reading to the end of section 10.2.

10.1.8 Balancing accounts and the trial balance

Ledger accounts like those in Figure 10.4 are a neat and a rational format for recording transactions as they occur. It remains to show how ledger accounts can be summarized and used to calculate profit or loss.

The summary is straightforward. First, each account is balanced – an entry is made on the side which is underweight, so that the account contains equal debits and credits. Then the account is ruled off and closed. Finally the balancing entry is made again beneath, on the side which was overweight. The effect is to summarize all preceding entries in the account with one entry on the side which was overweight.

The method and its significance is demonstrated in Figure 10.5 where the cash account is balanced. After all the transactions of the period, the business is left with £1,200 cash, and this is reflected in the balance of £1,200 DR on the cash account.

The account balances càn now be listed in a trial balance – so called because the book-keeper is on trial at this stage. If the sums are right and the principles of double entry have been observed, then the trial balance should list total debit balances equal to total credit balances.

Readers should balance the accounts in Figure 10.4 to verify that Figure 10.6 is an accurate trial balance drawn from those accounts. The trial balance relates to a specific moment. It is important to recognize this and we have therefore dated the trial balance at 31 December 1990.

Figure 10.5 Balancing the cash account

CASH			
transaction	DR £	transaction	CR £
A	1,000	B	200
D	300	E	50
H	350	G	100
		I	100
		BALANCE	1,200
	£1,650		£1,650
BALANCE	£1,200		

Figure 10.6 Trial balance at 31 December 1990

Account	DR £	CR £
Capital		1,000
Cash	1,200	
Rent	200	
Materials	100	
Advertising	50	
Debtors	50	
Creditors	–	–
Sales		700
Salaries	100	
	£1,700	£1,700

10.1.9 Profit and loss account and balance sheet

The discussion of the balance sheet in section 10.1.2 concluded with the idea that the balance sheet could be seen as collecting together

1 the net residue of past flows in and out of the business – for example, cash;
2 future flows in or out of the business – for example debtors or creditors; and
3 equity – the item which adjusts to make the balance sheet balance, and which itself can be seen as a future or potential outflow to the owners of the business.

These categories will cover a fair number of the balances in the trial balance in Figure 10.6.

The remaining balances must concern flows which are now complete and leave no residue in the business. These are the outflow of sales, and the inflows of goods or services which have been used up or passed through the business to emerge as part of what is sold.

> A simple definition of profit is: value of outflows, *less* value of inflows used.

We should therefore group the relevant balances together in a profit and loss account, which will enable us to determine profit for the period.

Figure 10.7 is an extended trial balance which allocates each balance in the original trial balance, either to the profit and loss account as representing a completed flow leaving no residue in the business, or to the balance sheet as representing a residue or a future or potential flow.

Figure 10.7 Extended trial balance at 31 December 1990

	Trial Balance		Profit and Loss Account		Balance Sheet	
	DR	CR	DR	CR	DR	CR
Account	£	£	£	£	£	£
Capital		1,000				1,000
Cash	1,200				1,200	
Rent	200		200			
Materials	100		100			
Advertising	50		50			
Debtors	50				50	
Creditors	–	–				
Sales		700		700		
Salaries	100		100			
Profit			250			250
	£1,700	£1,700	£700	£700	£1,250	£1,250

The allocation is simplistic – we have assumed for example that the rental period has expired and that all the materials have been used – i.e. that there are no residues of these items left in the business. Nevertheless the principles should be clear.

Readers should review Figure 10.7 and check the correct allocation of balances against the criteria outlined above.

Figure 10.8 is a simple set of financial statements based on the extended trial balance. Financial statements is the name generally given to profit and loss account and balance sheet together. Readers should attempt to follow figures from the original trial balance, through the allocation in the extended trial balance in Figure 10.7, and into the financial statements in Figure 10.8. Note that some of the original balances are lost in totals in the financial statements.

To appreciate the achievement in terms of system, elegance and economy, readers may also care to review the original list of transactions in section 10.1.5.

Figure 10.8 Financial statements for the year to 31 December 1990

Profit and loss account for the year ended 31 December 1990	£
Sales	700
Expenses	(450)
Profit	£250

Balance sheet as at 31 December 1990	£
Assets: Debtors	50
Cash	1,200
Total assets	£1,250
Liabilities	—
Net assets	£1,250
	£
Capital	1,000
Retained profit for the year	250
	£1,250

10.1.10 Two definitions of profit

The financial statements in Figure 10.8 reveal an interesting relationship. The balance sheet at 31 December 1990 shows net assets of £1,250. Net assets at the beginning of the business were £1,000, being the cash introduced by the owners. During the year net assets, and therefore equity, have increased by £250. This increase in equity is the owner's profit, and is the same as the profit figure in the profit and loss account, which was arrived at by comparing income and expenses.

The equality is not an accident. Figure 10.7 shows that it is a consequence of the double entry system. The debit required to balance and close the profit and loss account must be equalled by the credit for profit for the year in the balance sheet.

Nevertheless we are left with two definitions of profit. On a transactions basis, profit for a period is the excess of that period's income over expenses. On a balance sheet basis, profit for a period is the increase in net assets during that period.

The difference can be significant. Consider a business which buys a freehold property for £1,000,000 and operates as a school. After one year the profit and loss account, on a transactions basis, indicates that expenses have exceeded income and that the school has made a loss of £2,000. But looking at the net assets it may be that the property, although recorded at a cost of £1,000,000, is now worth £1,500,000.

Has the business made a small loss or a very large profit? It depends on the definition of profit.

We shall return to this problem, but meanwhile we shall concentrate on the measurement of profit on a transactions basis, through the profit and loss account.

10.2 Adjusting the records

Double entry book-keeping was developed to keep a track on things. For this purpose it is, in its way, elegant and efficient. It was not designed to produce periodic statements of profit, although it is the main source of information on which a statement of profit must be based.

In this section we examine why the book-keeper's trial balance must be adjusted before a statement of profit can be produced, and demonstrate the major adjustments that may be necessary.

10.2.1 Recording transactions and recognizing profit

> As measured on a transactions basis: profit for a period is the excess of income *from sales completed in the period*, over *related* expenses.

For profit purposes, income is recognized in the period in which the sale takes place. Expenses are recognized so far as possible in the same period as the sale to which they relate.

Compare this against the time at which transactions are recorded. If a book-keeper has evidence of a sale, he or she cannot lay it aside until the sale is complete. It must be recorded immediately, or the recording system fails in its purpose. Similarly the book-keeper must record expenditure as and when it happens, and not at some later stage when the input has passed through the business and emerged in a sale.

There is thus inevitably a difference between the time at which the transaction can be *recognized* as contributing to profit or loss, and the time at which it must be *recorded* by the book-keeper.

This means that the trial balance, which is based on the book-keeper's records, must be adjusted before profit or loss can be calculated. We deal with the major adjustments below. It should become apparent that many of them are matters of judgement, and not of hard fact.

The discussion will be related to the trial balance in Figure 10.9. We intend to produce financial statements for year 1. The preceding year was year 0. The following year is year 2. The adjustment and allocation of balances will be recorded in an extended trial balance in Figure 10.12 on page 273.

Figure 10.9 The Language School: trial balance at 31 December, year 1

Ledger account	DR £	CR £
Sales		124,000
Salaries	30,000	
Purchases	6,000	
Rates	4,000	
Utilities	3,000	
Sundry	7,000	
Debtors	5,000	
Creditors		3,000
Cash	4,000	
Fixed assets	110,000	
Long-term loan		10,000
Capital		30,000
Profit and loss account, 1 January, year 1		2,000
	£169,000	£169,000

10.2.2 Deferred income

Assume that the school requires payment in advance, and has therefore issued invoices or received cash for £2,000 worth of courses which will take place in year 2. The book-keeper has quite properly *recorded* the sale and the appropriate debtor or cash received. Nevertheless these sales cannot be *recognized* in year 1. They belong to year 2.

In the extended trial balance therefore only the sales completed in year 1, value £122,000, should be credited to the profit and loss account of year 1.

The remaining £2,000 should be credited to the balance sheet as 'deferred income'. In the balance sheet it represents a liability to deliver courses in year 2.

At the beginning of year 2 this credit can be transferred to the sales account, where it will add to the sales recorded in year 2.

Assuming that £1,000 of year 1 sales were recorded in year 0, sales for year 1 could be presented as:

	£	
sales *recorded* in year 1	123,000	
add year 1 sales recorded in year 0	1,000	(from year 0 balance sheet)
	124,000	(year 1 trial balance)
less year 2 sales recorded in year 1	(2,000)	(to year 1 balance sheet)
sales *completed* in year 1	£122,000	(to year 1 profit and loss account)

10.2.3 Deferred expenditure

Assume that the £30,000 debited to the salaries account includes £1,000 paid to a teacher for time spent preparing a course to be given in year 2. Arguably then, the courses given in year 1 have consumed only £29,000 of teachers' time.

Accepting this argument, we shall place £29,000 as a debit in the year 1 profit and loss account, and £1,000 as a debit in the year 1 balance sheet where it will represent an asset which can be used in year 2. To avoid scandal we should call the asset 'course material' or some such. The manoeuvre is demonstrated in Figure 10.12, the extended trial balance.

The effect is to defer recognition of the expenditure until year 2. In year 2 the debit will be transferred from the balance sheet to the salaries account, where it will be deducted from year 2 sales in arriving at year 2 profit.

The manoeuvre is clearly a matter of judgement. Many accountants would dispute that it is allowable at all. The material developed may be worthless, and the course in year 2 may never be given. Other accountants would perhaps permit the manoeuvre under the most stringent conditions. Our example is not intended to endorse the procedure, but to demonstrate it.

10.2.4 Stock

£6,000 has been debited to the purchases account in year 1, but we shall assume that goods purchased at a cost of £500 remain in stock at the end of year 1, ready for use in year 2.

The business will therefore wish to recognize expenditure in year 1 with a debit of £5,500 to the profit and loss account, and carry forward the remaining £500 as stock, an asset and a debit in the balance sheet. At the beginning of year 2, the debit in the balance sheet can be transferred to the year 2 purchases account, where it will be added to the purchases recorded in year 2.

The treatment is similar to the treatment of deferred sales, and thus purchases for year 1 can be seen as:

	£	
purchases *recorded* in year 1	5,800	
add opening stock (say)	200	(from year 0 balance sheet)
	6,000	(year 1 trial balance)
less closing stock	(500)	(to year 1 balance sheet)
material *used* in year 1	£5,500	(to year 1 profit and loss account)

A stock adjustment is uncontroversial in itself, but judgement is required. Is the stock still good for use? Is it still worth at least as much as the business originally paid for it? The business should only create an asset, stock, to the extent and value that it can use the asset.

In most schools, which do not trade in goods, stock may represent mainly brochures for future courses. These can be expensive and it may seem fair to carry them forward as an asset, to be charged as an expense against the future income they will generate.

On the other hand, some accountants would argue that expenditure on brochures should be recognized in the period in which it occurs. They may argue that future sales may never arise, or alternatively that carrying forward expenditure of this kind is the start of a slippery slope.

Undoubtedly some students who see advertising material in year 1 will only attend the school in year 2. Perhaps some advertising expenditure should also be carried forward? Where would it all end? Better just to recognize the expenditure now.

There are merits on both sides of the argument and neither is 'correct'. The answer will depend on circumstance, although all honest accountants would agree that it is better to err on the side of caution. If in doubt, expenditure should be recognized in the profit and loss account of the period in which it occurs.

10.2.5 Prepayments

Rates, and some other services, are generally paid for in advance. Assume that the £4,000 debited to the rates account includes £1,000 paid in respect of the first quarter of year 2.

The cost to be debited to the year 1 profit and loss account should therefore be only £3,000, and the remaining £1,000 should be debited to the year 1 balance sheet as an asset, known as a prepayment.

At the start of year 2, the balance sheet debit can be transferred to the year 2 rates account, where it will be added to the rates paid and recorded in year 2.

Readers should compare the terms 'prepayment' and 'deferred income'. Prepayments are always payments in advance *made by* the business. They are an asset because whatever the business has paid for, it may use in the future. Deferred income, as we know, is a payment *received* in advance by the business. It is a liability because the business is obliged to deliver whatever it has received payment for.

10.2.6 Accruals

The trial balance shows that the school has recorded £3,000 of bills for utilities (gas, electricity etc.). Utilities, and some other supplies, are generally billed after use. Assume then that the business has used a further £750 worth of utilities for which it has not yet received or recorded a bill.

Here the business will wish to recognize a total of £3,750 expenditure on utilities in the year 1 profit and loss account, being the £3,000 already recorded, and the further £750 which it has used but not recorded.

Double entry comes to the rescue. The school can debit the original

£3,000, plus an extra £750, to the year 1 profit and loss account; and balance the extra debit with a £750 credit to the year 1 balance sheet.

The debit in the profit and loss account will adjust the recorded expenditure upwards to an approximation of the amount used in year 1, while the credit in the balance sheet will represent the liability to pay for the amount used but not yet billed at the end of year 1. At the beginning of year 2, the credit in the balance can be transferred to the year 2 utilities account, where as a credit it will offset the debit which will be recorded when the bill is received.

The credit in the balance sheet at the end of year 1 is known as an *accrual* – that is an estimated liability to pay for goods or services used for which no bill has yet been received.

10.2.7 Provisions

Provisions are like accruals in all but name. The term accrual tends to be reserved for bills which can be predicted to arrive with virtual certainty, and where the amounts involved can be estimated with reasonable accuracy.

The term provision tends to be reserved for amounts which can only be guessed at, at the time of the balance sheet, or even for bills that may, with luck, never arrive. In any event, obviously whatever triggers a provision in year 1's financial statements must be an event in year 1. An example of a straightforward provision would be when a local building contractor has performed some work for the school during a period, but neglected to bill for his work by the end of the period. In this case the financial statements must include a guess as to the amount involved, which will be included in the profit and loss account as a debit or expense, and in the balance sheet as a credit or liability to pay.

Here we shall take the case of a student who suffered a minor electric shock in the language laboratory during year 1 and has taken steps to sue the school, which is not insured for such eventualities. Reviewing the case, the manager decides that if the student does not drop the case, he or she will be satisfied with an ex gratia payment of £250. This amount should be provided for in the accounts of year 1. In view of the uncertainties involved, the provision is known as a *provision for contingent liabilities*.

The procedure is to debit the year 1 profit and loss account with £250, thus reducing year 1 profit, and to credit the year 1 balance sheet with £250, representing the contingent liability.

Imagine that in year 2 the matter is settled by payment of £300. The credit entry for this transaction will be to the cash account. £250 will be debited against the provision in the balance sheet, eliminating the £250 previously credited. The remaining £50 will be debited in the year 2 profit and loss account, reducing year 2 profit by £50.

Imagine on the other hand that the student drops the claim altogether in year 2. In this case the school will be left with an unnecessary provision – a credit of £250 in its balance sheet. This credit will simply be released or transferred to the year 2 profit and loss account, thereby increasing year 2 profit by £250, after (unnecessarily as it happened) decreasing year 1 profit by £250.

Clearly judgement is called for in making provisions. Beyond that the process is uncontroversial. It is only prudent to provide for expected losses. But note that provisions are often extremely popular with new managers, or when profit figures in any case will be bad. Of course high provisions will reduce year 1's reported profit, but in year 2 perhaps some provisions can be released, which will boost year 2 profits, and thereby prove the genius of incoming managers or the capacity of the business to recover from temporary set-backs.

10.2.8 Bad debts – write-offs and provisions

Some debtors never pay. Where a particular debt is judged to be irrecoverable, the debit relating to that debt cannot be taken to the balance sheet. It is no longer an asset. Instead the debt should be written off, by taking the debit to the profit and loss account where it will reduce profit for the period and vanish like the debt itself.

A slightly more difficult case arises when management may know from experience that, say, 10% of debtors never pay, but they cannot identify which ones they will be. Here a provision for bad debts should be made. The procedure resembles the steps for the creation of any provision, and is illustrated in Figure 10.12 on page 273. A debit, of £500 in this instance, is made to the profit and loss account to recognize the loss, and a credit is made to the balance sheet, which is deducted from the value of debtors. If in a future period a debt is written off, then there is a credit to the debtor's account, to eliminate the debt, while the debit is made to the provision account, thereby reducing the provision, instead of the profit for the period in which the write-off takes place.

10.2.9 Fixed assets

Fixed assets are things which are fixed in the business, things acquired at a certain expense which the business intends to use over a number of years.

The first problem is to recognize a fixed asset when you see one. Obvious examples are buildings, furniture and equipment. Fixed assets need not be tangible objects: anything acquired for use over a number of periods can be a fixed asset. This would include the right to use a trade name, patent or copyright materials, over a number of years. Sometimes it is difficult to judge whether a fixed asset has been created or not – extensive building repairs could include an element of improvement that will serve the business for many years to come.

Once a fixed asset has been identified, the second problem is what to do with it. Fixed assets are generally acquired at a high cost and are intended to be used over a number of years. It is unreasonable to charge all of the high cost of a fixed asset against the profit of the period in which it is acquired. Besides, the fixed asset remains in the business at the end of the period, and therefore the debit representing the fixed asset should be placed in the balance sheet as, precisely, an asset.

On the other hand, fixed assets cannot remain in the balance sheet for ever. At some stage they will be used up, broken or scrapped. Fixed assets are acquired at a cost, and the cost must somehow be recognized in the profit and loss accounts of the periods in which the fixed assets are used.

This effect is achieved by provision for depreciation. The procedure is first to place the debit in respect of a fixed asset in the balance sheet, where the cost of its acquisition will not affect the recorded profit of the business. Then by instalments the debit in the balance sheet is transferred to the profit and loss account. This reduces the recorded profit of each year in which the asset is used, and simultaneously reduces the value of the asset in the balance sheet.

Before giving an example of the procedure, we explain the peculiar intangible fixed asset of goodwill.

10.2.10 Goodwill

Goodwill is an intangible asset which is not included in our example, but which readers may come across in the financial statements of their own business or those of a competitor.

Goodwill arises when one business acquires another business. Assume that business A buys business B. Business B has one single asset valued at £60,000 but since the business is thriving, business A pays £100,000 to take over B and secure not only its asset but also its future profits.

Business A's book-keeping for this transaction must involve a credit of £100,000 to cash, representing the money going out. It will also make a debit entry of £60,000 to represent B's asset coming in. A's books now do not balance. They need a further debit of £40,000 to balance the credit entry. This debit is made to a new account and called goodwill.

Goodwill is therefore the difference between the price paid for a business and the value of the separable net assets taken over. It is to some extent an artificial asset as we have seen, but nevertheless it resembles a fixed asset in that it represents expenditure made with a view to securing future profits.

10.2.11 Depreciation and amortization

If the cost of a fixed asset is to be charged to the profit and loss account over a number of years, it is important first to know or to estimate the cost, and the number of years involved.

A business can usually sell a fixed asset when it has finished using it. Let us assume that the business in Figure 10.9 has acquired a fixed asset for £110,000 in year 1, as shown in the trial balance. It expects to use the fixed asset for four years and then dispose of it for disposal proceeds of £30,000. The total expense on the fixed asset which the business must charge against its profit over the years involved is therefore £80,000. This is the *depreciable amount*. The *estimated useful life* of the asset is four years and so the simplest procedure is to charge the profit and loss account of each of the four years with £20,000, while simultaneously reducing the balance sheet amount of the fixed asset – its *net book value* – by £20,000 each year. The calculations and procedure are summarized in Figure 10.10.

Figure 10.10 Depreciation summary

	£
purchase cost	110,000
less estimated disposal proceeds	(30,000)
depreciable amount	£80,000
estimated useful life	4 years
annual depreciation charge	£20,000

	Profit and loss account	Balance sheet		
	charge for year	cost	(total depreciation)	net book value
	£	£	£	£
Year 1	20,000	110,000	(20,000)	90,000
Year 2	20,000	110,000	(40,000)	70,000
Year 3	20,000	110,000	(60,000)	50,000
Year 4	20,000	110,000	(80,000)	30,000

Note: estimated disposal proceeds may also be known as *residual value*.

At the end of year 4 we assume that the business disposes of the asset for £30,000 as expected. The book-keeping entries are:

DR cash £30,000, to record incoming cash.
CR fixed asset £30,000, to record outgoing asset.

The credit to the fixed asset account will eliminate the existing debit of £30,000 and close the account.

We have assumed that the disposal proceeds for this asset, and its useful life, must be estimated.

Some fixed assets, like the right to use materials, have a definite life and no disposal proceeds or residual value. The depreciation process for these assets is often known as *amortization*.

We have also charged depreciation evenly over the life of the asset. This is the *straight line method*. It is the easiest, but not the only way to spread the cost of an asset over its useful life. Some businesses may prefer to charge a fixed proportion (say 25%) of the net book value of the asset each period. This results in a high depreciation charge in early years and is known as the *reducing balancing method*.

Finally we have also assumed for simplicity that the business has only one fixed asset. In reality a business will have several classes of fixed assets each containing a number of individual items. The business must develop a depreciation policy appropriate to each class of asset, and apply the method to each asset in the relevant class.

10.2.12 Profits and losses on disposal

The annual depreciation charge is an estimate and as such is liable to error. If the error is such that net book value is less than disposal proceeds, then too much depreciation will have been charged and the business will record a profit on disposal to correct for this. If the error is such that net book value is greater than disposal proceeds, then too little depreciation will have been charged, and the business will record a loss on disposal to correct the preceding error.

It is important to realize that profits or losses on disposal do not reflect business acumen or the lack of it: they reflect adjustments to the depreciation charge. This is illustrated with numbers in Figure 10.11. We assume that three businesses, A, B and C, each acquire a fixed asset at a cost of £110,000 in year 1. Each charges depreciation in years 1, 2 and 3 and disposes of its asset for £50,000 at the beginning of year 4.

Figure 10.11 Profits and losses on disposal

Table 1: Profit or loss on disposal	A £	B £	C £
cost of purchase	110,000	110,000	110,000
total depreciation charged, years 1–3	(60,000)	(70,000)	(50,000)
net book value on disposal	50,000	40,000	60,000
disposal proceeds	(50,000)	(50,000)	(50,000)
(profit)/loss on disposal	£ —	£(10,000)	£10,000

Table 2: Total charged to profit and loss account

	£	£	£
depreciation, years 1–3	60,000	70,000	50,000
(profit)/loss year 4	—	(10,000)	10,000
total charge, years 1–4	£60,000	£60,000	£60,000

Table 3: Cost to business

	£	£	£
cost of purchase	110,000	110,000	110,000
disposal proceeds	(50,000)	(50,000)	(50,000)
effective cost	£60,000	£60,000	£60,000

Table 1 in Figure 10.11 shows that business A has estimated depreciation accurately and makes neither profit nor loss on disposal. Business B has overestimated depreciation and makes a profit on disposal of £10,000. Business C has underestimated depreciation and makes a loss on disposal in year 4.

Table 2 shows the combined effect on profit of depreciation and profit or loss on disposal, for each business over the four years involved. Each will ultimately charge the same total amount against profit.

Table 3 shows that the total amount charged to profit in each business represents the same objective total cost. The apparent profit of B and the loss of C are merely corrections of errors in estimation.

Table 3 also shows that the chore of calculating and providing for depreciation is worthwhile. The alternative to a policy of depreciation would have been for each business to recognize a huge cost, and drop in profit, in year 1, followed by a smaller, but still huge increase in income and therefore profit, in year 4.

10.2.13 Provisions, profits and money

Depreciation is a provision, and Figure 10.11 is illustrative of certain aspects of provisions generally.

Many people think that provisions involve laying money aside to pay for future liabilities, or in the case of fixed assets, to pay for replacement assets. Figure 10.11 shows that this is not the case. The different provisions made in A, B and C made no difference whatsoever to the cash the businesses had in hand.

Figure 10.11 also shows that provisions make no difference to long run profit – A, B and C each ultimately recognized the same expense of £60,000 over the four year period. The only difference made by the different provisions was the difference in timing. Business A recognized the expense in three equal instalments of £20,000. Business B recognized the expense in three instalments amounting to £70,000, followed by a correction of £10,000. Business C recognized the expense in three instalments amounting to £50,000, followed by a further instalment of £10,000.

Provisions therefore do not affect cash or long run 'physical' profits. They are solely a book-keeping device, affecting the accounting period in which costs are recognized.

Readers should review all of the adjustments dealt with in the sections above and confirm that their only effect is to delay or advance the recognition of income or costs. They cannot affect the ultimate occurrence of income and costs any more than changing the clocks in summer can affect the time the sun rises.

10.2.14 Depreciation and assets which increase in value

Some assets increase in value, so that their disposal proceeds can be expected to exceed their purchase cost. Should such assets be depreciated?

The finest minds in accountancy have strained over this issue and concluded that depreciation should be charged. The reasons seem to be: that no asset can live forever and therefore it is used up over time, and depreciation must reflect this; and/or that nothing comes for nothing – if a business is using an asset to make profits, it must reflect the use with a depreciation charge against profits.

We can offer no useful contribution to this debate.

10.2.15 Revaluing assets

The system of accounting we have presented shows assets in the balance sheet at their cost of acquisition (stock), or at the cost of acquisition less any amounts which have been recognized as an expense in the profit and loss account (fixed assets). This is known as the *historical cost convention*.

It is possible to adopt other conventions, or to modify the historical cost convention to allow for the revaluation of certain assets. Other conventions are not frequently adopted, but the revaluation of certain assets is a common practice.

The motive for this is simply to make the balance sheet mean something. Under the strict historical cost convention, the asset side of the balance sheet has virtually no objective meaning. Different businesses can carry precisely the same fixed assets at vastly different net book values, depending solely on their depreciation policies and, if prices are changing, the date of acquisition. If fixed assets are shown at valuation, then users of accounts can see the real value of the assets, and different businesses can be compared on an equal basis.

Revaluation is a simple book-keeping procedure. Assume an asset is currently shown at a net book value of £60,000. It is valued at £100,000. A debit to the asset account of £40,000 will ensure that the asset is in future shown at valuation of £100,000. The corresponding credit is entered in the balance sheet under the heading 'revaluation reserve'. Like other reserves the revaluation reserve will be part of the owner's equity. It is kept separate from other reserves because unlike most other reserves it represents a profit which has not yet been realized through a transaction. Readers will recall that this problem was referred to in section 10.1.10, which offered two definitions of profit.

10.2.16 The extended trial balance

The adjustments discussed above are recorded in the extended trial balance in Figure 10.12. Readers should study each adjustment or allocation to ensure that they understand and agree with what is happening, and refer where necessary to the section in which the adjustment is discussed. Readers in management positions may never have to prepare an extended trial balance, but they will almost certainly be called upon to approve or to suggest adjustments to accounts, or to interpret accounts which have been subjected to similar adjustments. It is important to understand how these adjustments are effected, what they mean, why they are necessary, what they reveal, and perhaps what they attempt to conceal.

In terms of the double entry mechanics involved, readers should particularly note and check how the net debits and credits of balance sheet and profit and loss account together, always reconcile across to the ledger account from which they are derived. Nothing, ultimately, is added or taken away.

The financial statements based on this extended trial balance are given in Figure 10.13 section 10.3 below, which deals with the presentation of financial statements. Before proceeding to section 10.3, however, it is worthwhile to take a last look at debits and credits in the light of our greater acquaintance.

10.2.17 Debits and credits: what they mean

Much of the initial difficulty with double entry arises from a mistaken conviction that debits and credits, being opposites, must be somehow opposed as 'good' and 'bad'. The mistake leads to utter confusion when we see that a debit in the profit and loss account represents an expense (bad), while a debit in the balance sheet represents an asset (good). Conversely a credit in the profit and loss account represents income (good), while a credit in the balance sheet represents a liability (bad).

It is possible to dismiss the analogy with good and bad as simply naive, but we can work through it, from first principles, to gain a better understanding, not just of debits and credits, but also of some fundamental aspects of business and accounts.

The discussion relates to debit and credit balances in the trial balance.

A debit records the value of an inflow. An ideal business would need no inflows. It would contrive to sell without the need to buy or use anything, and would therefore have no expenses and no assets. (The cash it generated would go out instantly to its owners.) A real business by contrast must use or hold inflows, in order to make sales. The contrast with the ideal shows that all inflows (debits) are, if you like, 'bad' insofar as they represent costs, but 'good' insofar as they represent a capacity to do business. A debit in the profit and loss account represents an inflow used up in making past sales, and is therefore recognized as an expense. A debit parked in the balance sheet as an asset preserves its dual nature. On the one hand it may be seen as a cost awaiting recognition as an expense. On the other hand it may be seen as a capacity to do business and generate profit in the future. Some assets partake more of one quality than of the other.

A credit records the value of a past or future outflow. Whether this is good or bad depends essentially on where it is going. An outflow to a creditor may be bad – it reduces the assets of the business. But an overflow to a customer is good – it represents a sale. And an outflow to the owners is also good, at least from their point of view.

Readers should review section 10.1.7 before proceeding. At that stage we were concerned to emphasize the point that a debit represents an inflow. We now acknowledge that all inflows are ultimately destined for recognition in the profit and loss account as expenses. The misnomers identified in section 10.1.7 are therefore explicable as representing the premature recognition of inflows as expenses.

10.3 Presentation of financial statements

Many businesses are required by law to produce and publish regular financial statements. Others may face a similar administrative requirement. In either case the form and content of the statements may be very strictly prescribed. We cannot therefore present one example as a model form for all and any financial statements.

Nevertheless all financial statements will contain the same kind of information, using broadly the same terms, descriptions, and formats, and therefore one example may serve as a general illustration.

Our example is given in Figure 10.13, where the financial statements are based on the extended trial balance in Figure 10.12. Readers should follow the commentary in section 10.3.1 and attempt to trace numbers in the financial statements back to their origin in the extended trial balance, to see how these are ultimately presented.

The comments in section 10.3.1 are principally explanations of terms and format. True financial statements will have detailed notes analysing items and amounts shown on the face of the profit and loss account and balance sheet. Notes are an integral part of financial statements and should not be ignored. The first note should deal always with accounting policies, stating whether the accounts have been prepared under the historical cost convention and

	TRIAL BALANCE		PROFIT AND LOSS ACCOUNT		BALANCE SHEET		
	DR	CR	DR	CR	DR	CR	
LEDGER ACCOUNT	£	£	£	£	£	£	*ADJUSTING ACCOUNT*
Sales		124,000		122,000		2,000	Deferred income
Salaries	30,000		29,000		1,000		Course material
Purchases	6,000		5,500		500		Stock
Rates	4,000		3,000		1,000		Prepayments
Utilities	3,000		3,750			750	Accruals
Sundry	7,000		7,250		250		Provision for contingent liability
Debtors	5,000		500		5,000	500	Provision for bad debts
Creditors		3,000				3,000	
Cash	4,000				4,000		
Fixed assets	110,000		20,000		110,000	20,000	Depreciation
Long term loan		10,000				10,000	
Capital		30,000				30,000	
Profit and loss account for year 1 at 1 Jan, year 1		2,000				2,000	Profit for year 1
			53,000			53,000	
	£169,000	£169,000	£122,000	£122,000	£121,500	£121,500	

Figure 10.12 The Language School: extended trial balance at 31 December, year 1

stating policies for the recognition of income, the valuation of assets, depreciation etc.

Our example contains figures for year 1 only. True financial statements will usually have a parallel column giving figures for the prior year or comparative period. Readers should be careful to distinguish which column relates to which year.

10.3.1 Commentary on financial statements

Comments are referenced to the financial statements in Figure 10.13.

1 *Turnover* is a generic name covering all things like sales from which a business gains its usual income. The word is useful – many businesses do not make sales as such (consider agencies and rental companies etc.). Choice of the word turnover is explained in Chapter 12.

2 and 3 *Cost of Sales* and *Gross Profit*: these terms derive from trading businesses which simply buy and sell goods, and allow a useful distinction between the gross profit obtained by buying and selling, and the net profit after deduction of other costs. Gross profit is often expressed as a percentage of sales. The *trading account* of a business contains only sales, cost of sales and gross profit – which may also be called trading profit. In our example cost of sales represents teachers' salaries and material used.

4 *Expenses*: given here in total – a note may disclose some or all of the details involved.

5 *Taxation*: tax is a large and legal matter that we cannot deal with in this text. Readers should note, however, that taxable profit is determined by legislation and not by the accounting conventions described in this chapter. No business decision should be taken on the basis of tax considerations only, but the timing and legal forms of certain transactions can have important tax effects. Professional advice on tax matters is generally worth paying for.

6 *Distribution* is the name given to any share-out of profit among the owners of a business. Where the business has shareholders, the distribution is called a dividend.

7 and 8 *Profit*: note that profit for the year is not necessarily the bottom line. In this instance the profit retained and brought forward from previous years has been added to the retained profit for year 1, so that the final total will agree with retained profit in the balance sheet.

9 *Fixed assets* are stated net of total depreciation. Note that in year 2 a further £20,000 depreciation will be charged so that total depreciation will be £40,000 at the end of year 2. A note on fixed assets and total depreciation should analyse the assets by type, and give details of additions and disposals during the period.

10 *Intangible fixed assets* should be stated separately, also net of total depreciation, and described in a note.

Figure 10.13 The Language School: financial statements for the year to 31 December, year 1

Profit and loss account for the year to 31 December, year 1	comment	£
Turnover	1	122,000
Cost of Sales	2	(34,500)
Gross profit	3	87,500
Expenses	4	(34,500)
Profit before taxation		53,000
Tax charge for the year	5	—
Profit for the year after taxation		53,000
Distributions	6	—
Retained profit for the year	7	53,000
Retained profit at 1 January, year 1		2,000
Retained profit at 31 December, year 1	8	£55,000

Balance sheet at 31 December, year 1

FIXED ASSETS	comment	£
Tangible assets	9	90,000
Intangible assets	10	—
		£90,000
CURRENT ASSETS	11	
Stock and materials	12	1,500
Debtors and prepayments	13	5,500
Cash		4,000
		£11,000
CREDITORS (amounts payable within one year)	14	(6,000)
NET CURRENT ASSETS	15	5,000
TOTAL ASSETS LESS CURRENT LIABILITIES	16	95,000
CREDITORS (amounts payable after more than one year)	17	(10,000)
		£85,000
CAPITAL AND RESERVES	18	£
Capital	19	30,000
Profit and loss account	20	55,000
		£85,000

11 *Current assets* are like a rope of sand – ever present in the business but never the same individual items. Stocks, debtors and cash are continuously turned over as the business goes on.
12 *Stocks and materials* should be analysed and described in a note.
13 *Debtors and prepayments* should also be analysed in a note. Debtors may be split into *trade debtors*, arising in the normal course of business, and *other debtors* arising as a result of loans made, insurance claims etc. Note that debtors are stated net of the provision for bad debts, which should be given in the note.
14 *Creditors* payable within one year includes *all* amounts payable within one year. The total should be analysed in a note. In this instance the total includes deferred income, accruals and the provision made, which should be described. Creditors as such (being the amount for which bills have actually been received, or which is known for certain) should be split between *trade creditors* or business suppliers, and *other creditors* such as overdrafts, tax payable etc.
15 *Net current assets* is current assets *less* creditors due within one year. Note that if this is a negative figure it should be presented as *net current liabilities*.
16 *Total assets less current liabilities*: current liabilities is another name for amounts payable within one year (see note 14 above). Note the confusing interplay of subtotals – the amount £95,000 comes from the £5,000 immediately above, and the £90,000 total fixed asset figure towards the top of the balance sheet.
17 *Creditors* payable after more than one year should be analysed in a note, giving the dates payable, rates of interest etc.
18 *Capital and reserves* may also be called *shareholders' funds* if the business is a limited company. Note that in terms of the accounting equation the balance sheet shows the equality of net assets and equity (both £85,000). Our example has only one reserve – the profit and loss account. Other reserves are possible – a revaluation reserve for example.
19 *Capital*: a note should describe the different kinds of capital and by whom it was subscribed (shareholders, partners etc.) and any additions or reductions in capital during the period.
20 *Profit and loss account*: note that this is the total balance on the profit and loss account which includes retained profits of year 1, and retained profit of previous years. It does not represent the retained profit for year 1 only (see notes 7 and 8 above).

10.3.2 Other financial statements

In recent years it has been recognized that traditional financial statements – profit and loss account and balance sheet – are not the only, or even the best, way of conveying certain financial information about a business. Some businesses have begun to offer supplementary financial statements to emphasize different aspects of the business. We deal with two of these, in broad outline.

1 STATEMENT OF SOURCE AND APPLICATION OF FUNDS

If a business purchases a fixed asset, or raises or repays a large loan, these are events of considerable significance. However, traditional financial statements give them very little emphasis. They are detectable only by a close reading of the notes to the financial statements, and a comparison of the balance sheet of one year against the balance sheet of the preceding year.

The statement of source and application of funds attempts to correct this situation by analysing where funds have come from (operations, sale of fixed assets, new sources of capital, reduction of bank account etc.), and where they have gone (purchase of fixed assets, repayment of loans, increase in bank account etc.).

There is no standard format for the statement, but given an awareness of its purpose and the terms involved, which are drawn from the standard financial statements, readers should be able to interpret the examples they encounter.

2 STATEMENT OF VALUE ADDED

A statement of value added is frequently prepared for distribution to employees. The idea is to present the business as a joint venture between its owners and its employees, which is of benefit to the community as a whole.

The statement begins with the value of sales, and deducts the costs of 'bought in goods and services', except labour.

The balance remaining constitutes the value added by the business. The statement goes on to show how value added is distributed between suppliers of labour (employees), suppliers of capital (owners), and taxes to the government which supplies bounty for all.

10.3.3 Interpretation of financial statements

This chapter has dealt only with the sources and preparation of financial statements. It represents background knowledge which is essential for readers who wish to interpret financial statements. It is not by itself adequate as a basis for the interpretation of financial statements. This requires some knowledge of the characteristics of business in general and of the business which particular financial statements attempt to describe. We deal with these matters in Chapter 11 and return to the interpretation of financial statements in Chapter 12.

Conclusion

Financial information about the performance and state of affairs of an enterprise is conventionally presented in the form of a profit and loss account or income and expenditure account, plus a balance sheet. To understand the form and significance of these statements it is necessary to appreciate their connection with the double entry system of accounting.

Recording financial information

The double entry system depends on the somewhat contrived view of a transaction as involving an inflow and an outflow of equal value. For every transaction, both flows must be recorded – the inflow as a debit, the outflow as a credit. Debits and credits regarding any item of interest may be collected under one heading where they constitute an account.

At any instant there will be a residue of inflows inside the business, and a number of future or potential outflows. These can be seen as the contents of the business and the claims on those contents. The two must be equal and the equality is represented in the accounting equation,
NET ASSETS = EQUITY.

Separate accounts can be summarized or balanced, and the balance on each account listed in a trial balance. By extending the trial balance, balances representing 'contents' and 'claims' can be assigned to the balance sheet. Other balances will represent completed outflows, or inflows which have passed through the business. These should be allocated to the profit and loss account so that the value of completed outflows can be compared against the value of inflows to determine the profit or loss made in a period.

This profit will be equal to the increase in net assets over the period.

The logic of the double entry system enables us to see the assets of a business in a favourable light, as representing a capacity to do business in the future, or in a less favourable light, as future costs to be charged against the profit of the business.

Adjusting the records

The period in which a transaction is recorded may differ from the period in which the business should recognize the transaction as contributing to profit or loss. The process involves judgement, and is done within the framework of the double entry system by shifting balances between the profit and loss account and the balance sheet. One important adjustment is depreciation, which allows a business to recognize the cost of a fixed asset over the period of its use.

Adjustments can affect the profit *reported* by a business for a given period. They cannot affect the profit *made* by a business, and in the long run the profits reported must equal the profits made.

Financial statements

Conventional financial statements are the profit and loss account (or income and expenditure account) for a period, and a balance sheet drawn up to represent the state of affairs at the end of the period. These are usually given with comparative figures for the previous period.

There will be a family resemblance between all such statements, but legislation or administrative requirements may govern their precise format and content.

The profit and loss account (or equivalent) shows sales completed in a period, less related expenses. The balance sheet puts flesh on the bones of the accounting equation, analysing assets, liabilities and equity.

Financial statements should be accompanied by detailed notes which should not be ignored. One important note should state the accounting convention and policies adopted for recognizing income and expenditure. The usual accounting convention is the historical cost convention which shows assets at the cost of acquisition, less any amounts charged to depreciation. It is possible to modify the historical cost convention and show certain assets at valuation.

A business may present additional statements emphasizing certain aspects which are not clearly demonstrated in the traditional financial statements.

The statement of source and application of funds emphasizes changes in assets and liabilities. The statement of value added shows how the value added by a business – the excess of its sales over its purchases – is distributed between employees, owners, and through taxes, the government.

Key terms and ideas

The main terms and ideas introduced in the chapter are listed below. Readers should review the list and refer to the chapter where necessary to ensure that they understand the meaning of the terms and the significance of the ideas they represent.

conventional financial statements
profit and loss account
income and expenditure account
profit/surplus
loss/deficit
balance sheet
equity/fund
accounting equation
assets
liabilities
equity
net assets
profit-increase in net assets
recording transactions
recognizing transactions
deferred income
deferred expenditure
stock
prepayments
accruals
provisions
contingent liabilities
bad debts – write-off
bad debts – provision

double entry system
transaction
inflow
outflow
debit
credit
(separate) account
ledger
balance
trial balance
extended trial balance
profit-transactions basis
reported profit
physical profit
historical cost convention
revaluation
revaluation reserve
asset as deferred expense
asset as capacity
debit as inflow
debit as expense
accounting policies
turnover
cost of sales
gross profit
fixed assets
goodwill
depreciation
amortization
disposal proceeds
residual value
depreciable amount
useful life
net book value
profit/loss on disposal
straight line method
reducing balance method
net profit
trading account
trading profit
distribution
current assets
trade debtors
trade creditors
current liabilities
net current assets/liabilities
statement of source and application of funds
statement of value added

Follow-up activities

1 After one year of operations a business has:

ASSETS:	cash	£500
	debtors	£600
	stock	£100
	equipment	£800
LIABILITIES:	bank loan	£500
	creditors	£100

What is the owner's equity?

Given that the owner started with capital of £1,000 and withdrew £100 in the course of the year, what is the profit for the year?

2 After a second year the business above has:

ASSETS:	cash	£600
	debtors	£700
	equipment	£800
LIABILITIES:	bank loan	£500
	creditors	£2,000

What is the owner's equity? Comment.

3 At the end of a period a business has a trial balance as follows:

	debit £	credit £
sales		20,000
purchases	5,000	
wages	4,000	
debtors	2,000	
creditors		6,000
fixed assets	7,000	
cash	9,000	
capital		1,000

Divide these balances between the profit and loss account and the balance sheet.

4 Adjust the division of the balances in activity 3 on the basis that:

1 half of the recorded sales are for lessons to be given in the next period.
2 £1,000 worth of purchases remain in stock at the year end.
3 half of the debts are probably uncollectable.
4 a bill for £1,000 is expected for repair work done in the year.

5 Depreciation: assume that the fixed assets in example 3 will be sold after ten years for £1,000. Adjust the profit and loss account to provide for depreciation.

6 Obtain the accounts of your own school or those of a rival (from Companies House).

What are the main assets of the school?

What are the attributes of the school which enable it to make a profit? How well are these attributes measured or represented in the accounts of the school?

What are the school's main liabilities or sources of finance? What return do the providers of finance receive?

11 CASH FLOW MANAGEMENT AND MANAGEMENT ACCOUNTING

Aims

The aims of this chapter are:

1 to introduce the topics of planning, decision-making and cash flow management.
2 to analyse the components of profit and to reassemble them in the form of the break-even model.
3 to show how break-even analysis can be used to predict the effect on profit of changes in the major planning variables.
4 to contrast planning considerations and decision-making considerations.
5 to develop and illustrate marginal analysis as the appropriate approach to decision-making.
6 to introduce and define the idea of relevant costs for decision-making, including the ideas of opportunity cost and deprival value; and to illustrate the use of these ideas.
7 to outline the classification of costs as direct costs, indirect costs, and overheads.
8 to show the ways in which cash flow and profit may differ, and to demonstrate the potential effects of this difference.
9 to introduce the techniques of cash flow forecasting and cash flow management.

Introduction

This chapter deals with three of the most important areas in which financial considerations impinge upon a business: planning, decision-making, and cash flow. While financial accounting, introduced in the last chapter, deals essentially with the past, each of these areas deals with the future. This is important: managers may be judged on their past, but their actions can only affect the future.

For each area, we develop a different way of looking at a business. For planning purposes we shall develop the idea of a business as a capacity, provided by incurring certain costs, which we hope to use for a series of transactions which will generate profit. This will be reflected in break-even analysis, which can be used to test the effect on profit of changes in the major variables of financial planning.

For decision-making we see a business as a series of separate transactions, each of which must be judged on its separate merits. We develop some rules for identifying and quantifying relevant costs for decision-making.

In respect of cash flow, we see a business as a reservoir in a circulating system of cash movements. We see how the system can run dry and collapse even though the business may be making profits, and we describe some ways in which cash flow can be controlled.

11.1 Planning

Planning involves the business as a whole – its people and organization, its marketing strategy and its environment. This section deals only with the business as an economic structure. In other words it assumes that prices, costs, and quantities sold are given or can be varied at will as the business plans to make a profit.

These are large simplifying assumptions, but in one respect they are justified. Changes in the environment, the organization, its people or its marketing strategy will feed through into changes in price and quantity sold, and into cost structure and cost levels. We need to know how changes in each of these variables will affect profit.

The following sections present a framework within which the problem can be addressed. We begin with this equation to define profit

$\pi = \mathrm{TR} - \mathrm{TC}$
(profit = total revenue *less* total cost)

and proceed to examine each element of the equation.

11.1.1 Total revenue

Total revenue is given by the simple equation

$\mathrm{TR} = \mathrm{P} \times \mathrm{Q}$
(total revenue = price × quantity sold)

This is always true.

From this we draw the conclusion that if prices are doubled, total revenue will double, or that if quantity sold is increased by 50%, total revenue will increase by 50%, and so on.

Readers can verify the arithmetic, but may dispute the conclusion. An increase in price will probably lead to a reduction in quantity sold. Alternatively a plan to increase quantity sold may necessitate lowering prices. You cannot change prices without changing quantity sold, and vice versa.

We accept the objection but feel entitled to ignore it in the present context. In a language school we are not speaking of astronomical changes in price, or of changing quantities sold by thousands or millions of units (even though in the text we may use large proportional changes to make the arithmetic clearer).

So we assume that price and quantity can be varied independently, and that changes in either will lead to directly proportionate changes in total revenue. This makes revenue rather uninteresting, but profit and costs are different.

11.1.2 Profit: revenue and costs

Profit we know is given by the equation:

$\pi = \text{TR} - \text{TC}$
(profit = total revenue *less* total cost)

We also know, or assume, that an increase in price will lead to a proportionate increase in total revenue: but will it lead to a proportionate increase in profit? The answer is no, because costs will not change as a consequence of any change in selling price.

But what if we increase quantity sold? Will profit increase proportionately? Again the answer is no, but this time because although total revenue and *some* costs will increase in proportion to the quantity sold (these are variable costs), other costs will not change in response to changes in quantity sold (these are fixed costs).

The next two sections explore the characteristics of fixed costs and variable costs.

11.1.3 Fixed costs

Fixed costs do not vary in proportion to quantity sold.

Examples in a school will usually be the cost of premises and the cost of administration. A school must have premises and administration of some sort, and once these are provided, the related costs will not vary if there is one student more or one student less. They may not vary if there are 100 students more or less.

But at some stage if a school continues to expand, it will fill up its premises or exhaust its administrative resources. At this stage it must expand its premises or hire additional administrative staff. The costs of its premises or administration, which were fixed until this critical stage was reached, will now jump to a new level and remain for the time being fixed at that level, irrespective of the number of students enrolled.

Figure 11.1 shows a graph of premises and administrative costs per year against student weeks per year. The total costs of administration and premises are £500,000 per year, and with this capacity the school can provide for up to 2,500 student weeks per year. From the graph we can read off the accommodation and administrative costs incurred if there are no student weeks (£500,000), if there are 2,500 student weeks (£500,000), and if there are sales of student weeks at some intermediate number (again £500,000).

Figure 11.2 overleaf shows a similar graph for the same school, perhaps one year later after it has expanded its premises and administrative resources (which now cost £750,000 per year) so that it can provide up to 5,000 student weeks per year. Note that the school cannot now go back – the costs incurred if there are no student weeks are now £750,000, and remain fixed at that level until the new capacity level of 5,000 student weeks per year is reached.

Figure 11.1 Fixed costs

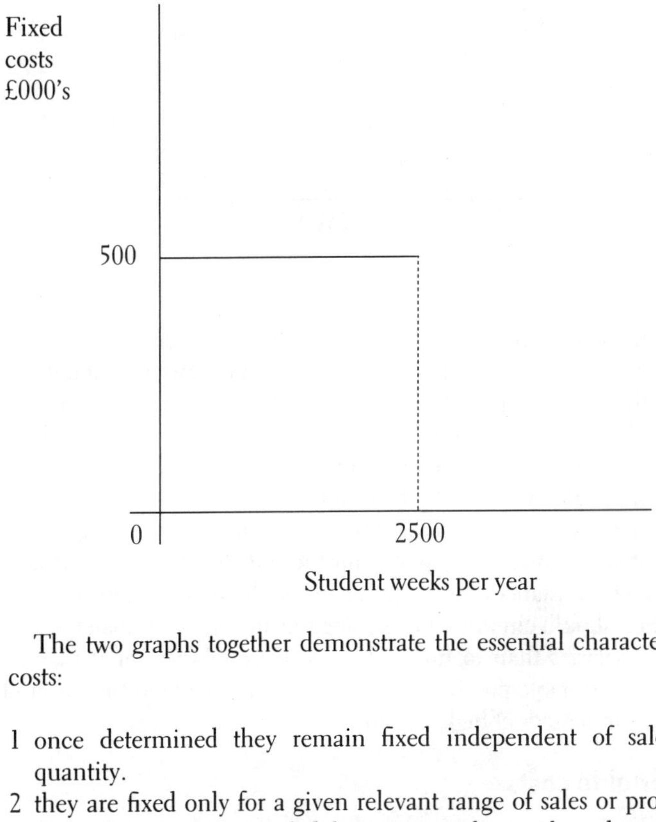

The two graphs together demonstrate the essential characteristics of fixed costs:

1 once determined they remain fixed independent of sales or product quantity.
2 they are fixed only for a given relevant range of sales or product quantity. Once that range is exceeded the entire graph must be redrawn.
3 no costs are fixed with respect to time. Fixed costs may change over time but at any one time they are fixed independent of sales or product quantity. Thus fixed cost changes over time must be reflected in a redrawing of the fixed cost graph.

It should be clear from the above discussion that costs are classified as fixed not by virtue of what they represent (rent, administrative salaries etc.) but by

Figure 11.2 Fixed costs after increase in capacity

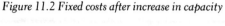

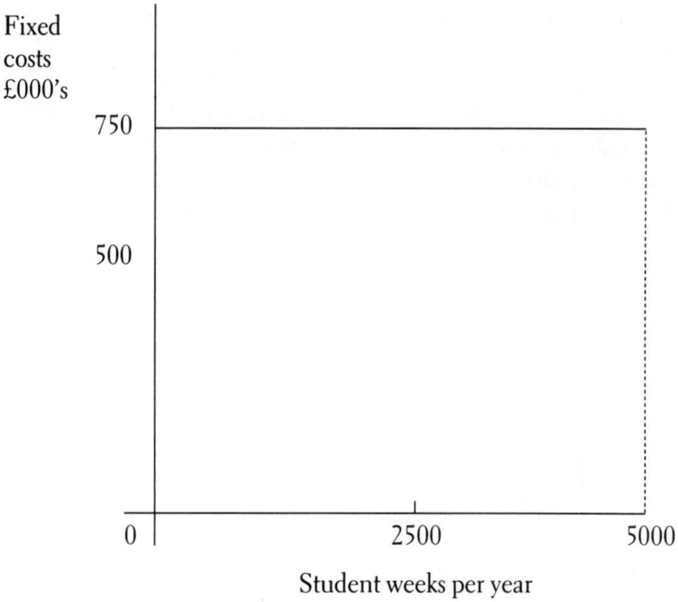

virtue of the difficulty of entering or withdrawing from arrangements. Half of the rent incurred in expectation of 500 students weekly cannot generally be repudiated if there are only 250 students weekly. Consequently rent is generally a fixed cost. On the other hand if a business could rent teaching space by the hour at short notice then it could adapt so that rent was no longer a fixed cost but a cost that varied with the number of students.

The point will not be pursued in the rest of our analysis below, but readers should note that costs which are easy to adjust in one direction (up or down) in response to circumstances, may be sticky or difficult to adjust in an opposite direction should circumstances change again. Thus it is easier to hire staff or increase salaries than to fire staff or decrease salaries, or it may be easier to dispose of suitable premises in periods of slack demand than to find suitable premises in periods of high demand.

11.1.4 Variable costs

Variable costs vary in direct proportion to quantity sold (or produced).

Some variable costs are very easily identifiable: consider a school which distributes free textbooks to students on each course. Each book costs £3 and each course lasts four weeks. Here the cost of books is directly proportional to the number of student weeks. In respect of books, 100 student weeks will cost £75, while 200 student weeks will cost £150 and so on. A graph of this cost is given in Figure 11.3.

Figure 11.3 Variable costs

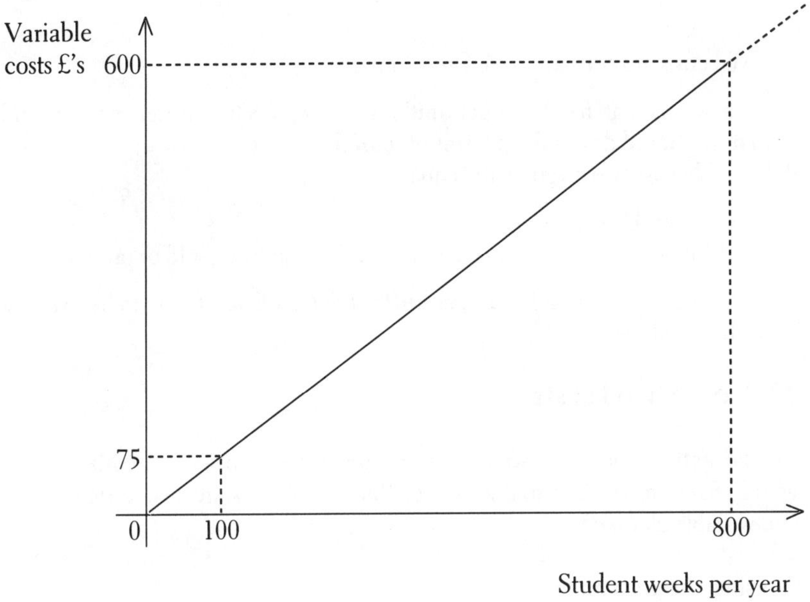

Other costs which should be variable can be identified logically, but the variable cost per unit is more difficult to quantify. Some of these may be quantified arbitrarily: in a school which provides food, the cost of ingredients can be expected to vary with the number of student weeks. It can be made to vary by a known amount simply by agreeing with the chef a reasonable sum per student for the purchase of food.

Other variable costs will only be quantifiable by estimation based on past experience. For example the cost of photocopying paper will probably vary with the number of student weeks, but it will not be possible to determine by immediate observation that each student week requires x sheets, or to impose an arbitrary allowance of x sheets per student week. It should be possible, however, to estimate a rough average usage of paper per student week, and to convert this into a variable cost per student week.

11.1.5 Fixed and variable costs: summary

1 Fixed costs attach to the enterprise as a whole. They do not change in proportion to changes in quantity sold or produced. In time they may change to a new level but at the new level they will not change in proportion to changes in quantity sold or produced.
2 Variable costs change in direct proportion to changes in quantity sold or produced. It may be possible to see a variable cost per unit, or to fix an arbitrary variable cost per unit. In some cases it may be necessary to estimate a variable cost per unit.

3 Fixed costs are given by the equation

$FC = k$
(fixed costs are constant over a given range).

This means that 'fixed cost per unit' is meaningless for further analysis, and that we should deal only in terms of *total* fixed costs.

4 Variable costs are given by the equation

$TVC = VCU \times Q$
(total variable cost = variable cost per unit × quantity sold or produced).

This means that variable cost *per unit* is the significant figure to be used for further analysis.

11.1.6 Mixed costs

To clarify the exposition, we have so far presented examples of costs that are wholly fixed or wholly variable. In real life many costs are a mixture of fixed and variable elements.

Consider these examples:

1 Cost of premises. In real life it may well be possible to enter short-term contracts to hire teaching premises in response to peaks in demand. In this case the graph of rental costs would appear as in Figure 11.4.

Figure 11.4 Step-fixed costs

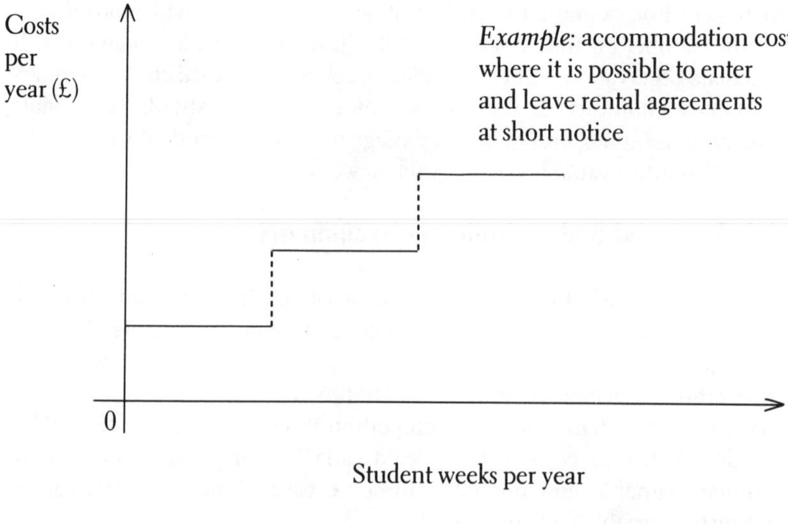

Figure 11.5 A kinked cost

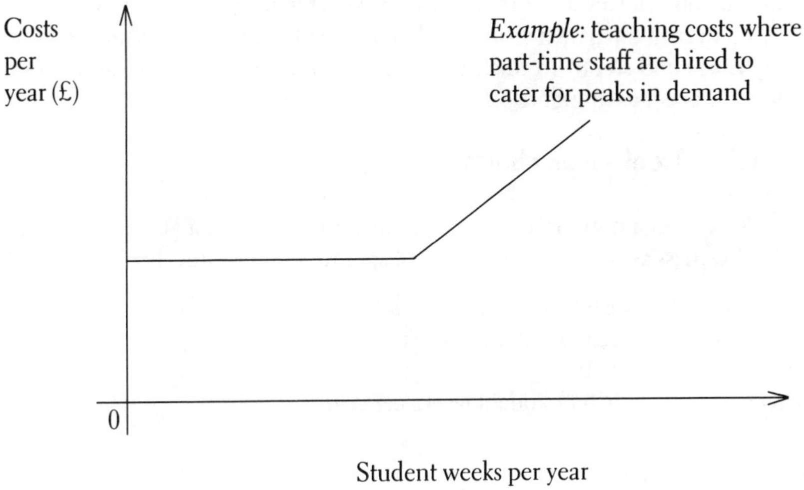

Figure 11.6 Mixed (semi-fixed or semi-variable) costs

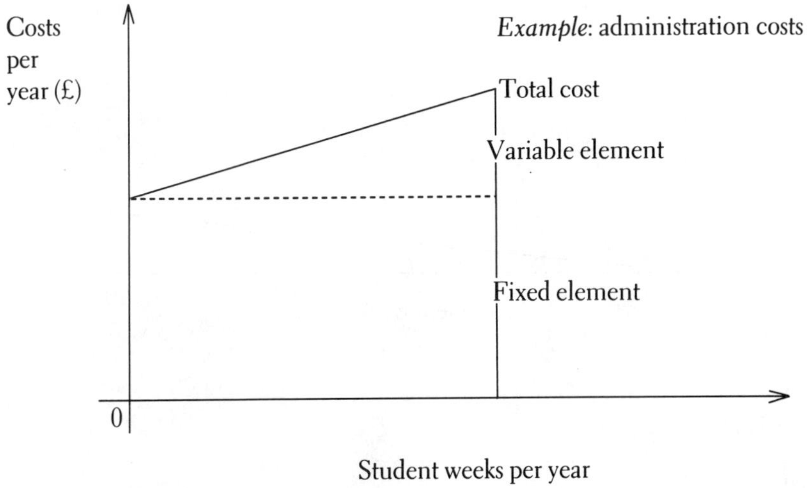

2 Teaching costs. It is no doubt possible to run a school of some kind staffed by teachers employed and released on a week by week basis. In this case, teaching costs would be strictly variable. At the opposite extreme, a school could be exclusively staffed by full-time teachers on indefinite contracts. In this case, teaching costs would be strictly fixed costs. A more likely practice between these extremes is to employ a core of full-time salaried teachers sufficient to cater for minimum or average demand, while relying on temporary teachers to provide for periods of peak demand. In this case the graph of teaching costs would appear as in Figure 11.5.

3 General administration costs. The cost of administrative staff and of the

resources they use will for the large part be fixed irrespective of the number of students. However it is reasonable to expect that more students will mean more overtime payments, more telephone calls, more stamps and stationery usage and so on. In this case the graph of general administration costs would appear as in Figure 11.6.

11.1.7 Break-even charts

We are now in a position to review our analysis and form a graphical picture of the business as a whole. First we must assume some figures. Let them be:

sales price	£100 per student week
variable cost	£20 per student week
fixed cost	£80,000 per year
capacity	2,000 student weeks per year

Figure 11.7 Variable costs

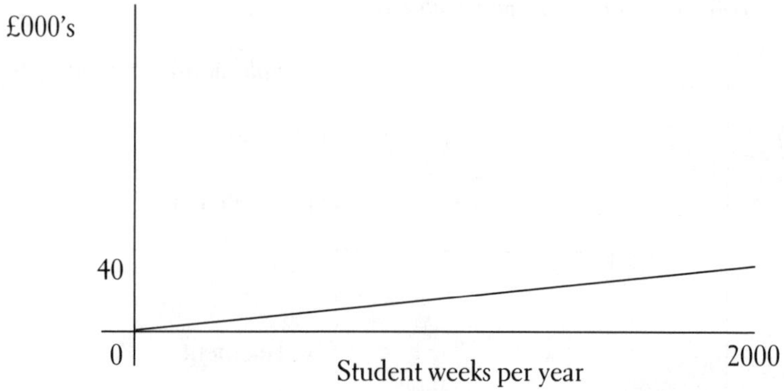

Figure 11.8 Fixed costs

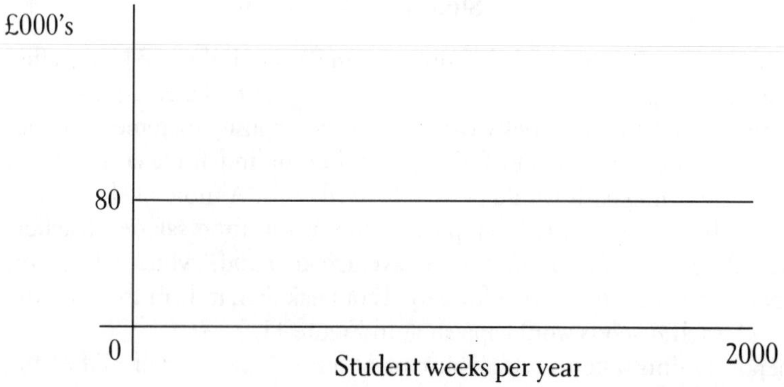

Figure 11.9 Total costs

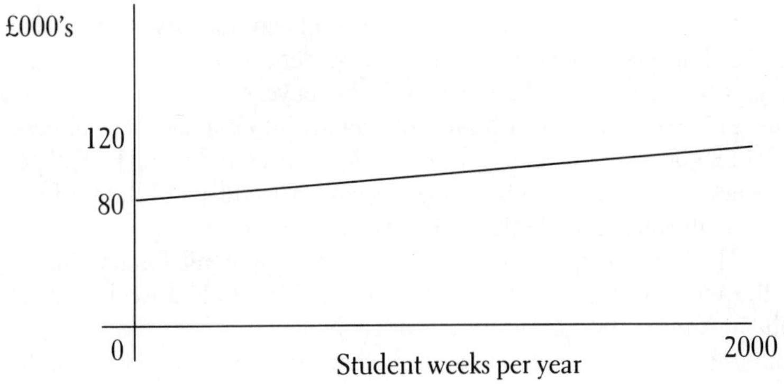

Figure 11.10 Total revenue

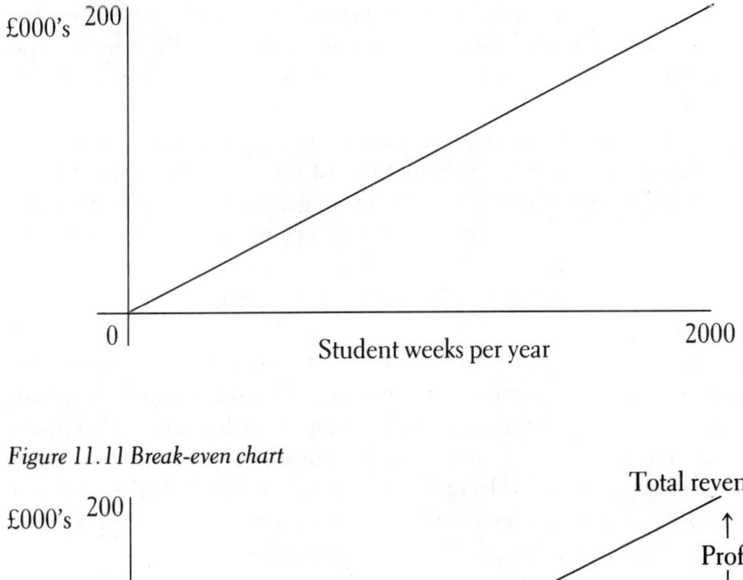

Figure 11.11 Break-even chart

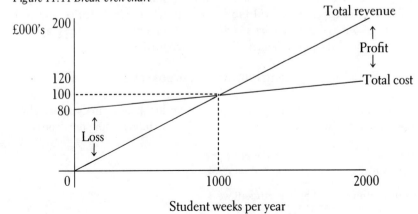

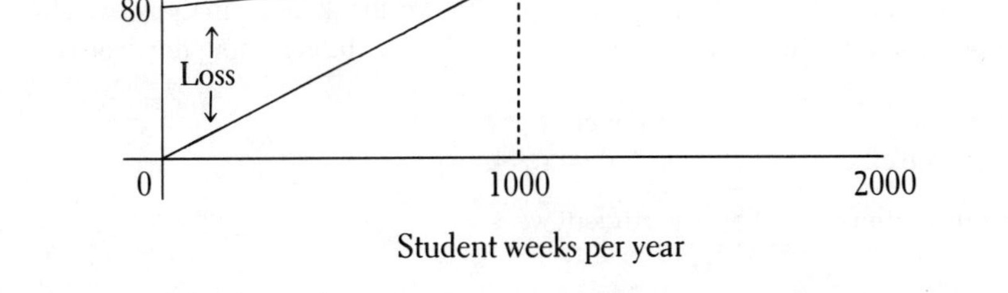

Figure 11.7 graphs variable costs, starting at nil for no student weeks and rising by £20 per student week to £40,000 for 2,000 student weeks per year.

Figure 11.8 graphs fixed costs. Since fixed costs do not vary with student weeks, the line starts at £80,000 for no student weeks and continues horizontally to £80,000 for 2,000 student weeks per year.

Figure 11.9 combines the two previous graphs into a graph of total cost, starting at £80,000 (the fixed cost) for no student weeks and rising by £20 per student week (the variable cost) to a projected total cost of £120,000 for a school full to its capacity of 2,000 student weeks per year.

Figure 11.10 is a graph of total revenue. Starting at nil for no student weeks, the revenue line rises by £100 for each extra student week sold, to reach the maximum revenue at capacity of £200,000.

Finally Figure 11.11 superimposes the revenue line of Figure 11.10 on the total cost line of Figure 11.9. This is called a break-even chart.

The break-even chart tells us a number of things. In particular it shows the level of profit or loss that the school can expect, given this price and cost structure, at any level of sales between zero and 2,000 student weeks per year. (This is the vertical distance at any point between the total revenue line and the total cost line.) Thus it shows us that the maximum loss the school could make is £80,000 per year, and that its maximum profit would be £80,000, with sales of 2,000 student weeks per year.

Most significantly, the break-even chart shows us the point at which the total cost line crosses the total revenue line. At this point costs and revenue are equal; and the school breaks even. By reading down from this point to the horizontal axis we can determine that the school will break even if it sells 1,000 student weeks in the year – that is, if on average it manages to fill 50% of its capacity. Below that level it will make a loss. Above that level it will make a profit.

In general break-even analysis can help us to determine in advance the effect on profit of changes in prices, or costs, or quantities sold. If we are setting up a school, break-even analysis can help us to determine what prices we must charge to break even at a given level of capacity, or alternatively at what level of capacity we will break even given a particular price and cost structure. But to use the analysis in this way, it is simpler to drop the graphical presentation and adopt a more mathematical approach.

11.1.8 Planning: contribution and break-even analysis

To develop a more mathematical approach to break-even analysis, we shall continue with the example used in section 11.1.7, representing the data as:

sales price	£100	per student week
variable cost	£20	per student week
contribution	£80	per student week

fixed cost	£80,000 per year
capacity	2,000 student weeks per year

'Contribution' is a new line in the data and represents a new idea. The idea is simple:

> contribution per unit is sales price per unit less variable cost per unit.

Both the name and the idea derive from the analysis presented in section 11.1.7. Below the break-even level, each student week contributes £80 (in this example) to cover fixed costs. Above the break-even level each student week contributes £80 to profit.

The idea of contribution simplifies calculation and reasoning – we now have to deal with only one number (contribution) instead of two (sales price and variable cost).

Using this idea we can readily calculate at what average level of capacity the school will break even. The fixed costs to be covered are £80,000. Each student week contributes £80, and therefore 1,000 student weeks will cover fixed costs, allowing the school to break even at an average of 50% capacity (1,000 student weeks is 50% of 2,000 student weeks).

We can repeat and vary the analysis with a further example: you have the option of setting up (or expanding) a school in one of two locations. A school in location A would operate under severe competition and would have to set its prices at general market levels. A school in location B could set its own prices for a premium product. Your best estimates of the data are as follows:

	A	B	
sales price	£85	?	per student week
variable cost	£25	£35	per student week
contribution	£60	?	per student week
fixed cost	£180,000	£250,000	per year
capacity	5,000	4,000	student weeks per year

At what level of occupancy will school A break even?
Let the school break even with Q students. Then at break-even point:

> total contribution = £60Q = fixed cost = £180,000
> and thus Q = 3,000 = 60% of capacity.

At what level of capacity will school A achieve a target profit of £42,000?
Let the target be achieved with R student weeks. Then:

total contribution = £60R = fixed cost + target profit = £180,000 + £42,000 and thus R = 3,700 = 74% of capacity.

We require school B to break even at 50% occupancy. What price level should be set?

Let the *contribution* per student week be £C. At 50% occupancy the number of student weeks per year will be 50% × 4,000 = 2,000. Then at break-even point with 50% occupancy:

total contribution = £C × 2,000 = fixed cost = 250,000
and thus C = £125.

Given that variable cost is £35, the sales price must be £125 + £35 = £160 per student week.

Similar calculations could be performed on almost any permutation of the data, both to test the effect of plans on profit, and to test the sensitivity of plans to unforeseen changes in the data. It should be relatively simple for example to verify that if the projected sales price for location A was overstated by 15% (i.e. its sales price was actually £74 per student week) then its break-even point would rise to 3,673 student weeks per year – about 73% of capacity.

Break-even analysis is therefore a simple but surprisingly powerful aid to planning. But note that as with all the analytical techniques discussed in this chapter it does not make decisions for us. Analysis contributes to clearer vision, but it cannot be a substitute for managerial or entrepreneurial judgement.

11.1.9 Break-even analysis: some practical problems

It would be false to persuade readers of the virtue of break-even analysis and leave them with the impression that its application in real life will be quite as simple as the initial presentation of principles given above. In real life there will be problems and pitfalls.

The first problem concerns data. In general the data we have concerns the past, and planning concerns the future. In view of changing prices and even a change in the structure of the business, data concerning the past may no longer be relevant.

Even given relevant data, a second problem arises with its analysis. This arises particularly in any attempt to analyse costs into fixed and variable elements. In real life costs do not come neatly labelled as fixed and variable. Most costs are a mixture of the two. However in the context of a language school, this problem is not as severe as it may be in other industries. The largest costs – accommodation and teaching – can normally be analysed into fixed and variable elements by inspection. Other costs – commissions, food, textbooks and student outings – may readily fall into the variable category. Remaining costs will almost certainly contain a large fixed element and a comparatively small (or very small) variable element. Remember that a cost which contains a variable element for *usage* (e.g. electricity) is not necessarily a cost which will vary with *student hours*. (For electricity the cost may vary with student hours in a residential school, but in a school which provides only teaching premises, electricity will almost certainly be a fixed cost.) Remember also that we are ultimately interested in the total cost line, and not in an itemized analysis of each constituent cost. Thus logic tells us that more student hours probably means more usage of postage stamps, but unless this variable element is comparatively large and easily identifiable (each student receives a 2 kilo registered package of pre-course information . . .), it is probably simpler to treat postage as a fixed cost, or to leave it with all other costs which cannot be readily broken down into fixed and variable elements and treat them statistically as in Figure 11.12.

Thirdly and most importantly, the mathematical or graphical model that emerges in real life may be considerably more complex than the one we have presented in Figure 11.9 where total costs and total revenues are both represented by straight and continuous lines. We know that as a result of its component parts, the total cost line may well be discontinuous, with sudden jumps to higher levels (see Figure 11.4), or kinked (see Figure 11.5).

Figure 11.12 Estimating cost analysis

Having extracted the self-evidently fixed or variable elements of costs, the quarterly management accounts of your school show the following residue of costs which you cannot easily analyse:

quarter	student weeks	costs
1	500	£20,250
2	700	£20,375
3	700	£20,500
4	1000	£20,875

These points can be plotted on a graph or scatter diagram as below, and an estimated cost line drawn through the points which in this instance would indicate that these costs contain a fixed element of £19,000 per quarter and a variable element of £2.00 per student week.

Scatter diagram

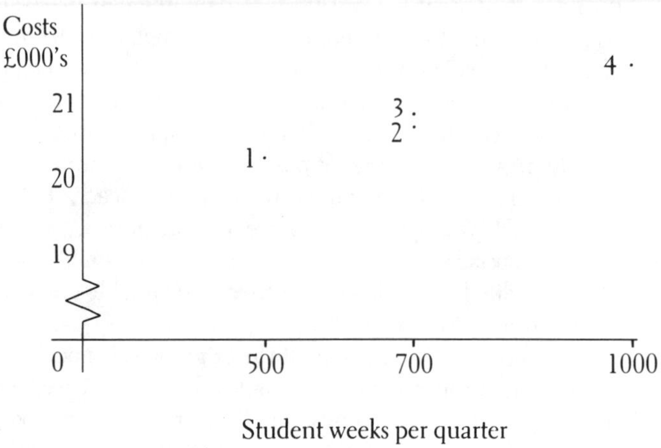

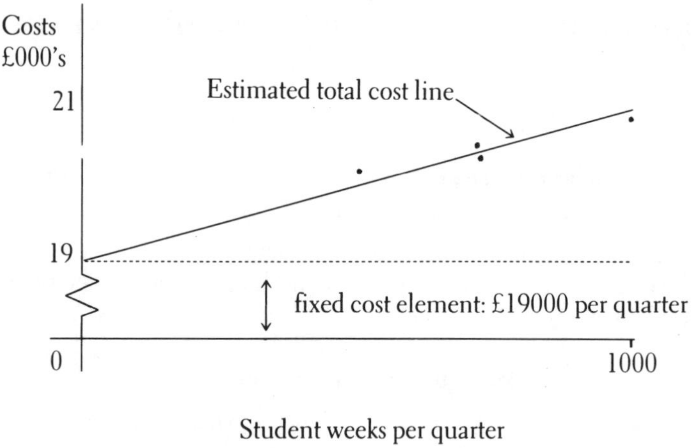

from estimate: increase in total costs: £2000
increase in student weeks: 1000

∴ estimated variable costs: £2 per student week.

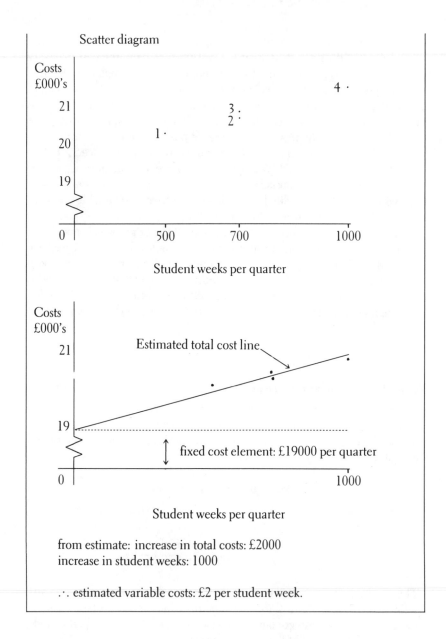

Equally, the revenue line in real life may prove to be kinked or even curved. Figure 11.13 demonstrates how this situation may arise.

Figure 11.13 A kinked or curved revenue line

It may be that a school runs two or more courses at different prices. Here it becomes necessary to estimate the sales mix at different levels of activity, and hence calculate the revenue expected. A simple example is given in the table below.

	course A	course B	total units sold	total revenue
sales price	£60	£100		£
units sold:	250	250	500	40,000
	500	250	750	55,000
(capacity)	1,000	—	1,000	60,000

Although only three points are given here, it is possible to join them on a graph and read off estimated total revenue at intermediate levels of sales. The graph is given below.

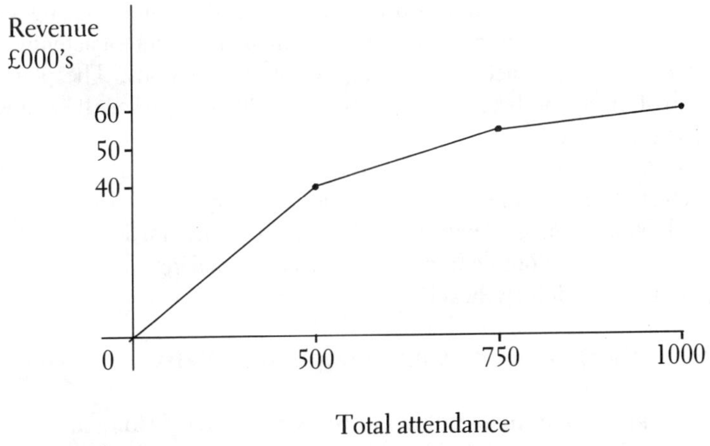

A final problem in applying break-even analysis may have already occurred to some readers. Consider a school which provides the following sales by quarter:

first quarter	1,300	student weeks
second quarter	1,600	student weeks
third quarter	1,700	student weeks
fourth quarter	1,400	student weeks
TOTAL for year	6,000	student weeks

This is well within the school's capacity of 6,400 student weeks per year. Yet there is a flaw. The school sells a time-based product. Capacity of 6,400 student weeks per year implies a capacity of 1,600 student weeks per quarter. In the third quarter this capacity limit is exceeded and the school must revise its sales forecast to 5,900 student weeks in the year.

Subject to this check (which may need to be done on the basis of monthly or even weekly capacity limits) the school can continue with straightforward break-even analysis. But it may be reluctant to forgo the extra sales. How should it plan or decide to deal with them? The question will be left to readers as an exercise at the end of the chapter. It requires decision-making techniques which have not yet been introduced.

11.2 Decision-making

Just as the planning section of this chapter dealt only with the economic framework of the business, so this section deals only with the cost aspects of decision-making. Costs are clearly not the only criteria for decision-making, but decisions impact on costs and whatever may be the decisive factors, it is always necessary to take account of costs.

We have drawn a distinction between planning and decision-making which may seem arbitrary or unnecessary. But they are in fact different activities and require different approaches. Planning concerns intentions. The planning approach starts at the beginning and considers the long term. It frequently anticipates a long run of similar transactions.

Decision-making concerns immediate choices. The decision-making approach starts in the middle of events and considers the short term. It deals with each transaction as unique and to be assessed on its individual merits.

The following sections demonstrate the decision-making approach, and the problems to which it is applicable.

11.2.1 Short-term decisions: marginal analysis

We have emphasized the usefulness of break-even analysis for planning. But the same analysis is not applicable to short-term decision-making.

An example should make this clear. We determined that the school in section 1.8 would break even at 50% capacity (i.e. at 1,000 student weeks per year), charging £100 per student week. Assume that the school is now operating, and that for the forthcoming month it has spare capacity of 40 student hours and no hope of filling that capacity. Assume also if you like that the school has never met its 50% break-even target and is doomed to make a loss by charging its dwindling number of students only £100 per week (though this assumption is not a necessary part of the analysis). An agent telephones and offers to provide 40 student weeks for the forthcoming month at £30 per student week (net of his large commission). Does the school accept or reject this business?

From a long-term or planning point of view the offer is obviously ludicrous. The school would never plan to take on business at £30 per student week. It is already making a loss at £100 per student week, and in any case would never even cover its fixed costs by taking business at £30 per student week.

Nevertheless, faced with the decision now, the school should take the business. Why? Consider the data: the school has spare capacity and so accepting these students at £30 per week does not entail turning away other students at £100 per week. Furthermore the school is offered £30 per student week against variable costs of £20 per student week. No other costs will change because they are fixed costs. Each student week, even at the long-term uneconomic rate of £30, will make a positive contribution of £10, and therefore the school should accept the business.

We can demonstrate this point in another way. The school can either accept or reject 40 student weeks at £30 per student week. The effects of the choice can be tabulated as:

	ACCEPT	REJECT
additional revenue	£1,200	—
additional costs	£800	—
additional profit	£400	—

(The additional costs represent variable costs of £20 per student week.)

We have used the word 'additional' above in its obvious and ordinary sense. However accountants and economists would generally prefer to use the word 'marginal' in this context, subject to the definition:

> Marginal cost (or revenue) is the cost (or revenue) which one extra specified unit of activity will incur (or generate).

The relevant unit of activity must be specified or determined by the decision-maker. It may be a student week, in which case marginal cost will be equal to variable cost (unless the student week in question crosses a discontinuity in the total cost line – see Figure 11.4 on page 288).

However the decision may concern an entirely different unit of activity – for example whether to take on an extra class, or whether to employ an extra teacher.

Marginal analysis – the comparison of marginal costs and revenues – is the basic approach to short-term decision-making where planning considerations are no longer relevant. The next section develops two examples of marginal analysis in practice.

11.2.2 Applications of marginal analysis

A major problem in applying marginal analysis is to avoid the slip into average costing, which is not appropriate to *any* rational discussion.

Consider a school which employs full-time teachers on indeterminate contracts under which they are paid £15,000 to teach 1,000 hours per year. All teachers are fully employed and additional students are being turned away. Should the Director of Studies employ another full-time teacher, or employ his wife on a part-time basis at £30 per hour?

At first sight this is an open and shut case. A full-time teacher appears to cost £15 per hour while the part-time alternative costs £30 per hour. However, adopting a marginal analysis we see that a full-time teacher simply costs £15,000 for the following year. There is no question of asking for a refund if the teacher is required to teach less than 1,000 hours. The real question then is, how many extra hours will be required in the year?

A marginal analysis of this problem could be represented as:

hours required	cost of full-timer	cost of part-timer
1–499	£15,000	less than £15,000
500–1,000	£15,000	£15,000 or more

If the expected unit of activity (number of extra hours) is anything less than 500, then the Director of Studies is justified in paying £30 per hour instead of employing a full-time teacher.

The last example involved comparing only the marginal cost of two alternatives. The next example invites comparison of both marginal revenue and marginal cost.

Imagine a school which can employ teachers on monthly contracts for £1,000 per month. Each teacher will teach one class for a month, but for reasons of space no class can contain more than 10 students. Students pay a purely exemplary price of £150 per month. No other costs or revenue are relevant. There are 63 student applicants for the forthcoming month. How many classes should be given?

The global or average approach would probably offer this analysis:

		£
projected income:	63 students at £150	9,450
expense:	7 teachers at £1,000	7,000
profit:		£2,450

Therefore proceed with seven classes of nine students.

The marginal approach would offer this analysis:

student numbers	marginal income £	marginal cost £	profit (loss) £
1–10	1,500	1,000	500
11–20	1,500	1,000	500
21–30	1,500	1,000	500
31–40	1,500	1,000	500
41–50	1,500	1,000	500
51–60	1,500	1,000	500
61–63	450	1,000	(550)

Three students, and their proffered fees of £150 each, are therefore rejected, and the school proceeds with six classes of 10, and a profit for the month of £3,000.

11.2.3 Relevant costs for decision-making

A chapter on costs will naturally include problems and the relevant costs for addressing each problem (frequently with a statement that no other costs are relevant).

However, business problems seldom arise in such convenient packages.

Decision-makers must search for relevant information and reject irrelevant information. Relevance is apparently a matter of common sense, but management accountants have developed a definition of relevant costs for short-term decision-making:

> Relevant costs are all future differential cash flows which are affected by the decision.

It is worth labouring the elements of this definition. Relevance concerns the *future* since decisions cannot reverse the past. Relevance to a decision between alternatives is concerned with *differentials* between the alternatives. Where the alternatives do not differ there is no basis for a decision between them. Relevance concerns *cash flows* because cash (and not accounting profit or any other arbitrary measure) is the objective measure of a business transaction. By extending the definition of relevant costs to *all* future cash flows we can also take account of relevant income, which in the context is treated simply as a negative cost.

11.2.4 Relevant costs: opportunity costs

Choosing to undertake one activity will often (but not always) mean that we cannot undertake another activity. If we are faced with mutually exclusive business opportunities, then the relevant costs of one opportunity will include the profit lost by the consequent inability to take the alternative opportunity.

This is a slightly alien concept because it always involves an alternative, which may not be explicitly stated. You are employed for £20,000 a year, but could set up your own school and gain profits of £24,000 a year. Remaining in employment therefore 'costs' you £4,000 a year (by comparison with its unstated alternative of self-employment). You set up your own school and your 'profit' is £4,000 a year (by comparison with its unstated alternative of remaining in employment). The matter is clearer if the statement is expressed at greater length : *the decision* to remain in employment *as opposed to becoming self-employed* has cost you £4,000.

The idea involved is known as opportunity cost:

> The opportunity cost of a decision is the positive net cash flow lost by inability to take the best alternative decision.

Opportunity costs only arise when decisions are mutually exclusive. If a decision excludes no other decision with cash flow consequences, then it has nil opportunity cost. This can happen. But note that a decision to spend money excludes the decision to save it.

Since opportunity costs are distinctly related to decisions, they are always distinctly relevant for decision-making.

11.2.5 Irrelevant costs: sunk costs

Some costs are so irrelevant that they have their own name, sunk costs:

> Sunk costs are past costs or costs which are irrevocably committed by past decisions.

Since sunk costs by definition cannot be affected by a current decision, they are by definition irrelevant to a current decision.

This point enables us to contrast relevant costs for decision-making against relevant costs for planning. If your school is committed for the year to a rent of £1,000 a month for premises, the fact is irrelevant when you are making a costing decision in mid-year. It *was* extremely relevant when you were planning before the start of the year and before you entered the commitment.

The main problem in recognizing sunk costs and dealing with them as such is probably emotional. On the one hand it may be hard to accept that so much past effort and expense should be treated as worthless. On the other hand it may be hard to forgive a project which has already swallowed thousands and promises to yield only hundreds. In both cases, however, the relevant costs are only the future cash flows.

11.2.6 Relevant costs: an example

The new Director of Studies at the Dartmouth Institute is determined that the school should build a reputation for providing new, high quality, specialized courses. He has in mind beginning in the current period (year 1) with one of two options : course A or course B.

The Financial Director opposes this initiative. She is content that the school is already operating very profitably and is invariably full with its normal courses. She doubts the long-term value of the initiative and believes that neither of the options will add to profit in year 1.

The information you have been able to gather is as follows:

fees: course A and course B would each generate fees of £12,500 in year 1.

classrooms: both course A and course B envisage taking 20 students, and occupying two classrooms. Each course would last for one month. As noted, the school is usually full with students taking normal courses in classes of 10. Each normal class generates fee income of £6,000 per month. The variable cost of all classes (normal classes as well as A and B classes) is £200 per month, excluding the matters dealt with below.

teaching: all staff are full-time salaried staff. Normal classes have a varying mixture of teachers, some on Grade I salaries of £12,000 per year (£1,000 per month), some on Grade II salaries of £18,000 per year. Course A would require two teachers for the month of its duration. These would be Grade I teachers. Course B would require two teachers, both of them on Grade II salaries. No additional teachers would be needed as a consequence of holding either course, but for course A the school's marketing manager would be required to contribute to workshop sessions on business topics for approximately half of the course time. The marketing manager is paid £24,000 per year and would have to cancel a projected seminar on marketing which would yield the school net income of £200.

computer room: the school has recently invested in an electronic learning centre, or computer room, for which equipment is on long-term lease at a cost of £1,000 per month. Course A would occupy the facility for 25% of its available time during the month in which the course is held. Course B would not use the facility. Students in normal classes currently use the facility as a free optional extra, but it is not yet featured in the school's publicity material.

vehicles: students on course A would require full-time use of the school's minibuses, each of which is depreciated at £2,400 per year. The mileage incurred is not expected to exceed mileage in normal use, but the school would need to hire a driver for the month at a cost of £800. Course B would not use the school's vehicles.

special data: course B would require up-to-date information from a specialized economic database. For year 1, during which time the course would take place, the school has purchased an annual subscription at a cost of £1,200. Course A would not use the information and there are no plans to use the information in connection with any other course.

books: adequate books for both courses are in stock. Each course will require

20 books. The books for course A were bought for £2 each. These books have now been dropped from the publisher's list and are no longer used in the school. Course B will use one of the standard textbooks currently used by normal classes in the school. The books in stock were bought for £2.30 each, but the wholesale price is now £2.50 per copy.

artist's materials: course B would use up a supply of artist's materials which were bought several years ago, at a cost of £400, for courses which the school has now dropped. Similar materials would now cost £600. The materials in stock are in good condition and could be returned to the supplier for £300.

Decision I: prepare relevant costings to help the Director of Studies decide whether to offer course A or course B in year 1 only. (Readers are recommended to attempt this *before* reading the notes below.)

We are required to decide between course A and course B. Comparing the cash flows, we have:

fees and variable costs: equal for each course. Not differential cash flows and therefore irrelevant.

classrooms: equal usage for each course and therefore irrelevant.

teaching: no additional teachers will be required therefore no additional cash flows. Therefore an irrelevant cost.

marketing manager: salary is irrelevant since it would be paid anyway. Loss of £200 net seminar income is an opportunity cost of course A.

computer room: a sunk cost and therefore irrelevant. No opportunity cost through exclusion of use by normal students, since this is a free extra to the courses, which was not described in their publicity material.

minibus: depreciation is not a cash flow. Mileage (a potential cash flow in respect of fuel) is expected to be normal and is therefore not a differential cost of course A. However £800 for the driver is a relevant cost against course A.

special data: sunk cost and therefore irrelevant.

books: for course A a past cost therefore sunk and irrelevant. No alternative use and therefore no opportunity cost. For course B original cost of books is again sunk and irrelevant, but the books must be replaced for normal courses. Relevant cost of books for course A therefore 20 × £2.50 = £50.

artist's materials: original cost sunk and therefore irrelevant. Replacement cost irrelevant since no other course uses the materials and course B is to be held in year 1 only. Opportunity cost is £300 lost by not returning materials to supplier.

To summarize and compare, the relevant costs are:

	course A	course B
	£	£
marketing manager	200	—
minibus driver	800	—
books	—	50
artist's materials	—	300
Total relevant cost	£1,000	£350

The Director of Studies would therefore prefer course B on cost grounds.

Decision II: prepare relevant costings to help the Director of Studies persuade the Financial Director that holding course B in year 1 only will increase the profit of the school.

We are now required to choose between course B and the normal classes which it would displace. Comparing the cash flows, we have:

fees: course B £12,500, *two* normal classes £12,000.
variable costs: not a differential cost.
teaching: not a differential cost.
special data: sunk cost.
books: now no longer a differential cost. Course B would use 20 books, two normal classes would use 20 books.
artist's materials: opportunity cost remains £300.

To summarize and compare, the relevant costs are:

	course B	two normal courses
	£	£
fees	12,500	12,000
artist's materials	(300)	—
net relevant income	£12,200	£12,000

Course B will therefore generate additional positive cash flows of £200 and is justifiable on cost grounds.

Decision III: the Director of Studies resolves to go ahead with course B in year 1, and to offer the same course once annually thereafter. He believes that in year 2 and subsequently the price of course B could be safely increased to £13,500, but no other price changes are expected. The Financial Director remains opposed. Prepare relevant costings to enable her to demonstrate that on this basis course B will reduce profits both in year 1 and in subsequent years.

Here we must establish two sets of relevant costs: one for course B in year 1, and a second for course B in subsequent years. Both sets of costings should implicitly contrast course B and its best alternative – two ordinary classes. Reviewing the costs for the final time we have:

fees: course B, year 1 £12,500, year 2 £13,500.
classrooms: in each year course B would necessitate losing fees from two normal classes: opportunity cost of space £12,000 in each year.
variable costs: not a differential cost between course B and normal courses.
teaching: not a differential cash flow.
special data: data specific to year 1 remains a sunk cost. No opportunity cost because use does not demand replacement. Therefore no relevant cost in year 1. However, for each subsequent year, up-to-date information specific to that year will have to be purchased at a cost of £1,200.
books: not a differential cost.
artist's materials: course B is now to be held annually. Use of the materials in year 1 now requires replacement for year 2, and so on. Relevant cost for each year is now the replacement cost of £600.
To summarize, relevant costs are now

	course B year 1 £	course B subsequent years £
fees	12,500	13,500
classrooms	(12,000)	(12,000)
special data	—	(1,200)
artist's materials	(600)	(600)
net relevant cost	(£100)	(£300)

On cost grounds, therefore, course B is now demonstrably not preferable to the alternative of two normal classes.

Readers should review the examples and note how items which have a cost relevant to one decision may be irrelevant to another decision. They should also note how items which may be relevant to two decisions may assume a different relevant cost in each decision (see artist's materials in decisions II and III).

This problem is dealt with in the following section.

11.2.7 Deprival value

The relevant costing of artist's materials in section 11.2.6 may be clarified if we introduce the concept of deprival value or value to the business (the terms are synonymous).

Before proceeding to a definition of deprival value which is confusing at first sight, it may be helpful to examine the logic behind the idea, which is relatively simple.

First the name: a business has an item in stock and proposes to use it for a project. Using the item in the project will deprive the business of the item and hence we are interested in the item's deprival value.

Now the measurement. We know from opportunity costing (section 11.2.4) that the opportunity cost of an item is the net cash flow lost by not putting the item to the best alternative use. There are two alternatives to using the item in the project under consideration: one is to sell it forthwith; the second is to use it in another project. The best of these alternatives is the one that will generate the highest positive net cash flow. Prima facie this is the opportunity cost of the item.

But assume that it is possible to replace the item at its replacement cost. The best alternative to using the item in the project under consideration is now excluded only if the positive net cash flow of the best alternative is lower than the replacement cost. In other words if we can replace the item and still make a profit from the best alternative then the best alternative is not excluded and the relevant cost of the item is only its replacement cost.

The logic is summarized in the definition:

> Deprival value is the *lower* of
> 1 replacement cost
>   and
> 2 the higher of
> 2A cash flow from alternative use
>   and
> 2B proceeds of immediate sale.

The cash flow from alternative use is frequently known as 'economic value'.

11.2.8 Direct costs, indirect costs and overheads

The classification of costs as direct, indirect and overhead is essentially pragmatic. It will bear little analytical weight but can be useful.

Direct costs are costs of whatever goes directly into a unit of production. In a school this would include teachers' time and materials distributed to students.

Indirect costs are related to production but less directly. In a school this could include teaching materials which are not used up in any one class.

Overheads are all other accounting costs, including administration, depreciation and so on. Overheads may be split into production overhead and administration overhead.

The definitions are somewhat fuzzy at the margin but that does not matter. Since the classification is not the basis of any further analysis, you may assign borderline costs to any category that seems to you most reasonable, provided the same convention is observed by your colleagues.

There are two advantages in this kind of classification. First, it is easy to apply. You can list all the costs in your accounts, like salaries, rent, advertising or cleaning, and assign each one immediately to the appropriate category.

The second advantage makes the classification useful as well as easy: it tends to correspond with natural divisions in the organization. Nobody ever heard of a fixed cost department or a variable cost department, because they don't exist and would make no sense if they did. But a production department (responsible for direct costs), a support services department (responsible for indirect costs) and an administration department (responsible for overheads), or equivalents under whatever name, do seem to make good sense as a way of dividing functions and responsibilities within the organization.

Direct costs, indirect costs and overheads therefore present a useful classification of costs once we begin to look at a business as an organization of responsible people, rather than purely as an economic entity. We shall return to this topic in the next chapter.

11.3 Cash flow

In the discussion so far, we have made two implicit assumptions:

1 that profit is sufficient to guarantee the financial health of a business; and
2 that revenues and costs are instantly realized in cash, or that a business is indifferent to when they are realized in cash.

In a perfect world these assumptions would hold, but in the real world they do not.

First, a business needs cash as well as profits. In the short-term if a business has cash, it can afford to wait for profits. If it has no cash, it is finished – instantly.

Second, revenues and costs are not instantly realized in cash. This is the main reason why profit is not related to cash, and why profit alone will not guarantee financial health. And given the importance of cash, a business cannot be indifferent to when its revenues and costs are realized in cash.

The cash receipts and payments of a business constitute its cash flow. The remaining sections of this chapter demonstrate how and why cash flow differs from profit, and the effect of that difference, and go on to suggest ways in which cash flow can be controlled.

11.3.1 The relative autonomy of cash flow and profit

From the discussion of accounting profit in Chapter 10, it should be clear that profits and losses are not directly related to positive or negative cash flows. The main factors which cause differences between profit and cash flow are:

1 fixed asset purchases and sales.
2 introduction of new capital.
3 repayment of loans and distribution of profits.
4 changes in working capital.

The first three of these factors, and their effects on cash flow, are relatively clear. The fourth factor introduces a new term, and its effect on cash flow is more subtle.

To define the new term: working capital is contrasted with fixed capital. By an unstated application of the accounting equation, both terms represent, in fact, assets:

> Fixed capital is (that part of capital which is tied up in) fixed assets – buildings, plant and machinery etc.
> Working capital is (that part of capital which is tied up in) assets which circulate through the business as part of normal trading activity – particularly cash itself, debtors and stocks.

Using the term capital to represent assets is not entirely perverse in this context. Fixed assets are generally financed from some fixed source of capital – owners' equity or long-term loans. Other assets are often financed from more temporary sources – overdrafts and creditors.

The effects of changes in working capital are subtle but may be dramatic.

11.3.2 Cash flow, profits and growth: an example

The Mathews Academy specializes in teaching English for Defence Studies to staff officers from around the globe. Its Principal, Colonel Mathews, has concluded an agreement with his staff under which, by an unfortunate error, all income remaining after payment of other costs for the month is distributed as salary or bonus. The school breaks even exactly. All costs are paid in cash at the end of the month in which they are incurred. Fees of £1,000 per student per month are received one month in advance. The school takes its first bookings in January and begins operations in February. It begins with no cash and an overdraft limit of £150,000. The school grows rapidly, and its monthly cash flow is shown in Figure 11.14. At 31 May Colonel Mathews despite his lack of profit has a healthy £250,000 in the bank.

His rival Colonel Johnstone has established an alternative academy, and has taken care to ensure that payments to his staff vary so that after payment of all other costs, there is a residue of 10% of fee income. In short his net profit is 10% on sales. Colonel Johnstone pays all his costs at the end of the month in which they are incurred. He attracts the same number of students as Colonel Mathews and charges the same fees of £1,000 per student per month. He believes that since his clients are sovereign governments of friendly states, it is safe to allow them to defer payment in cash until the month following the course. Like Colonel Mathews he begins operations in February with no cash and an overdraft limit of £150,000.

His cash flow is as shown in Figure 11.15. At the end of June, Colonel Johnstone – who runs the profitable school – has exceeded his overdraft limit. Colonel Mathews – who makes no profit – sits on a mountain of cash. Except for the timing of receipts, and the profitability of the failed enterprise, there is no difference between the two businesses.

Points illustrated:

1 positive cash flow can arise even when there are no profits. Conversely negative cash flow can arise when there are profits.
2 growth – in general a good thing when the business is profitable – may have unforeseen and catastrophic effects on cash flow. Conversely, decline may have beneficial cash flow effects.

Figure 11.14 Mathews cash flow – January – June

DATE	31.1	28.2	31.3	30.4	31.5	30.6
no. of students enrolled	0	50	100	150	200	250
fees rec'd at £1000 per student	£ 50,000	£ 100,000	£ 150,000	£ 200,000	£ 250,000	£ 250,000
total payments	—	(50,000)	(100,000)	(150,000)	(200,000)	(250,000)
net cash inflow/(outflow)	50,000	50,000	50,000	50,000	50,000	—
opening cash balance	—	50,000	100,000	150,000	200,000	250,000
closing cash balance	50,000	100,000	150,000	200,000	250,000	250,000

Figure 11.15 Johnstone cash flow – January – June

DATE	31.1	28.2	31.3	30.4	31.5	30.6
no. of students enrolled	—	50	100	150	200	250
fees rec'd at £1000 per student	£ —	£ —	£ 50,000	£ 100,000	£ 150,000	£ 200,000
total payments	—	(45,000)	(90,000)	(135,000)	(180,000)	(225,000)
net cash inflow/(outflow)	—	(45,000)	(40,000)	(35,000)	(30,000)	(25,000)
opening cash balance	—	—	(45,000)	(85,000)	(120,000)	(150,000)
closing cash balance	—	(45,000)	(85,000)	(120,000)	(150,000)	(175,000)

11.3.3 Controlling cash flow : an illustration of the principles

Assume now that Colonel Johnstone persuades his bank manager to relent. He points to the underlying profitability of his business and promises to reduce his overdraft to nil by the end of the year. Both businesses continue to trade, but since both have reached capacity, for the rest of the year each takes only 250 students per month.

By the end of the September, since there is no growth or decline, the cash flows of both businesses have stabilized. Mathew's bank balance remains at a constant £250,000, while Johnstone's overdraft is steadily reducing. However, Mathews now decides that he needs at least £400,000 to purchase a fixed asset. Johnstone realizes that six months, each with £25,000 positive cash flow, will not clear his £175,000 overdraft by the end of the year as promised. Both are operating at capacity and cannot expand. In view of the competition between them, neither feels that he can raise the price of his course. How can each guarantee the cash he requires?

In October, Mathews decides to make all his payments in arrears – the month *after* the expense is incurred. Johnstone on the other hand decides to demand payment from his clients in the month during which the course is provided. The cash flow consequences are shown in Figures 11.16 and 11.17 overleaf. In summary, after one year Mathews, who makes neither profit nor loss, and started with £ nil in the bank, now has £500,000. Johnstone, who has consistently made profits, ends the year with £225,000.

Points illustrated:

1 a business will gain cash permanently and sometimes substantially by extending the period of credit it takes. Conversely it will lose cash by paying more promptly.
2 a business will gain cash by bringing forward the date at which it collects the cash due to it. Conversely it will lose cash by extending the period of credit it offers.

11.3.4 Practical steps

Practical cash flow management may be analysed into four steps:

1 estimate the importance of cash to the business.
2 control working capital.
   – establish a policy for taking credit from suppliers.
   – control the credit extended to purchasers.
   – reconcile the bank account.
   – control cash flows and stocks.
3 plan and prepare for cash movements through a cash flow forecast.
4 maintain flexibility in funding arrangements.

Figure 11.16 Mathews cash flow – July – December

DATE	31.7	31.8	30.9	31.10	30.11	31.12
no. of students enrolled	250	250	250	250	250	250
fees rec'd at £1000 per student	£ 250,000	£ 250,000	£ 250,000	£ 250,000	£ 250,000	£ 250,000
total payments	(250,000)	(250,000)	(250,000)	—	(250,000)	(250,000)
net cash inflow/(outflow)	—	—	—	250,000	—	—
opening cash balance	250,000	250,000	250,000	250,000	500,000	500,000
closing cash balance	250,000	250,000	250,000	500,000	500,000	500,000

Figure 11.17 Johnstone cash flow – July – December

DATE	31.7	31.8	30.9	31.10	30.11	31.12
no. of students enrolled	250	250	250	250	250	250
fees rec'd at £1000 per student	£ 250,000	£ 250,000	£ 250,000	£ 500,000	£ 250,000	£ 250,000
total payments	(225,000)	(225,000)	(225,000)	(225,000)	(225,000)	(225,000)
net cash inflow/(outflow)	25,000	25,000	25,000	275,000	25,000	25,000
opening cash balance	(175,000)	(150,000)	125,000	(100,000)	175,000	200,000
closing cash balance	(150,000)	(125,000)	(100,000)	175,000	200,000	225,000

11.3.5 The importance of cash

There is a rich literature on the cost of money, supported by theory and complex mathematics. For general purposes it is sufficient to know that each business has its own specific cost of money. This may be as low as the interest that could be gained on cash deposits. It may be the interest of an overdraft. It may be the profit that further investment in the business could generate. In extreme cases the cost of a lack of cash could be infinite – the collapse of the entire business. While it may be difficult to estimate the cost of cash numerically, it should be relatively simple at least to estimate the significance of the cost of cash. This will not remain constant in all circumstances, but it will be the benchmark against which the cost of control measures should be measured.

11.3.6 Creditor payment policy

Most suppliers offer an unspecified period of credit. For these suppliers the business should institute a policy. A suitable policy might be: 'payment at the end of the month following receipt of invoice', which implies that six weeks is the average period of credit taken. Advantages of a creditor payment policy:

1 payments are not made unnecessarily promptly.
2 the payment procedure – raising and despatching cheques etc. – may be done in bulk, with cost advantages over ad hoc procedures.
3 total amounts payable, and date of cash transfer, are determinable in advance. If necessary emergency measures may be taken on a basis of reasonable priority.

EXCEPTIONS

As noted, some suppliers may impose their own terms of trade, and these will form exceptions to any creditor payment policy. Other exceptions may be made voluntarily. Where a business is a large purchaser, then it may negotiate special terms with its suppliers where volume, discount and credit terms are the major variables. A preference for discount may lead the business to shorten the period of credit it normally takes, and so on. Criteria for policy exceptions:

1 is the exception necessary to ensure (continuing) supply? Otherwise,
2 what is the value of the discount (for early payment) or the extra period of credit (for later payment)?
3 what are the costs of exceptional procedures – both financial and in terms of disrupted routine?

11.3.7 Credit control

A school, as supplier, may determine its own credit policy as to the extension of credit. However, there are significant business considerations in the establishment of a credit policy which go beyond the straightforward preference for cash. These include:

1 the nature of the product. Schools provide courses, which must be arranged in advance. Students expect delivery as promised. On the other hand, attendance by the student cannot be enforced. Payment in advance – probably non-refundable – is therefore an advantage for planning purposes as well as for credit control.
2 the market and competition. A school in competition should consider its credit policy as part of its overall marketing strategy. Thus a large discount for accelerated payment for courses may not necessarily justify itself in pure

cash management terms, but may be justified as a means of expanding turnover or encouraging repeat business. Conversely, onerous requirements for cash in advance may be good in terms of cash management, but bad overall if they drive away customers.

Given the general tendency of debtors to postpone payment, a credit policy requires active enforcement. This will involve regular procedures to:

* list debtors and due dates
* review and update the list
* remind overdue debtors with increasing urgency

and these steps should be subject to managerial review to ensure that they are done effectively and efficiently.

A key indicator of the success of credit control is the length of credit extended, or 'days' sales in debtors'. To illustrate by example, assume a business makes sales of £365,000 in a year, or £31,000 in a month. Ignoring weekends, holidays etc., we may say that the business makes £1,000 of sales per day. Now if debtors are £42,000, this represents 42 days' sales, and this is a fair estimate of the average length of time debtors take before making payment in cash. A more active credit control policy would reduce this period, while a slacker policy would allow the period to lengthen.

11.3.8 Bank reconciliation

The crucial cash balance is not the balance on the cash account of the business but the bank balance. It is the bank which will grant or withhold funds, and through which payments are made.

We know from private life that the bank's account balance is frequently different from the balance of our own account records. A bank reconciliation merely identifies the causes of the differences. Typically a bank reconciliation will start with the bank balance and list the items to be added or subtracted before arriving at the cash book.

A business at the limit of its credit facilities may well need to reconcile its bank account daily.

11.3.9 Cash floats and stocks

As noted above, cash held physically in the business (rather than in the bank) is not a significant figure to the bank through which payments are made. Clearly a business will need to keep some cash in the form of notes and coins or even as advances to staff to cover incidental expenses. However, the amount and number of these floats should be strictly controlled. By the same argument, all cash and cheques received should be very promptly banked.

A business must keep a reasonable stock of the goods and materials it needs in order to operate. However, stock held in advance of use represents cash spent in advance of necessity. Stocks should therefore be held at a minimum, but cash flow benefits of low stocks should be compared against the business costs. Low stocks imply more and smaller orders (i.e. higher ordering costs and lower discounts for bulk). In addition, where there are long delivery times, low stocks carry the risk of a 'stock out' and consequent loss of trade or efficiency.

11.3.10 Cash flow forecast

The mechanics of preparing a cash flow statement are straightforward. It is customary to pick a day at the end of a period (week, month, year) and to determine that all cash movements in the period take place on that day.

The top line of the statement represents cash received. The simplest way to estimate this is to begin with the volume of sales expected in the period, to multiply by price to reach a monetary figure, and to assign that amount, in proportion determined by experience, to the periods in which payment is expected. Note how this is done in the examples for Mathews and Johnstone.

Regular expenses should then be listed as in the profit and loss account, and amounts allocated to the period in which they will be paid. Rent, rates and utilities are the major items which tend to come in quarterly lumps. Other major items which may have a devastating effect on liquidity are tax payments and quarterly accounting for VAT.

Finally, non-trading cash flows should be inserted. These could arise in connection with the sale or purchase of fixed assets, the repayment of loans, the distribution of profits, and so on.

Given totals for expected receipts in each period, and expected payments in each period, then the net cash flow for each period may be calculated. Then each period's net cash flow may be added to (or taken from) the opening cash balance to determine the closing cash balance – which becomes the next period's opening balance, and so on.

Uses of the cash flow forecast:

1 to test the cash effect of operating plans, particularly through working capital requirements.
2 to determine the viability or timing of discretionary payments (e.g. in connection with capital expenditure).
3 to determine the viability of loan repayment dates or schedules.
4 to demonstrate that the business is responsibly planned and run. Many banks make overdraft facilities conditional on the presentation of a cash flow forecast.

11.3.11 Funding arrangements – overdrafts and loans

Loans are generally cheaper than overdrafts, in part because they are normally advanced against security. This makes loans a suitable source of finance for fixed assets. But for working capital (cash) requirements, an overdraft is preferable for two reasons:

1 working capital requirements tend to fluctuate. Loans, being fixed, must be fixed at the highest level of requirement and therefore involve unnecessary costs when cash requirements are temporarily lower.
2 loans are accompanied by inflexible repayment schedules which frequently do not coincide with periods of cash surplus.

Conclusion

This has been a long chapter, reflecting the importance and the difficulty of the subjects covered. It is divided between planning, decision-making and cash flow management. Each major section developed a specific way of looking at a business.

Planning

For the planning analysis a business is pictured as an entity which incurs fixed costs in order to provide capacity. The business plans to use that capacity for a series of transactions, each of which will generate a contribution to fixed costs and ultimately to profit. Break-even analysis uses a graphical or mathematical expression of this idea which allows managers to test the effect on profit of changes in prices, costs and quantities sold.

Decision-making

In the context of decision-making a business is seen as a series of discrete transactions, each of which can be assessed, without reference to past or sunk costs, on the basis of its own marginal costs and revenues. Each decision is seen as excluding an alternative (even if the alternative is to do nothing), and consequently relevant costs for decision-making include opportunity costs – the lost benefits of the excluded alternative.

Cash flow

In dealing with cash, a business is presented as a reservoir in a circulating system. Long-run profits should ensure that cash continues to circulate, but in the short run, revenues and costs are not simultaneously matched by inflows and outflows of cash. If the outflows of a period exceed the inflows, then the system may run dry and the business will collapse. The section showed the techniques of cash flow forecasting and working capital management.

Key terms and ideas

The main terms and ideas introduced in the chapter are listed below. Readers should review the list and refer to the chapter where necessary to ensure that they understand the meaning of the terms and the significance of the ideas they represent.

planning
fixed costs
relevant range
sticky costs
variable costs
total fixed costs
variable cost per unit
mixed costs
step-fixed costs
kinked costs
semi-variable costs
semi-fixed costs
break-even chart
contribution
break-even analysis
fixed element of a cost
variable element of a cost
cost estimation
scatter diagram
decision-making
marginal costs
unit of activity
average costs
relevant costs
opportunity costs
sunk costs
deprival value
replacement cost
economic value
direct costs
indirect costs
overheads
cash flow
working capital
fixed capital
importance of cash
cash flow forecast
credit control

Follow-up activities

1 A school has the following simplified cost structure:

fixed costs	£500,000 per year
variable costs	£100 per student

Projections for the following year indicate:

student enrolments	1000
average fee per student	£1,200

a) What profit for the year is expected?
b) What would be the effect on profit of:
  i) a reduction of £100,000 per year in fixed costs?
  ii) an increase of £50,000 per year in fixed costs?

iii) doubling student fees (assuming this could be done without loss of trade)? Would profits double?
iv) halving student fees (assuming no effect on volume)?

2 List the main annual expenditures of your school and classify the expenditures as fixed or variable. Over what range would the fixed costs remain fixed? How much in the way of time and disruption would it take to alter any of the fixed costs?
3 Obtain or estimate last year's actual figures for the expenditures you have listed, and for the volume of sales (probably student weeks) in the period. Hence estimate a variable cost per student week.
Estimate the average fee per student week, and use this to calculate the break-even point of the school.
4 What information should, or could, the school record to facilitate or improve the estimates you have made?
5 Under what circumstances is it preferable to try to turn a fixed cost into a variable cost? Under what circumstances would you attempt to turn a variable cost into a fixed cost? Is there scope for such rearrangements in your school?
6 Take the cost and revenue figures you estimated in activities 2 and 3. Update them for any known or expected price changes and for any revised plans that the school may have. Estimate how and when these expenditures and revenues will be reflected in cash flows and hence produce a monthly cash flow forecast for the year to come.
Is the cash flow even throughout the year?
Are there any months in which the cash flow is negative?
What resources or facilities does the school have to survive periods of negative cash flow?

12 USING FINANCIAL INFORMATION AND BUDGETS

Aims

The aims of this chapter are:

1 to argue the need for budgeting and to demonstrate how budgets are prepared and used.
2 to discuss the ways in which management information may be presented in order to help managers monitor and control the business.
3 to emphasize the idea of operating capacity and show how capacity can be estimated.
4 to consider the cost and value of information.
5 to introduce the techniques and problems involved in the interpretation of financial statements.
6 to show the behavioural effects of using financial information as a basis for assessing the performance of managers.
7 to outline the contents of a business plan.

There is also an appendix dealing with the basic organization of a financial information system.

Introduction

This chapter is pragmatic. It builds on the more schematic views of a business presented in the previous two chapters, and shows how the knowledge developed there is put together, used and interpreted in the information a manager may generate, receive or request.

The underlying theme is that financial information is ultimately only useful insofar as it serves as a basis for judgement and action.

12.1 Budgets

Budgets are not popular among many pragmatic managers. Some arguments they may advance:

1 budget preparation diverts time and effort from real management now, towards imaginary management of a hypothetical future.
2 actual results always vary from budget, hence:
a) budgets are dangerous nonsense – 'there are lies, damned lies, and budgets'.
b) even more time is wasted trying to explain variances from budget.
3 in a school, everyone knows that the real jobs of management are getting students in and keeping costs down – 'you don't need a fancy plan, you just need to get on with it'.

These arguments have some force. But there are stronger arguments to demonstrate that budgets are vital even to the smallest business.

Defining a budget as the financial expression of a business plan, it is clear that a budget can fulfil these functions:

1 *coordination*: a plan, worked out in advance, allows a business to avoid the contradictions and bottle-necks that arise from uncoordinated activity. In a larger school, a lack of coordination would allow the marketing manager to mount a campaign in Brazil, just as the Director of Studies is developing materials especially for Swiss bankers. In a smaller school, it may allow the proprietor to overlook the fact that a demand peak in July may require clerical overtime in June, or that growth will require additional working capital.
2 *rational allocation of resources*: without a plan, cash is spent on a first-come first-served basis and other resources are similarly used. Budgeting allows a rational assessment of needs and priorities.
3 *delegation*: once agreed, a budget represents delegated power to deploy resources. Without further reference to higher authority, the administration may go ahead and purchase the minibus, the Director of Studies may employ additional teachers, the senior teacher may purchase needed materials, and so on. There is a saving in management time.
4 *control*: the budget represents a charted course. Regular monitoring of actual progress against budget permits a series of minor non-disruptive adjustments to bring the school back on course. When external shocks dictate a radical change of course, regular budget monitoring reveals the situation earlier and gives more time to adjust.
5 *motivation*: agreed budgets provide a target and some managerial commitment to meeting the target. Empirical studies show that actual performance improves when a reasonable target performance is explicitly set and agreed.
6 *raising finances*: no reasonable bank or lender will advance funds on the basis of a half-baked scheme on the back of an envelope. No reasonable borrower would commit herself on such a basis. The interests of both parties are served by the existence of a formal business plan and budget.

12.1.1 Budget preparation : organizational aspects

Given that a budget is intended to coordinate, delegate and motivate, it is important that all interested parties should be represented at the appropriate stage of budget development. Consider a plan to extend student numbers. This involves:

1 an assessment of the market.
2 teaching resources and materials.
3 student residential, feeding and entertainment requirements.
4 teaching premises, cleaning, maintenance etc.

It is likely that different people within the organization will all have relevant knowledge, constraints and preferences differently affected by the plan. Consequently all should be represented or consulted as the plan is prepared. Precise procedures for this cannot be laid down in the abstract, but it is clear at least that a budget will probably be the work of a committee rather than an individual.

12.1.2 Computation and presentation

A budget must begin with a sales forecast. The variables are student numbers and unit prices. The constraint is the capacity of the school.

Given the best estimates of these variables (a large assumption), then the projected income of each period can be calculated as follows:

period	January	February	March	April	(etc.)
student weeks	800	850	900	920	
price	100	100	120	120	
income (£ 000's)	80.0	85.0	108.0	110.4	

Next, costs must be estimated and assigned to each period. Since the number of teachers and their rates of pay may well vary with the number of students (as temporary teachers arrive and leave in response to demand) teaching costs are best projected in a similar way to the revenue projection above, taking care to allow for salary reviews, grade increases and so on.

Other costs may be classed as fixed, variable or discretionary. Fixed costs will include rent, administrative staffing etc. These may be estimated with reference to past experience, planned savings, expected price changes and other relevant factors. They may be evenly assigned to each period, although care should be taken to ensure due allowance for seasonal factors (extra help or expense in the gardens over the summer) or for 'trips' in fixed costs occasioned by changes in demand (temporary clerical or kitchen staff for example).

Variable costs will include those which are strictly variable on an 'engineering' basis (costs of certain materials should naturally vary with the number of students). They will also include costs which can be made variable on an arbitrary basis. Thus a school may allow £5 or £6 per student week as entertainment cost or materials expenditure. These costs should be calculated and assigned to the relevant periods.

Discretionary costs are those costs which may be increased or decreased, advanced or retarded, without immediate effect on the operation of the business. The most obvious examples are marketing excursions, advertising, speculative course development and certain kinds of fixed asset investment. These should be assessed in terms of business need, and the expenditure assigned to the best and most convenient period.

In parallel with this process, the business should consider its programme of fixed asset replacement and investment. What fixed asset changes will be occasioned by decrepitude, projected student or staff needs or other causes? How will fixed asset changes affect revenue expenditure? How should fixed asset acquisition be timed in view of need, availability of funds and possible disruption of operations during installation?

The result of these estimates and calculations will be draft revenue and capital budgets. The revenue budget will be in the form of a profit and loss account, totalled for the entire budget period, with income and expenditure assigned to each control period (week, month or quarter) within the overall budget period. The capital budget will include only capital expenditure, again totalled for the entire budget period, with specific expenditures assigned to the relevant control period.

The projections must now be reviewed and assessed. Do the managers responsible for execution of the plan agree that it is complete, coherent and feasible? Does the plan generate sufficient profit in line with the strategy of the business and its owners' requirements? Finally a cash flow forecast must be prepared on the basis of the draft budgets. Will permanent or temporary extra finance be required at any stage? Will it be available? At what cost? Will the business be able to make any capital (loan) repayments as they fall due? Will there be sufficient cash to make any necessary tax or dividend payments? The budget must be revised until all of these questions are answered satisfactorily.

12.2 Management reports

With the budget prepared, the business must take steps to monitor its progress against interim budget targets. On the basis of this regular comparison, managers may take corrective measures of control, or if necessary revise the budget in whole or in part. (Budget-actual comparison is part of a continuous feedback loop. Actual variances from budget may indicate errors in forecasting or budgeting techniques as well as performance failures.)

Figure 12.1 is a typical management report. While it is not a bad report, it is not presented as a model. Management reports should be specific to particular organizations. No single form of report can cater for all management needs. The number, nature and frequency of management reports will vary with need, and the costs and benefits of the information they convey. Any form of management report should provoke (and answer) a number of questions.

Figure 12.1 Management report

PROFIT AND LOSS ACCOUNT FOR MARCH 1992

	Actual	Budget	Prior year
Student weeks	396	425	430
	£	£	£
Fee income	32,917	33,984	31,969
Direct costs	14,792	13,848	12,791
Administration	7,218	6,894	6,416
Premises	4,254	3,210	3,947
Selling	521	430	308
Depreciation	1,703	1,653	675
Vehicle running costs	90	135	151
Other	2,560	160	200
Total branch costs	31,138	26,330	24,488
Branch profit	1,779	7,654	7,481
Central overhead	3,000	3,000	2,400
Net profit (loss)	(£1,221)	£4,654	£5,081

COST ANALYSIS	Actual	Budget	Prior year
	£	£	£
Direct costs			
Teachers' salaries	14,089	13,120	11,720
Materials	703	728	1,071
	£14,792	£13,848	£12,791
Administration			
Salaries and wages	5,272	4,926	4,607
Office utilities	1,094	948	1,058
Travel and entertainment	313	274	166
Miscellaneous	539	746	585
	£7,218	£6,894	£6,416

Figure 12.1 Management report (*continued*)

Premises			
Rates and insurance	458	656	579
Gas and electricity	505	930	887
Maintenance	2,821	1,278	2,132
Cleaning	470	346	349
	£4,254	£3,210	£3,947
Selling			
Advertising	300	250	—
Commissions	221	180	308
	£521	£430	£308
Depreciation			
Fixtures and fittings	1,490	1,440	588
Motor cars	213	213	87
	£1,703	£1,653	£675
Other			
Bad debts	2,560	160	200
—	—	—	—
	£2,560	£160	£200

12.2.1 Who is it for?

Figure 12.1 is a general purpose report, for one school in a group of several schools. The group managing director might receive a report merely listing the actual and budgeted profit of each school, allowing him or her to review overall results, and follow up variances if necessary with the appropriate manager(s). Otherwise in the hierarchy, the marketing manager could specify a report detailing only student numbers and fees. The building manager could specify a report dealing only, and in greater details, with premises costs. Other individuals and their specific needs may be imagined, but as a general rule reports should be tailored to the needs of the user.

12.2.2 Is all the information relevant and necessary?

At best irrelevant information beyond the scope of the manager's responsibilities or interests will waste a manager's time. At worst it will bury what is relevant and the entire report will be binned or filed unread.

12.2.3 Does the report present all the necessary and relevant information?

As a general purpose report, Figure 12.1 obviously lays itself open to any number of minute objections on this score. But within the context of its general purpose design, and its necessary elimination of small detail, it is possible to point out some notable absences:

1 there is no indication of the school's capacity and hence of the potential revenue it is losing by not filling that capacity. This problem is considered in section 3 below.
2 certain costs can reasonably be expected to vary with the number of students. It would be useful if the budget were *flexed* to show what the expenditure should have been, given the actual number of students. Thus the variance attributable to control (as opposed to volume) would be isolated.
3 similarly the variance in the income includes a price increase effect masking the volume fall effect. The report could separate these effects.
4 there is no capital budget report. Arguably the same information is given through the depreciation line (differences in fixed asset value will reflect in differences in the depreciation charge), but this presentation reduces the monetary effect of unbudgeted fixed asset changes in proportion of the monthly depreciation charge to fixed asset value.

12.2.4 What useful information does the report convey?

Figure 12.1 essentially tells us that profit is lower than budget. This is partly the effect of a fall in volume (mitigated by a rise in average price – perhaps a change in student mix). It is partly the effect of a rise in costs (or perhaps the absence of a commensurate fall in costs). These different effects, requiring very different responses, are unquantified. There is also a substantial unbudgeted provision for bad debts, relating in fact to an overseas agent. It may be that the fall in volume is directly occasioned by the dispute with the agent, in which case a commentary should be added to make the relationship clear. In general, management reports should *always* be accompanied by a brief commentary explaining variances and perceived relationships of this nature.

12.2.5 Is the report entirely accurate and reliable?

Error should always be considered as a possible cause of variances. In Figure 12.1 we may note that the figure for rates and insurance appears to have fallen, considerably. This apparent fall is in fact the result of a failure to accrue. Accruals and the failure to account for changes in stock are the most common cause of error in periodic reporting. A business may well decide to live with such errors, provided they are not large, to save itself the time and trouble occasioned by full accruals procedures at the end of every month or quarter.

12.2.6 Is the information timely?

Information has value only in so far as it may constitute a basis for action. The report in Figure 12.1 is given monthly. The business may require some information on a daily or weekly basis (e.g. cash or debtor balances), and other information only on a monthly, quarterly or even annual basis. In any event it is important that the information should arrive promptly while it remains of relevance. The highest relevance and the highest value attaches to information concerning the future which may still be affected by management action. Language schools, which take bookings in advance, have much of this future information readily to hand. They should make use of it.

12.3 Capacity

A language school will generally face high fixed costs and low variable costs. Unlike firms in many other industries, schools can only produce for immediate demand. They cannot build up a stock of lessons for future sale.

In consequence, managers must be concerned above all to ensure that facilities, expensively obtained, are used as intensively as possible. The management report in Figure 12.1 is of little help in this task. It does not show the capacity of the school, nor the extent to which this is being used, or left unused.

There are two reasons for this. One is that accountants are creatures of habit and tend to supply only the information they have always given. The information they offer is generally important, but managers should not assume that it is complete or sufficient. Managers should request the information they need.

A second reason why a figure for capacity is rarely calculated, is that any figure is open to question or ridicule. One may always squeeze an extra student into each class, or keep the school open one hour longer. This point is of no significance. The intention is to establish a basis of comparison rather than a scientifically verifiable number.

Figure 12.2 represents a capacity calculation for a school with twenty-five rooms, each capable of accommodating fifteen students. Since the calculation must start somewhere, it begins with the assumption that all rooms could be used round the clock, every day of the year. This is plainly unrealistic – there is no market for lessons in the middle of the night, or (perhaps) at weekends or on bank holidays, and some rooms must be used for non-teaching purposes. Note that allowance for these factors alone appears to eliminate almost 75% of the space and time the school has paid for.

Figure 12.2 Capacity

	rooms		days		hours		class size	total
maximum	25	×	365	×	24	×	15	3,285,000
weekends and holidays			(120)					
lunch and nighttime					(12)			
non-teaching rooms	(5)							
	20		245		12		15	882,000
policy limitations:								
class hours					(3)			
class size							(5)	
CAPACITY (student hours)	20		245		9		10	441,000
student weeks @ 15 hours per student week								29,400
maximum student presence (any hour)								200

There may be other limitations on the use of space and time. Our example assumes that for policy reasons the school has decided to limit class size to a maximum of ten students and to operate sessions of three hours in the morning, afternoon and evening. Even these modest limitations eliminate a further 50% of the space and time at the students' disposal.

The resulting figure of 441,000 student hours per year will probably never be attained. It may even be exceeded if the school discovers a market for weekend courses, but it does represent a reasonable target against which actual performance may be measured.

Even the process of calculation in itself is worthwhile if it serves to remind managers of one of their basic business tasks – to develop profitable use of the resources available to them.

Once the figure is calculated, then it should be regularly reviewed. Would it be possible to create more than twenty teaching rooms? Would it be worthwhile even to reduce class-size and charge a premium for specialist attention? These are marketing questions, but managers should ensure that the regular accounting system provides them with the data to provoke the questions and to contribute to their solution.

Given a figure for capacity, each monthly or quarterly management report should state the capacity taken up, once again as a reminder of the possibilities for improvement. Without this information management reports can become nothing more than a litany of cost overruns, which in itself can be counterproductive. An emphasis on costs alone may easily lead to reductions in quality or in capacity which could destroy the enterprise as a whole.

12.4 The cost and value of information

The discussion so far has encouraged readers to seek more and better information for planning, decision-making and control, and to treat the accounting system as a basic source of much of this information.

However, no information is free. It takes time to collect and analyse data, and to summarize and present information. It takes more time to consider and use information. Time, in this instance as much as any other, represents money.

Readers should therefore consider not only whether the information they receive is sufficient, or sufficiently clear, but also whether it is excessive or irrelevant. The value of information to be set against its cost, is the value of the improved decisions to which it contributes.

Both the cost and the value of information are hard to calculate with any precision, but they should not for that reason be ignored. Before accepting information as it is managers should ask themselves how, if at all, it helps them, and what would be lost if they did not have it. Before requesting information, managers should know how they plan to use it, and what they will gain from using it.

12.5 Interpretation of accounts

Chapter 10 demonstrated that financial accounts are a product – almost a by-product – of a system actually devised simply for recording transactions. The value of financial accounts for any other purpose, is limited by their origins in this system. Nevertheless financial accounts are often our only source of information on a business, and must be pressed into further service.

Figure 12.3 Summary financial statements

	A	B
	£	£
Turnover	10,000	10,000
Profit before interest	205	171
Interest	5	21
Net profit	£200	£150
Fixed assets	900	733
Current assets	830	830
Current liabilities	(730)	(730)
Net current assets	100	100
Total assets less current liabilities	1,000	833
Loan	50	210
	£950	£623
Equity	£950	£623

Figure 12.3 is a summary of the financial accounts of two businesses. Which is doing better?

On first inspection it seems no contest. Both make sales of £10,000, on which A makes a profit of £200 while B makes only £150. But profit depends not just on the profit of each sale, but also on the number of sales made, which should be related to the facilities at the disposal of the business. And profitability is related not just to sales, but to the return obtained by the owners on the amount of capital they have tied up in the business.

Profitability alone, however, cannot be the sole criterion in assessing a business. We also need to assess how robust a business is – how safe it is in the short term, and how flexible it may be in the future.

The main question therefore resolves itself into a number of subsidiary questions, which we address in detail below. Readers should follow the discussion with close reference to Figure 12.3.

12.5.1 Which business is making more profitable sales?

A is making net profits of £200 on sales of £10,000 – a net profit of 20%. B makes 15% net profit on sales. On this scale, A is a clear winner. But A has more assets than B, and therefore should be making more sales as well as more profits. How do the businesses compare on this scale?

12.5.2 Which business is making more intensive use of its assets?

A has total assets less current liabilities of £1,000. Using these assets it makes sales of £10,000 in a year. We can say that it turns over its assets 10 times every year. B, with total assets less current liabilities of £833, also makes annual sales of £10,000. It turns over its assets 12 times every year.

B then is making more intense use of its assets. If A could equal B's rate of activity, then A could increase its profits.

12.5.3 Which business is making more profitable use of its total capital?

A is financed by £1,000 – being equity of £950, plus loan capital of £50 (note that in accordance with the accounting equation, this total of £1,000 corresponds with A's total assets less current liabilities of £1,000). To this total amount of capital A produces a return in the form of net profit (to owners), £200; and interest (to lenders), £5: total return £205. A therefore is making a total return on capital of 20.5%. By the same calculation (171 ÷ 833 × 100%), B is also making a total return on capital of 20.5%.

Note that B's higher level of activity (turnover of assets) has compensated for the lower profitability of its sales. In simpler terms, we may say that profit = (profit of each sale) × (number of sales).

12.5.4 Which business is more profitable to its owners?

A's owners receive net profits of £200, this in return for investing their capital of £950. A's owners therefore receive a return on their capital of 21.05% (being 200 ÷ 950 × 100%). By the same calculation B's owners receive a return of 24.08%.

From 12.5.3 above we know that both businesses are making equally profitable use of their *total* capital (or total assets). Nevertheless because B's owners are using more of other people's capital, they are able to enjoy a higher return on their own capital. This is known as the gearing effect, the name derived from a fairly simple analogy.

12.5.5 Flaws in the above analysis

While the analysis above is not difficult to comprehend, it is a little naïve. The main problem concerns the valuation of assets. We know from Chapter 10 that fixed assets are shown under the historical cost convention, at cost less accumulated depreciation.

In a time of changing prices, then, it is quite possible that A's fixed assets of £900 represent the same physical plant, machinery and premises as B's fixed assets of £733, the difference being merely that A's fixed assets were purchased later than B's fixed assets. A therefore only appears to have a greater asset base than B, and simultaneously A's profits suffer because it is obliged to make a higher depreciation charge.

Some accounts attempt to compensate for this by showing fixed assets at valuation (generally higher than the usual 'cost less depreciation'). The increase in asset value (a debit) is equalled by the creation of a revaluation reserve on the credit side of the balance sheet. But this is at best partially satisfactory.

Another problem with fixed assets is that it is not necessary to own them in order to use them – they may be rented or leased. If not owned, assets are not shown in the balance sheet. Thus while B shows a lower fixed asset value in its balance sheet than A, and appears to be using its assets more intensively, it may be that B is actually using *more* assets than A. Any simple comparison is therefore vitiated. This effect is known as off-balance sheet financing.

12.5.6 Financial health – gearing

Our questions so far have been concerned with financial performance. Questions of financial health are basically 'How safe is this business?'.

One longer-term measure of health is gearing, defined as:

either: debt ÷ equity
or: debt ÷ (equity + debt).

(Effectively these ratios measure the same thing. The precise definition adopted is a matter of personal preference or convenience.)

High gearing as we have seen can boost the profitability of shareholders' capital. But this comes at a cost. High gearing leaves little margin of safety in the case of a downturn in profits. In addition, at higher levels of gearing it becomes progressively more difficult and more expensive to raise further loan capital for expansion.

12.5.7 Financial health – the current ratio

In Chapter 10 current assets were defined as cash and assets close to cash (debtors and stock). Current liabilities are those which must be settled in cash within a year.

The current ratio is defined as current assets ÷ current liabilities. A low current ratio (especially a ratio less than 1) indicates that the business may have difficulty in meeting its liabilities as they fall due.

Thus a high current ratio is good – but not entirely so. High levels of cash, for example, may indicate that the business is complacent and has run out of ideas for investment. A high level of debtors may simply indicate a failure of credit control (see Chapter 11 on cash flow). High stocks may indicate a downturn in sales.

On the liability side, a language school will generally receive payment in advance. Its current liabilities will therefore include deferred income (cash or debtors in respect of future courses). High deferred income represents as it were a long order book – a sign of health. Nevertheless, as technically a current liability, high deferred income will depress the current ratio.

12.5.8 Interpretation of accounts – summary

1 Financial accounts are generated by a system designed to record historical information. They are not initially created for interpretation and therefore should be interpreted with care.
2 The principal difficulty in assessing performance arises from the ambiguity of balance sheet asset values.
3 There is no single key or critical indicator by which a business may be assessed. Each indicator, in addition to reflecting the ambiguities inherent in the underlying information, also reflects only one aspect of the business. It is unlikely that all the signals will be simultaneously positive, and while from one point of view a signal may be positive, from other points of view it may be negative.

12.6 Managerial performance

In a large organization, the managers of separate divisions may be assessed on the performance of their division. This gives them an appropriate measure of independence, responsibility and reward. The measure of performance however, must be fair, and it must be one which encourages managers to act in the best interests of the organization as a whole. These twin objectives are difficult to satisfy simultaneously.

12.6.1 Fairness

The assets at managers' disposal are frequently not of their choosing, and not comparable with those of other managers. One, for example, may enjoy the use of a freehold building while another may have to pay a high rent. One may have modern equipment – and suffer a high depreciation charge – while another has older equipment which is already fully depreciated.

It is possible to correct for such inequalities, by for example charging each division an imputed rent, or by eliminating depreciation from the profit figure on which they are assessed. But it is difficult to do this fairly and without adversely affecting the behaviour of managers.

Managers who face an imputed rent have little incentive to find or negotiate a lower actual rental cost. Managers who face no depreciation charge may feel free to splash out on new assets and equipment. Managers whose performance measure is affected by depreciation may run down the assets of their school or division to enjoy the temporary benefits of a low depreciation charge.

12.6.2 Overheads

The problem of managerial behaviour becomes acute on the question of overhead allocation. Assume an organization with, say, two schools and a separate head office.

Head office overhead costs need not be allocated to the separate schools at all. Theoretically this is fine, except that the managers of the two schools may now make plans which completely ignore the need to cover central overheads. Moreover the head office will undoubtedly provide some services, and to the managers of each school these will appear to come free of charge. They may take unnecessary and uneconomic use of those services.

Assume then that head office costs are allocated on the basis of usage of head office services by each school. Aside from the cost of collecting statistics for usage, the organization as a whole may face problems if operating managers decide that they can fulfil certain head office functions more cheaply themselves. The purpose of the head office is subverted and overall costs will probably rise.

Alternatively overheads may be allocated on some purely arbitrary basis – say one school has 20 teachers while the other has 30 teachers, so overheads are allocated on a 40:60 basis. Now the managers face an overhead cost which is independent of usage (affecting their use of the service), while the head office may see for each school an entirely arbitrary net profit after overheads which may adversely affect decisions about the strengths and weaknesses of each school and its respective manager.

12.6.3 Accounting and behaviour

It is clear from the discussion that where accounting information is used to spur or assess behaviour, the effects are not entirely predictable. The underlying situation may be manipulated to produce more rosy figures, or the figures themselves (what they include and what they exclude) may not be enough to encourage behaviour in the best interests of the organization as a whole.

Some of these problems are insoluble in terms of numerical technique. Managers should be aware of their existence, and capable of exercising compensating judgement.

12.7 Raising finance and the business plan

To begin or expand a business requires funds. A substantial part of these funds may be brought in from outside sources. Whether these sources are banks for commercial businesses, or sponsoring authorities for public sector organizations, they will need to be convinced that the enterprise is a worthwhile and relatively safe investment. This requirement should be met by provision of a business plan.

Most of the elements of a business plan have been introduced and illustrated in the course of this and the preceding chapters, especially those on marketing. A basic business plan should contain:

1 a summary of the proposal: how much is required and for what.
2 a brief discussion of the people involved: their experience, qualifications and (projected) responsibilities.
3 a marketing plan.
4 a budget forecast for at least the first year of operations.
5 a cash flow forecast for the same period.
6 a projected balance sheet after one year's operations.
7 a statement of the major assumptions or estimates, and the degree of risk attached to them.

Major enterprises, both in the public and the private sector, may have their own procedures under which managers may submit applications for central funds. For those who must apply directly to external sources of finance, help is at hand. In the UK the major banks are anxious to attract business custom. Many have managers or departments which specialize in dealing with new or growing businesses. Many provide information packs, including pro-forma budget and cash flow statements, with notes on how these should be prepared.

With this help, readers should be able to do much on their own, but those who are considering a major business venture should use the services of a good independent accountant. A good accountant should offer helpful criticism of the plan and assumptions, and check the rigour of calculations and presentation. More importantly they should advise on matters that this book cannot deal with: forms of business organization (partnership or limited company), and business and personal taxation.

Conclusion

This chapter has dealt with the financial reports a manager may generate, receive or require, and how they should be assessed and interpreted.

Budgets are the key to managerial control in any business. They serve a variety of purposes including coordination, delegation and rational assessment of the organization's activities. Budget preparation is essentially teamwork.

Management reports are regular comparisons of actual performance against budget. They permit a process of gradual correction, either of performance or of the plan itself in the light of changing circumstances. Management reports should contain all that is necessary and no more than is necessary. They should always contain a commentary. Ideally they should be tailored precisely to the needs of the recipient.

A flaw in many management reports is their excessive concern with actual costs and neglect of the opportunity cost of unfilled capacity. Although capacity is hard to quantify exactly, it is feasible to determine an order of magnitude, and managers should be constantly aware of the cost of unfilled capacity.

In requesting or receiving information, managers should recall that all information comes at a cost. Information must pay for itself as an aid to better planning and decision-making.

The performance of a business is ultimately summed up in its accounts or financial statements. Interpretation of accounts is not entirely a matter of science and numbers. Profitability and financial health may be measured in a number of ways and the signs are seldom unambiguously good or bad.

Where accounting information is used to assess the performance of divisions or their managers, we should be aware that this will affect the behaviour of managers in ways that may not be conducive to the overall good of the business. Accepting that it is not possible to produce an entirely fair or faultless method of accounting, managers must sometimes opt for the lesser evil and rely on judgement to correct for this.

A final, perhaps a first, use of financial information is in raising finance for a business venture. The business plan which supports a request for funds should contain information and projections on the personnel, organization, marketing and financial aspects of the business. Readers should by now be able to go a long way in constructing this for themselves, but should not neglect the professional advice of accountants and help of bank managers.

Key terms and ideas

The main terms and ideas introduced in the chapter are listed below. Readers should review the list and refer to the chapter where necessary to ensure that they understand the meaning of the terms and the significance of the ideas they represent.

budget
variance
sales forecast
discretionary costs
capital budget
capacity
flexed budget
off-balance sheet financing
business plan
overhead allocation
basis of allocation
net profit percentage
asset turnover
return on capital
gearing
revaluation reserve
current ratio

Appendix: Accounting systems

Accounting systems are important for two reasons:

1 they preserve information about assets and liabilities, and thus help to ensure the security of assets and the integrity of the business.
2 they collect information on the basis of which decisions are made.

It is therefore vital that accounting systems provide complete and accurate information. Systems must be specific to the business. No single grid or pattern can be imposed without reference to the circumstances of the business. However it is possible to state some general principles or requirements of a sound accounting system. The problem is particularly acute in language schools, where many students pay substantial amounts in cash.

1 Segregation of duties

This means that whoever handles assets (particularly cash) should not, in principle, have access to related records. Thus whoever raises invoices or records sales should not also have access to receipts. Whoever raises the payroll should not also have access to wages or salary cash. In small organizations this principle may have to be breached, but the dangers and temptations are clear. The absence of an asset will be noticed if there is a record of its one-time existence. If the record is altered then the asset may vanish without trace.

2 Independent check

Errors are bound to creep into any human activity or calculation. Two independent individuals are unlikely to make the same error. In principle, therefore, activities and calculations should be subject to independent check.

3 Audit trail

Errors in aggregation arise because items are wrongly included, or because they are wrongly excluded. An audit trail is the chain of references between a figure in a final report, and the initial documentation of amounts which compose that final figure. The trail should work both ways: it may be true that a figure in a report can be supported by initial documentation, but that does not establish that the figure in the report summarizes *all* the initial documentation that it should. To trace from report to document or transaction, it is sufficient to ensure that a proper system of referencing and filing is imposed. To trace from document or transaction to report is more difficult. It may involve pre-numbering of documents with checks for completeness of sequence. It may simply involve thorough search and rigorous procedures to ensure the inclusiveness of documents processed.

4 Back-up and fail-safe mechanisms

The records of a business are its collective memory and intelligence. Loss or destruction of records may be quite literally disastrous. Systems, and particularly computer systems, should incorporate safeguards against accidental loss or destruction of information, and should provide for the reconstruction of information that may nevertheless be lost or destroyed. Costs associated with the loss of information should be insured against.

5 Reconciliation

Frequently there will be two or more independent records of the same thing, such as:

- ⋆ bank statement and cash book balance.
- ⋆ total debtors and individual debtor listing.
- ⋆ fixed assets in the accounts, fixed assets recorded in an independent register, and fixed assets physically present in the business.

These records will invariably differ from time to time as one is up-dated before the other, and so on. Where separate independent records exist they should be regularly reconciled with an explanation of the differences.

Follow-up activities

1 What are the main operating activities in your school (teaching, recruiting, buying, selling, student accommodation, cleaning, cooking etc.)?

Who is responsible for the appropriate performance of these activities?

Who should be present or represented when budgets are prepared or approved?

2 In preparing or reviewing the annual budget of a school, what would be the main interest of the following people:

senior teacher
employed principal
marketing manager
accommodation officer
treasurer or accountant
bank manager
proprietor

How would these interests combine or conflict?

3 For each of the individuals above, and for those identified by you in activity 1, identify the information they would need in order to perform and improve their work.

How frequently would they need the information? How accurate or detailed would the information need to be?

How expensive would it be to gather and present the information?

How much of an improvement would it make to the overall working of the school?

4 Imagine that you are the manager of your school, and that a rival school known to you is owned by the same parent organization. The organization will obviously wish to reward the managers of its different schools on the basis of their performance.

How would you wish your performance to be measured?

What special circumstances of your school should be taken into account when comparing your performance with that of the manager of the rival school?

How do you think that the organization would wish to measure your performance? What difference would this make to the way that you did your job, or to the way in which you presented your plans and results?

BIBLIOGRAPHY

ACAS, *Disciplinary and Other Procedures in Employment*, (Draft Code of Practice) London: ACAS, 1985.

Adair, J. (ed), *A Handbook of Management Training Exercises (Vol. 1)*, London: BACIE, 1978.

Ansoff, I., *Corporate Strategy*, Harmondsworth, Middlesex: Penguin, 1984.

Armstrong, M., *Handbook of Personnel Management Practice*, London: Kogan Page, 1977.

Arnold, J. and Hope, Tony, *Accounting for Management Decisions*, London: Prentice Hall International, 1990.

Arnold, J., Hope, Tony and Southworth, A.J., *Financial Accounting*, London: Prentice Hall International, 1985.

Atkinson, G.G.M., *The Effective Negotiator*, London: Quest Research Publications, 1977.

Beckhard, R. and Harris, R.T., *Organizational Transitions: Managing Complex Change*, Reading, Mass.: Addison-Wesley, 1977.

Belbin, M., *Management Teams: Why They Succeed or Fail*, London: Heinemann, 1981.

Bell, M. *Guidelines for the Evaluation of TAFE Programmes*, Australia: Technical and Further Education, 1982.

Bowers, R., 'Project planning and performance', in British Council (1983).

Bramley, P., *Evaluation of Training: a Practical Guide*, London: British Association for Commercial and Industrial Education, 1986.

British Council, *Language Teaching Projects for the Third World, ELT Documents 116*, Oxford: Pergamon Press and the British Council, 1983.

Broadbent S. (ed), *Twenty Advertising Case Histories*, London: Holt, Rinehart & Winston, 1984.

Bush, T., *Theories of Educational Management*, London: Harper and Row, 1986.

Clark, J.L., *Curriculum Renewal in School Foreign Language Learning*, Oxford: Oxford University Press, 1987.

Cowell, D., *The Marketing of Services*, London: Heinemann, 1984.

Davidson, H., *Offensive Marketing*, Harmondsworth, Middlesex: Penguin, 1987.

Davies, J.L., and Morgan, A.W., 'Management of higher education in a period of contraction and uncertainty'. In O.Boyd-Barrett, T. Bush, J. Goodey, I. McNay and M. Preedy (eds), *Approach to Post School Management*, London, Harper and Row, 1983.

de Board, R., *Counselling People at Work: an Introduction for Managers*, Aldershot: Gower, 1983.

Drennan, D., 'How to make the bad news less bad and the good news great'. *Personnel Management Magazine*, August 1988.

Drucker, P.F., *Managing for Results*, London: Heinemann, 1964.

Enderud, H., Administrative leadership in organised anarchies, *International Journal of Institutional Management in Higher Education*, Vol. 4, No. 3, pp. 235–253, 1980.

Eva, D. and Oswald, R., *Health and Safety at Work*, London: Pan Books, 1981.

Everard, K.B. and Morris, G., *Effective School Management*, London: Paul Chapman, 1985.

Fisher, R., and Ury, W., *Getting to Yes*, London: Business Books, 1991.

Flenley, A.J., *Innovation in English language teaching in Japanese Senior High Schools*, Unpublished MATEFL Dissertation, Centre for Applied Language Studies, University of Reading, England, 1988.

Fullan, M., *The Meaning of Educational Change*, New York: Teachers College Press, Columbia University, 1982.

Griffiths, I., *Creative Accounting*, London: Unwin Hyman, 1987.

Guest, D., and Kenny, T. (eds), *Textbook of Techniques and Strategies in Personnel Management*, London: Institute of Personnel Management, 1983.

Handy, C.A., (2nd edition) *Understanding Organizations*, Harmondsworth, Middlesex: Penguin, 1978.

Handy, C.A., *Taken for Granted? Understanding Schools as Organizations*, London: Longman & Schools Council, 1984.

Handy, C. and Aitken, R., *Understanding Schools as Organizations*, Harmondsworth: Penguin, 1986.

Harrison, R., *Training and Development*, London: Institute of Personnel Management, 1988.

Havelock, R.G., *The Change Agent's Guide to Innovation in Education*, Englewood Cliffs, N.J. 'Educational Technology Publications', 1973.

Heller, R., *The Supermarketers*, London: Sidgwick & Jackson, 1988.

Henrichsen, L.E., *Diffusion of Innovations in English Language Teaching: The English Language Exploratory Committee's Promotion of C.C. Fries's Oral Approach in Japan, 1956–1968*, PhD. dissertation, University of Hawaii at Manoa, 1988.

Henrichsen, L.E., 'Factors which facilitate and/or inhibit the innovation-implementation process'. Paper delivered at TESOL Convention, San Antonio, March 1989.

Hirsch, M.L. and Louderback, J.G., *Cost Accounting*, Kent Publishing Company, 1986.

Honey, P., *Improve your People Skills*, London: Institute of Personnel Management, 1988.

Hopwood, A., *Accounting and Human Behaviour*, London: Haymarket Publishing, Accountancy Age Series, 1974.

Hyman, R., *Strikes*, (3rd edition) London: Fontana, 1984.

Kennedy, C., 'Innovation for change: teacher development and innovation'. *ELT Journal*, 41/3: 163–71, 1987.

Kenney, J. and Reid, M., *Training Interventions*, London: Institute of Personnel Management, 1986.

Lewis, C., *Employee Selection*, London: Hutchinson, 1985.

Long, P., *Performance Appraisal Revisited*, London: Institute of Personnel Management, 1986.

Maslow, A.H., 'A theory of human motivation'. *Psychological Review*, 50: 370–96, 1943.

Maslow, A.H., *Motivation and Personality*, New York: Harper & Row, 2nd edition, 1970.

McCabe, C., The External Evaluator – Inspector or Management Consultant? *Evaluation and Research in Education*, Vol. 1, No. 1, pp. 1–8, 1987.

McDonald, M.H.B., *Marketing Plans*, London: Heinemann, 1984.

McGregor, D., *The Human Side of Enterprise*, New York: McGraw-Hill, 1960.

Megranahan, M., *Counselling: a Practial Guide for Employers*, London: Institute of Personnel Management, 1989.

Miller, R., *Perspectives on Educational Change*, New York: Appleton-Century-Crofts, 1967.

Miles, M.B. (ed), *Innovation in Education*, New York: Teachers College, 1964.

Mullins, L.L., *Management and Organisational Behaviour*, London: Pitman, 1985.

Mumford, A., *Management Development*, London: Institute of Personnel Management, 1989.

Naisbitt, J. and Aburdene, P., *Re-inventing the Corporation*, London: Macdonald, 1985.

Nicholls, A., *Managing Educational Innovations*, London: Allen & Unwin, 1983.

Paisey, A., *Organization and Management in Schools*, London: Longman, 1981.

Pedlar, M., Burgoyne, J. and Boydell, T., *A Manager's Guide to Self-Development*, New York: McGraw-Hill, (2nd edition) 1986.

Pigors, P., and Myers, C.S., *Personnel Administration*, Maidenhead: McGraw Hill, 1977.

Plumbley, P., *Recruitment Selection* (4th edition). London: Institute of Personnel Management, 1985.

Randall, G., Pakcard, P., and Slater, J., *Staff Appraisal*, London: Institute of Personnel Management, 1984.

Robertson, I.T. and Smith, M., *Motivation and Job Design*, London: Institute of Personnel Management, 1985.

Robinson, K., *Effective Performance Interviews: a Self-Help Guide*, London: Institute of Personnel Management, 1983.

Rodger, A., *The Seven Point Plan*, London: Institute of Industrial Psychology, 1952.

Rogers, *Diffusion of Innovations*, New York: Collier-Macmillan, (3rd edition) 1983.

Rogers, E.M. and Schoemaker, F.F., *Communication of Innovations: a Cross Cultural Approach*, New York: The Free Press, (2nd edition) 1971.

Skilbeck. M., *School-based Curriculum Development*, London: Harper & Row, 1984.

Taba, H., *Curriculum Development: Theory and Practice*, New York: Harcourt, Brace and World, 1962.

Tomlinson, B., Managing change in Indonesian high schools, *ELT Journal*, Vol. 44, No. 1, pp. 25–37, 1990.

Torrington, D.P. and Champman, J., *Personnel Management* (2nd edition) Hemel Hempstead: Prentice Hall International, 1983.

Torrington, D.P. and Hall, L., *Personnel Management: a New Approach*, Hemel Hempstead: Prentice Hall International, 1987.

Trump, J.L., 'Influencing change at the secondary level' in Miller (ed), 1967.

Tyler, R.W., *Basic Principles of Curriculum and Instruction*, Chicago & London: University of Chicago Press, 1949/1973.

Ungerson, B., *How to Write a Job Description*, London: Institute of Personnel Management, 1983.

West, A., 'Recruitment and Selection' in Guest, D. and Kenny, T. (eds), 1983.

White, R.V., *The ELT Curriculum*, Oxford: Basil Blackwell, 1988.

Wilkinson, T. (ed), *The Communications Challenge*, London: Institute of Personnel Management, 1989.

Winkler, J., *Pricing for Results*, London: Pan, 1987.

INDEX

References in italics indicate figures